DISPATCHES FROM THE DEEP WOODS

DISPATCHES
FROM THE
DEEP WOODS

John G. Mitchell

University of Nebraska Press

Lincoln and London

Copyright
© 1991 by John G. Mitchell
All rights reserved
Copyright information on individual
selections appears on pages ix–x, which
constitute an extension of the copyright page.
Manufactured in the United States of America
The paper in this book meets the minimum require-
ments of American National Standard
for Information Sciences – Permanence of Paper
for Printed Library Materials,
ANSI Z39.48-1984.
Library of Congress Cataloging in Publication Data
Mitchell, John G., 1931-
Dispatches from the deep woods / John G. Mitchell.
P.   cm.
Includes index.
Summary: Describes the various types of forests
found in North America, their importance
to the environment, the threats to their survival,
and what can be done to save them.
ISBN 0-8032-3146-6 (alk. paper)
1. Forest conservation – United States.
2. Forest ecology – United States.
3. Forests and forestry – Unites States.
[1. Forests and forestry.
2. Forest ecology.
3. Forest conservation.]
1. Title.
SD412.M57   1990
333.75'16'0973 – dc20
90-36842 CIP AC

For Link, Boo, Dinko,
Mangamoonga, the Big Indian,
and the Druids of the Hollow

CONTENTS

Acknowledgments, ix

Preface: Tree-Hugging in America, xi

The Hiding-Place Tree, 1

War in the Woods I: Swan Song, 13

War in the Woods II: West Side Story, 56

The Tree Army, 100

U.P., 119

Papa Country, 131

Unfinished Redwood, 141

Lord of the Eastern Forests, 164

Paradox in the Pemi, 171

The Man Who Married the Mountains, 182

*Yankee Forest for Sale: By the
BTU, (1981) 209*

*Yankee Forest for Sale: By the
Acre, (1989) 258*

*In Wildness Was the Preservation
of a Smile, 277*

Index, 299

ACKNOWLEDGMENTS

The following pieces are reprinted courtesy of *Audubon* magazine from the issues indicated:

"The Hiding-Place Tree," May 1986. Copyright © 1986 by John G. Mitchell.

"War in the Woods I: Swan Song," November 1989. Copyright © 1989 by John G. Mitchell.

"War in the Woods II: West Side Story," January 1990. Copyright © 1990 by John G. Mitchell.

"The Tree Army," originally published as "FDR's Tree Army," November 1983. Copyright © 1983 by John G. Mitchell.

"U.P.," November 1981, originally published in a somewhat different form. Copyright © 1981 by John G. Mitchell.

"Unfinished Redwood," September 1988. Copyright © 1988 by John G. Mitchell.

"Lord of the Eastern Forests," March 1988. Copyright © 1988 by John G. Mitchell.

"The Man Who Married the Mountains," originally published as "Measurer of Mountains," July 1985. Copyright © 1985 by John G. Mitchell. Portions describing the work of the Adirondack Council are adapted from "A Wild Island of Hope," copyright © 1989 by John G.

Mitchell, which appeared in the Fall 1989 issue of *Wilderness* magazine.

"Yankee Forest for Sale: By the BTU (1981)," originally published in a somewhat longer version as "Whither the Yankee Forest," March 1981, copyright © 1981 by John G. Mitchell.

The following two pieces are reprinted courtesy of *Wilderness* magazine from the issues indicated:

"Paradox in the Pemi," Winter 1982. Copyright © 1982 by John G. Mitchell.

"In Wildness Was the Preservation of a Smile," Summer 1985. Copyright © 1985 by John G. Mitchell.

"Papa Country" appeared originally as "Hemingway Country" in the May/June 1987 issue of *American Land Forum*. Copyright © 1987 by John G. Mitchell.

"Yankee Forest for Sale: By the Acre (1989)" appeared originally as "Mountain Views, Bargain Prices" in the July/August issue of *Harrowsmith*. Copyright © 1989 by John G. Mitchell.

In preparing these pieces for publication in their original forms, the author incurred a huge debt of gratitude to the following individuals.

At *Audubon*: Kathleen Fitzpatrick, Jennifer Reek Gilliland, Schellie Hagan, Mary McCarthy.

At *Wilderness*: T. H. Watkins, editor, and Patricia Byrnes.

At *Harrowsmith*: Thomas H. Rawls, editor.

American Land Forum is no longer with us. My thanks to Charles E. Little, the founding editor, for having given me the opportunity to participate in that brilliant experiment.

And finally, for assigning me so often to the forest beat and for granting me the freedom to pace it off my way, unrestrained by institutional policies or preachments, my thanks to Les Line, the editor of *Audubon*.

PREFACE:

TREE-HUGGING IN AMERICA

R eaders unfamiliar with the term *tree-hugging* deserve an explanation right off the bat. Tree-hugging is the theory and practice of revering arboreal species both individually and as they may occur in natural combinations, as in a wild forest. There are some folks (as Aldo Leopold once observed in another context) who can get along in this world quite well without hugging trees and forests in theory, and some who cannot. These dispatches are the accolades, the alarums, the excursions of one who cannot.

Where or when the term first emerged upon a printed page is beyond my area of expertise. I know only that it appears to have sprung from the noun form, *tree-hugger,* the latest in a long line of sobriquets applied over the years to describe certain types of conservation-minded citizens. As in daisy-sniffer or bird-watcher. Or bog-trotter (for backpacker) or sneakerface (a pejorative form of "little old lady in tennis shoes," applicable to either sex). Some of my friends in the environmental community do not care for any of these expressions because, I am told, they represent language that is lacking in dignity. That may be, though I suspect that some of my friends take themselves too seriously. I have a better idea. Let us take American forests seriously—as many of us as can possibly be induced to do so. Why? Why, because if we don't, sooner or later we won't have anything left to hug but ourselves.

The pieces in this book were originally published in magazines during the 1980s. Most appeared first in *Audubon*. Some are short; a few are quite long. I have tried to arrange them so that the alarums are buffered here and there by the accolades. Among the latter are a couple of pieces that may reveal, at least indirectly, how I came to be one of those who cannot live without hugging trees. "The Hiding-Place Tree," with its focus on the Ohio Valley, and "Papa Country," set in northern Michigan, explore the kinds of woods into which I was thrown at a formative age. For acquiring a proper appreciation of America's diverse woodlands, one cannot do any better than to begin with the great mixed deciduous forest that marches from southern New England and the Middle Atlantic states to the edge of the long-gone prairie, or with that other forest that rolls across the piney, birchbark edge of the North Woods. I was lucky to know both, and early; and therein became groomed to display, when at last I got there, the fullest measure of reverence for the big-tree country of the Far West.

There are a few pieces here that poke into dusty corners of forest history to stir up the ghosts of people who made that history. "The Man Who Married the Mountains" is one of these. It tells the story of Verplanck Colvin, the surveyor of the Adirondack wilderness in New York State. Another in this genre, "In Wildness Was the Preservation of a Smile," evokes the life and times of Robert Marshall, whose efforts to keep at least some of our forests forever wild ranged from those same eastern peaks to the interface of woodland and tundra in Alaska. A third entry in the historical mode, "The Tree Army," recounts some of the days and nights of the Civilian Conservation Corps, which helped patch up our forests during the bleak Depression years.

And finally—the perilous news, the alarums, dispatches from the sylvan battlefronts. Always it seems, somewhere in America, there is a forest in trouble. The Redwoods. The North Woods.

The puckerbrush. The old-growth. If it isn't the Forest Service stumbling around in the trees, it's the timber industry playing the market, or the energy industry looking for cellulose fuel, or the environmental "industry" appearing to wrap its arms around every last tree on the face of the earth. Of such stories as these, the reader may note that several come in pairs. "War in the Woods" starts as an excursion to Flathead Country, Montana, then winds up, in Part Two, in the ancient rainforests of Washington State. The "war," of course, is the one that will determine whether, by the end of this century, there are to be some old-growth conifers still standing outside of parks and wilderness areas, or none at all. In the "Yankee Forest" duet, we go to the other side of the country and back almost a decade to a time when it appeared that woodstoves and powerplants might turn central New England into some kind of electric Kool-aid acid test. Yet by 1989, the fuelwood crisis had moved to the back burner. Up front, a new threat was boiling—the potential conversion of vast tracts of timberland into condo villages and wilderness ranchettes.

One crisis in the woods goes away, only to be replaced by another. But perhaps we can handle that so long as the ranks of the tree-huggers among us keep growing, as they clearly have been in recent years. I remember a time when it wasn't altogether acceptable in certain circles to be a theoretical hugger of trees. I remember—this was about a quarter-century ago, when I was a staff writer for a national newsmagazine in New York City—being singled out by my colleagues as a rather unusual fellow. I was tabbed as a "consie," a daisy-sniffer. Some sophisticate suggested I should take my office up to Central Park. Then someone pasted a sign on my door. It said, "Mitchell loves trees more than people." Then, I didn't deny it. But I would now, because it's only half true.

THE HIDING-PLACE TREE

In the good old days before buttons and digits replaced Ma Bell's alphabet dial, the hottest telephone exchange in America was *Sycamore*-7. I have no data to support that bald-faced statement against the counterclaims of those who favored *Butterfield*-8 or *Plaza*-1 or *Pennsylvania-whatever-it-was*. I just know. I know it had to be the hottest exchange because everyone who didn't have a *Sycamore*-7 wanted one. I wanted one because I liked the snarling doggy sound of it. I wanted one because it conjured up a die-cast lucky image of my favorite tree.

How a rational youngster could possibly come to be enamored of the sycamore should be no mystery to those who are familiar with the tree's delightful peculiarities. First there is this strange matter of the sycamore's reptilian bark. The tree, in effect, sheds its skin—not quite, but almost—like a snake. Could any young scout or scalawag fail to be impressed by that singular achievement? What other North American tree appears to spring straight from the Age of Dinosaurs bearing, as the writer Rutherford Platt described it, "the imprint of antiquity"? Mottled and patchy, the light-brown bark flakes and falls in thin, jigsaw pieces, revealing a new off-white to somewhat-greenish layer underneath. It is a haunting and beautiful thing to walk among winter sycamores on a moonlit night. A good imagination can take those blotchy branches and turn them into pythons in the sky.

Next, in order of peculiarity, is the sycamore fruit, commonly known as the buttonball—a small, brown, hairy, tufted sphere with a long wick stem like the fuse of a cherry bomb. For autumnal classroom combat, for interdicting the academic reflections of friend or foe seated a few rows in front of you at study hall, nothing—neither acorn, nor pignut, nor buckeye—could quite match the ballistic perfection of the buttonball. It was a forgiving weapon in my time; it seemed to float through the air, and a direct hit on the wrong target never drew blood, as the buckeye sometimes did. Still, the buttonball commanded much respect on our boyhood battlefields, and you can be sure that those without the means of obtaining a good supply of the fruit were simply inviting a first strike as well as total disruption of the balance of terror.

Of other notable properties I am not quite sure which should come next in the ranking—the astonishing size of the tree or its tendency to cultivate and survive cavities in old age. Size strikes most sycamore admirers as the ultimate attribute. Such is the tree's affinity for the rich alluvial soils of creek bottoms and riverbanks that, in the right situation, it can grow to heights overtopping the giants of most deciduous species and to basal circumferences girthier than all but the stoutest of western conifers and the southern bald cypress. Some guidebooks list the sycamore as the biggest tree, from the standpoint of overall size, in the eastern United States. I believe it. On my scratch pad, the American sycamore—*Platanus occidentalis* if you prefer the taxonomic, or simply "buttonwood" if you don't—is the undisputed king of the forest. Your royal majesty Sylvanus Rex, I like to call it. The hiding-place tree.

Which brings us to the cavities. Show me an ancient sycamore without a gaping hole in its trunk and I'll show *you* a fraud, an impostor, an arboreal aberration. To be a proper sycamore with two or three centuries of life behind you is to be disemboweled, all this girth and heft and cloud-scratching elevation hunkered over and partly around an empty gut, a cellulose cavern hollowed by rot, a home for squirrels or possums or coons or wood ducks or chimney swifts. Or, in long-gone frontier times, for pigs or horses or men. Our pioneer folklore is chock-a-block with accounts of settlers stashing their families in sycamore hollows while log cabins were abuilding nearby. Later, with a proper roof over his own head, the frontiersman converted his hollow sycamore into a stable, or a silo for cornpatch grain. With breast-high circumferences occasionally running on past forty feet, you can imagine how big some of these cavities got to be. Not far from Ohio's Scioto River in frock-coat days stood a sycamore into the hollow of which thirteen men could ride their horses—and did, with room for two more of each. And on the banks of the Ohio River, near Marietta, settlers encountered a sycamorean cave sufficient to swallow forty men, albeit unmounted. Not that solving the housing shortage was, or is, the sycamore's sole utilitarian purpose. In other practical matters, its hard, coarse-grained wood has been used for boxes, barrel staves, butcher blocks, and assorted furnitures. For all its peculiarities, the sycamore is a serviceable tree.

More often than not in the woods or yards by the houses where I lived over the years, there was an American sycamore or two. Not in the sandy pinelands of eastern Massachusetts where I once served time, or among the orchards of the San Joaquin, or high and dry in the Land of Enchantment; and sadly, too, not even here and now in deciduous Connecticut, though a few specimens are scattered in other folks' woods and one whopper reigns by a roadside in the next town north. Alas, no tree can have both style and ubiquity. Yet this tree's natural range is more extensive than most, spreading from New England across the lower Great Lakes states to Iowa, down into east Texas along a wavering isohyet on the wetter side of the ninety-fifth or -sixth meridian, east across Georgia in a march to the sea, and north along the littoral, where the salt air does little to encourage record growth. Practically dead center in this vast domain is the

Ohio Valley. The heartland of American Sycamore Country. The seedbed of giants past and present. The realm of my very first hiding-place tree.

I do not recall that it was a terribly large tree. Size can get so distorted when you try to measure it through the half-remembered visions of your youth. But it wasn't a small run-of-the-mill sycamore either, for I believe that three or four youngsters could stand behind it unseen by someone approaching from the other side. The tree leaned out over the trail that ran through our hollow—our topographical hollow—on its way from Duck Creek to O'Bryonville. About halfway between its base and the first big branch was a hole big enough to put a dog through, and that's where we hid our manifestos of scorn for the redheaded Jimmie O'Connor, who had been trespassing in our woods to help himself to buttonballs. Actually, a third party happened to own the land where the sycamore shed its fruit and received our messages, but that was a nevermind. It was "our" hollow, and Jimmie O'Connor had no business being there.

O what delight I took composing those notes of scorn and defiance for Red O'Connor, then slipping down the trail after school and reaching up on tiptoe, the fingers just edging over the lip of the cavity, feeling the texture of the wood, and then the folded message, a page from my loose-leaf, dropping into place among the relic hulls of squirrel fodder. "Did you get your mail yet?" I'd say to O'Connor in the schoolyard the next day, though only if a teacher were nearby, for the redhead was older than I, bigger, faster on the draw; and while somewhat lacking in allies at school, he had no shortage of them at home. He liked to remind me that his dad could beat my dad, and he was probably right. His dad was as big as a horse and drove cement trucks for the city roads department. In any event, O'Connor never responded directly to my literary insults. "You'll get yours," is all he said. And one day I did. One day after school I slipped down the trail through our hollow with an especially virulent message clutched in my hand, walked around the backside of the tree, assumed the tiptoe posture with the upraised arm and proceeded to edge the note toward the cavity. I had done it so often, the motions were automatic. Not this time. Where the hole should have been, my fingertips came up against an immovable object. I looked up. Sonofabitch. Red O'Connor's first strike. He had plugged up the hole in the sycamore with cement, and a message had been etched upon it while it was still wet. "Get yur mail yet?" is all it said.

Over the years I have been back to the boyhood woods from time to time, but never far enough along the trail to see whether the sycamore expelled the filling, or buried it under a layer of bark; or to ascertain if the tree still lives. I suspect it does. What's twoscore years to Sylvanus Rex?

There was another important sycamore in my life, years later and miles away in the Empire State. This one spread its crooked branches just beyond the front door, one or two overreaching limbs going so far as to encroach upon the airspace of The Neighbor Lady who lived across the street. It was a grand old tree, and the source of much labor-intensive effort at leaf time. Especially for The Neighbor Lady, whose fetish for tidiness was not at all compatible with her location downwind from, as well as under, my leaf-shedding sycamore tree. The Neighbor Lady called it a plane tree, a *London* plane tree. And a *dirty* tree. It was the plainest, dirtiest tree she had ever seen, she said, and I ought to give serious thought to having it removed. I let that unkind suggestion pass, promising instead to lop off the branch that intruded most offensively upon her premises. Of course I had no intention of lopping off a branch, and The Neighbor Lady knew it. Promises, she said. From our window that autumn I watched her sweeping the sycamore leaves off her front tarmac (macadam being tidier than grass and garden). The Neighbor Lady took great pride in her tarmac, which looked like a great black bed with hospital corners. After the leaves had fallen, she stood on a stepladder swatting the overreaching branches with a broom, to precipitate the fall of the buttonballs and bring the autumnal shedding to a tidy conclusion. Apart from that, The Neighbor Lady and I got along well enough. As she forgave me my trespasses, so I forgave her all but one. I could never forgive her for calling my sycamore a London plane tree.

There is much understandable confusion as to the relationship between the American sycamore and the London plane. For years, I held the common stateside belief that the London plane tree—this scrawny pole in the sidewalk, this urban ornamental, this thing not of the forest but of the street—is some kind of poor and distant Old World cousin to our native buttonwood. Imperfect knowledge compelled me to scorn the Londoner as a mere vassal in the awesome shadow of Sylvanus Rex. Yet how wrong I was, how utterly naive, to discount and discredit this tree, for it is a direct descendant of the American sycamore—not a cousin, but son and daughter; not a spiky pole, a skinny bole, but a giant in the parklands of southern England, some specimens even rivaling buttonwood champs extant in the United States. So consider now some of the events bracketing the botanical accident that brought us the Londoner, *Platanus acerifolia,* in the first place, a tree not as holey as the sycamore, not quite as flaky, but one that has probably brought more shade and joy to western cityfolk than any other tree in the world.

In the beginning, whenever that was, the great taxonomist in the sky gave us of the division Spermatophyta, the subdivision Angiospermae, the class Dicotyledoneae, the subclass Archichlamydeae, the order Rosales, the family Platanaceae, and the genus *Platanus.* Of *Platanus,* certain learned *Homo sapiens,* well versed in Greek, Latin, and hair-splitting botany, have identified about ten species distributed in North and Central America, southeastern Europe, and across Asia Minor into the Indian subcontinent. Of these, three occur in the United States: the American, the Californian (*P. racemosa*), and the Arizonan (*P. wrightii*), the latter so closely related to the Californian that some experts discount the distinction altogether. Fortunately hair-splitting has fallen on bald times of late, so that it is altogether possible to reduce to three the number of *Platani* that are significantly widespread as well as sufficiently distinct—namely, our all-American *P. occidentalis,* the Eurasian *P. orientalis,* and the hybrid Londoner *P. acerifolia.*

A word about nomenclature. A good part of our confusion over plane trees might be traced to the classical origins and modern uses of the words *plane* and *sycamore*. Plane arrives upon the Middle English tongue by way of ancient Greece, from a word meaning "broad," as in broad leaves. And broad leaves almost all plane trees have in spades, the American's sometimes running to ten inches or more to rival even the broad-leafed catalpa and bur oak. Nothing complex in that, except for the fact that in Scotland and northern England, where true *Platani* are rare, there is a species of maple known officially as *Acer pseudoplatanus,* the maple with the leaves of a plane tree. And that's exactly what the Scots call this maple—a *plane*. Damn! You know why? Because the English call it—and sometimes the hybrid Londoner, too— a *sycamore*.

Now, as for *that* word, it likewise leaps at us from the Mediterranean to the Middle English to the taxonomic. *Sycomorus. Ficus sycomorus*. The fig tree with the leaves of a mulberry. If one can forget the fig for a moment, one might note that there is some resemblance between the leaf of the mulberry and that of the plane tree. If one cannot forget the fig for a moment, then consider that *F. sycomorus* is a species indigenous to Mideastern lands thought by Biblical scholars to be the precincts of the Garden of Eden. And remember what happened at the gates of the Garden of Eden? Adam had to cover his shame with a fig leaf. A leaf resembling that of the sycamore. If I recall my Genesis correctly, Eve had to put on a broadleaf or two or three herself. Ah, *sycomorus,* the hiding-place leaf.

Probably the first true *Platanus* to be noted by literate folk was the Oriental, a much beloved shade-thrower in the sunny precincts of Bulgaria, Greece, Yugoslavia, and points east. The Oriental was and is somewhat shorter than the American, rarely topping a hundred feet in height but at the same time capable of producing a proportionately larger crown. The ancient Persians and Greeks were especially fond of the Oriental. Once, on his way into battle, Xerxes is said to have detoured his legions that they might spend half a day admiring his favorite plane tree. And on the Grecian isle of Cos, the great Hippocrates supposedly lectured on matters of medicine in the shade of a giant Oriental. Possibly he had a word or two to say on the harmful effects of inhaling the tiny hairs or spicules that flake from the plane tree's leaves and fruit balls. The ancients suspected the spicules of causing a bronchial catarrh not unlike hay fever. No matter. Esthetics took precedence over public health as the ancients went right on conducting their business under the plane tree's branches.

In Renaissance times, the Scots and the English began to complicate the world's arboreal verities by importing specimen trees from the mainland. Among the first to arrive, from the Balkans, was that plane-leafed maple, *Acer pseudoplatanus*. This was followed—we are dealing now in decades, of course—by the Oriental plane. Its popularity as an ornamental probably had a full century's head start on English soil before the arrival of one of the very first American imports from Virginia, namely our old friend Rex, the hiding-place tree. Who exactly brought the first one over and where in England it might have been planted are details unknown to the tracers of origins. What *is* known, however, is that by 1670 the Orient and the Occident had met and together had begat the London plane tree. Some historians believe that a gentleman who served as gardener to Charles I contrived the hybrid in a nursery at Lambeth Church, London. Others say the hybrid made its debut in the botanical gardens at Oxford. Me, I prefer the Irish version, which gives no credit to an English gardener but rather to a chance cross-seeding in the soil of some casual plot where the two parent species were growing side by side.

There may be a stronger measure of consensus as to how the London plane became the predominant tree of its namesake city and of scores of cities throughout the Western world, for the secret of its success was clearly its resistance to air pollution. London in the late eighteenth century was a wilderness of chimney pots and withering conifers, of nevergreen evergreens poisoned by sulfuric mists and sootfall from the city's multitudinous coal fires. Here were the pine, the yew, the spruce, and the fir—"the very worst kind of plants," noted one landscape writer, "that could possibly have been selected for the London atmosphere"—embracing daily deposits of soot and dying; and there, amidst the singing nightingales of Berkeley Square, were those newfangled hybrid planes, their glossy leaves easily washed by rain, their root systems tolerant of the compacted condition of urban soil. *Voilà!* At last a living tree to defy the downscale side of human progress.

According to the last unofficial census, more than half the trees in London nowadays are hybrid planes; and possibly the oldest and most striking are the specimens planted at Berkeley Square in 1789. Elsewhere in the English-speaking world, the Londoner is about as ubiquitous as a tree can get. Frederick Law Olmsted ordered huge stocks of hybrid planes to garnish his American greenswards, including New York City's Central Park. Today, the island of Manhattan may well have a higher proportion of hybrids than London has.

Still, there is this lingering confusion. Once, on a visit to England, I stopped by the general office at Kings' College, Cambridge, to ask permission to trespass across a college meadow. I wanted to see a big hybrid, said to be one of the oldest in the Commonwealth, situated on the other side of the River Cam. Permission was granted, though the secretary with whom I spoke said she believed the tree belonged to Clare College rather than Kings'. I crossed the river and followed a meadow path straight along the edge of the Cam. The tree was very big indeed. Its ponderous branches were secured to the trunk by cables. And yes, it *was* Kings' tree, not Clare's, for its base stood firmly planted just inside a fence separating the two colleges. On my way out, I stopped again at the office to thank the secretary and to say that she needn't worry about the tree being claimed by another college.

"O, good!" she said. "I'm *so* glad it's ours."

"Yes, and it's one of the biggest plane trees in England."

"O?" she said. "Don't you mean a sycamore?"

I tried to explain. How the sycamore means one thing in America and another in England.

"O," she said, all that controlled British enthusiasm draining out of her in a rush. "I'd been led to believe we spoke the same language."

The reigning world champion American sycamore, the big daddy of them all, is rooted these days in Ohio soil, hard by a tributary of the Muskingum River, about midway between Columbus and Cleveland. I have never seen this tree, but according to my colleague the Ohio writer John Fleischman, it measures more than 48 feet in circumference, is 129 feet tall, and spreads its crown across 105 feet of airspace. The champs come, and the champs go. Until a few years ago this tree was only a contender, the crown then riding atop a Kentucky sycamore. This was dreadful news for citizens of the Buckeye State, since Bluegrassers also claimed possession of the world champion Ohio buckeye. It wasn't enough for Ohioans to know that Ohio grew the largest Kentucky coffee tree. If they couldn't have the buckeye back, bygawd they'd have the sycamore. And they got it when the champ in Kentucky went down for the final count.

For many years West Virginia had a top sycamore contender on Blennerhassett Island, in the Ohio River just downstream from Parkersburg—a specimen so big some folks believed it was an anchor that kept the three-mile island from floating away. Overall size, however, was not the distinguishing element of this particular tree. What set this one apart, what inspired so many fantastic stories, what ensured a place for it in the history books, was its hollow trunk. Until it went down for its own final count in 1953, this Blennerhassett sycamore just had to be the all-time undisputed champion hiding place of the world.

Four hundred years old it was at the end. *Four hundred years*. To think of it—a seed from a buttonball, drifting on the wind, falling to the riverine effluvia, germinating, sprouting. Now only Indians pass along this river; Europeans won't be seen here for a hundred years or more. In England royal gardeners are importing the Oriental plane tree from the faraway shores of a wine-colored sea. Bloody Mary is burning her Protestant bishops at the stake. William Shakespeare isn't a glimmer yet in his papa's eyes. The leaves come, the leaves go. The sycamore is fat and saucy as it reaches for the sky. Now in England they are importing the Occidental plane tree from Virginia. Here, along this river, blue-eyed, buckskin Virginians are passing by. Here's young George Washington, the cherry-tree killer, come to survey the lands between the Kanawhas. George glides by in his pirogue; the sycamore winks at him through the widening hole in its underbelly.

The hole in the tree is soon filled with myth and legend and bald-faced apocrypha. It is said to be the trysting place of star-crossed Indian lovers—a Capulet from Shawneetown, a Montague from the wigwam-balconies of the Mingo. It is the refuge of settlers hiding from Indians. It is Margaret Blennerhassett's post office. Ah, Margaret. The hole in the tree has a tale to tell about that, about *her*. And parts of it really happened. This much is known:

She was an Irish beauty, that Blennerhassett woman. Married to her own uncle Harman, she was, and the cause of much scandal and gossip back home in Killorglin. Seeking a new life together, they had come across the sea and down the big river to build a Palladian castle in the wilderness. They would have a fan-shaped lawn sweeping down to the water, formal gardens and curving piazzas, drawing rooms inside with Oriental rugs and Venetian mirrors. It was (said those who dropped by) a terrestrial paradise, a notion of Eden. Among those who dropped by in 1805 was Aaron Burr.

Remember Burr? The one who slew Al Hamilton in that duel at Weehawken and then defrocked himself right out of the vice-presidency. After that, almost everyone except Gore Vidal forgets about Aaron Burr. But the Blennerhassetts don't forget. They can never forget. Burr is on his way downriver, hoping to repair his reputation at New Orleans. The Blennerhassetts befriend him, invite him to dinner. It is a tragic mistake. Soon the aristocratic couple are caught up in Burr's scheme to lead an army of frontiersmen into Mexico and crown himself emperor. That in itself is a long and complicated story having little or nothing to do with sycamore trees. Suffice it to say that it is a story with a very unhappy ending for all parties concerned—charges of treason, the Palladian castle sacked by militia, Blennerhassett imprisoned, trials, acquittals for both men, a life of wandering and impoverishment for Harman and Margaret.

Enough of this. Back to the sycamore of Blennerhassett Island, before the fall. And this part is legend. For how could a hot-blooded, black-eyed hypnotist such as Burr fail to be attracted to a beauty such as Margaret? Impossible. That being the case, what are the two of them to do? Hanky panky? The legends do not go quite that far. Adultery, though widely practiced, was not then an acceptable notion in the young nation's folklore. Much more fashionable was an exchange of glances or, better yet, of scented notes. But where to leave them, where to read them away from the watchful eye of Uncle Harman? Ah, *sycomorus,* the hiding-place tree, just a few hundred yards down the bridle path. What a good imagination can do with *that!* Open your mind, now, and perhaps you will see Aaron Burr as I have seen him, skulking about the great tree, looking over his shoulder at the castle, furtively darting his lace-cuffed hand into the gaping cleavage of the sycamore, the envelope please, the paper pressed against his nose. It was never like this with Jimmie O'Connor, I promise you.

Over the winking years, the hollow sycamore of Blennerhassett Island was pressed into apocryphal uses other than providing romantic postal service. In time, it became a way station on the underground railroad for runaway slaves. A plucky band of Confederate raiders fought their Alamo here. It was a hanging tree; its hollow, Death Row. Then, as the legends fell away, visitors came to the island to have their pictures taken at the mouth of the cavity. They might be doing that yet if some coon hunters or trotliners hadn't come in from the cold one night and lit that fire in the hole, and the wind rising, and then the whole tree a blazing pyre. I'm sorry I never got to know that one. So what else can I say except—Requiescat, Rex, in ashes and apocrypha. May the seeds of your tufted buttonballs multiply and replenish the earth.

WAR IN THE WOODS I:

SWAN SONG

The people once more are at war in the woods, at war with themselves to decide who will control the forest's present and future. As in most wars, propaganda is cheap. There is much buzzing talk of spotted owls and sawmill shutdowns, old-growth and overmaturity, men out of work, bears out of habitat, appeals, lawsuits, log hauls, log exports, allowable sales, sediment loads, sustained yields, spiked trees, and statistical chicanery. It is a nasty sort of war, about as ugly as a conflict can get short of bona fide bloodshed, and not a few of the participants are beginning to fear that the next round could bring it to that.

This is not the first struggle for control of the nation's forests. A century ago people began to speak of the need for a system of preserves and then proceeded to cudgel each other with details. Out of that scrap came an agency that in time would be known as the U.S. Forest Service. There were skirmishes over the years about this and that, and a big blowout in the 1960s over harvest practices on some of the national forests, most notably the Monongahela in West Virginia and the Bitterroot in Montana. And out of *that* battle came the National Forest Management

Act of 1976, which was supposed to resolve controversies but only multiplied them.

It is not a simple thing to sort out why folks are back in the trenches again. Or maybe it is too simple, in that they never left. Still, there are forces at work in these winding-down years of forestry's first century in America—forces that did not exist a decade ago and that now exacerbate traditional animosities between those who look into a forest in order to see trees and those who see only timber.

First, there is this force that is known as the Market. In the forest-products industry the Market now decides how fast a corporation will harvest its timber in order to tickle its stockholders or turn away leveraged raiders. As a result, the merchantable timber in a number of corporate forests is just about gone. A decade ago industry people bragged that their hothouse "supertrees" would soon be ready to fill the supply line. But that was before the Market decreed a faster cut of the timber on hand. And now we discover that these other trees, the clones, aren't turning out to be quite as super as their breeders predicted. So the companies are saying they must plug up their gaps with Nature's trees from the national forests. Or else—meaning pink slips down at the mill.

The second force is the Forest Service's national forest management planning process, a legacy of the 1976 legislation and of a policy that would have each federal forest do its fair share of satisfying the nation's need for food, fiber, energy, water, soil stability, fish and wildlife, recreation, and esthetic values, or—in the immortal words of the Service's founding father, Gifford Pinchot—to provide "the greatest good to the greatest number in the long run." That such a dream can please only some of the people some of the time is an inevitability that at last is beginning to dawn on the Service's bureaucrats, now that their overdue forest plans are ripe for public challenge; now that the planner has juggled his timber base with his critical habitats and riparian zones and roadless areas that may or may not become uppercase-*W* Wilderness; now that some people want more fiber to place on the altar of the Market, while others stand up to be counted for practically anything else, including the right of a senile tree to die of old age.

As it turns out, a lot of people are standing to be counted in favor of arboreal antiquity, because that is the thrust of the third force giving such powerful momentum to the war in the woods. It is this uncommon idea that for some trees, particularly in the Pacific Northwest, life begins not at forty but at four hundred. It is this belief that forest ecosystems containing the last of the ancient trees deserve protection from the chains and skidders of the timbermen. Such an idea is viewed with the greatest contempt by many of the rural people who earn their keep from the woods and by the sweat of the brow, as well as by Market folks who sweat only in their boardrooms when they hear that the other side is out to stop them from turning these ancient trees into twenty-foot logs. Sure, there are other forces at work here, but these are the ones that seem to have stretched it out to such shrill extremes.

In the spring and summer of 1989 I went into the war zone, to the northwestern woods, to the Flathead Country of Montana. I wanted to discover, if I could, why people of differing persuasions feel as they do about forest issues and about each other, and why the tensions and suspicions—and the hatreds, too—have become so deeply embedded in the regional condition. I wanted to sort out some of the claims of the combatants about the good and bad impacts of harvesting old trees or just plain hugging them, and maybe test those furious certitudes against the pecking order of my own prejudices and preconceptions.

Now it is done. This is the story I have to tell.

1. LAY OF THE LAND

The Swan broods at the heart of the Flathead Country, these mountains astride their valley, where a river runs through it. The headwaters rise at eight-thousand feet, gushing out of the Gray Wolf Glacier, taking a sip from the Angels' Bathing Pool and those spangled lakes that sequin the afternoon shadow of the peak known as Daughter of the Sun. Then down she goes into the valley to gather her creeks, Rumble and Jim and Fatty and Goat and Lost and Soup; seventy-five miles of gathering creeks all the way to Bigfork on Flathead Lake. In places the valley is just wide enough, wall to wall, to occupy a cross-country bushwhacker the better part of a long afternoon, if he stays off the logging roads. On one side, east, rise the serrated peaks of the Swan Range; west, the Mission Mountains. A state highway skewers the valley, keeping the river at a distance and giving the twist to a couple of settlements called Condon and Swan Lake, whose residents seem delighted that all of their names, in aggregate, couldn't begin to fill one page in a metropolitan telephone directory. With the Mission Mountains Wilderness right up there in big-sky view, and the Bob—the Bob Marshall Wilderness—hunkered just over the crest of the Swan Front, some folks in Condon like to say they can go out the back door and, without ever scuffing pavement, step right up to the way it *all* used to be, when trees were trees instead of timber.

As if it weren't enough that a range, a river, a valley, a village, and a lake should all have to share the name of the same bird, the Swan had to get itself declared a ranger district as well, one of several such districts constituting the 2.3-million-acre Flathead National Forest in northwestern Montana. There are five national forests in Montana west of the Continental Divide, including Flathead, and three in Idaho north of the Salmon River, and together these lands embrace one of the richest timber resources in the United States. The Inland Empire, old-time boosters used to call the region, or a part of it anyway. It was an empire built for the most part by big railroads, little mines, and a lot of lumber.

Ownership patterns in the Swan reflect the railroad legacy, even though you won't find a mile of functional track in the whole valley. It all goes back to the top-hat times of yesteryear, when the federal government was dangling free land upwind of the railroader's nose. To get the budding Northern Pacific Railroad tracking from old St. Paul to Puget Sound, Honest Abe Lincoln and his Congress conceived a carrot of nearly thirty-nine million acres of federal real estate, saying "Come and get it!" Long after the Northern got it—this being the largest single grant of public land in U.S. history—various mergers, divestitures, takeovers, and exchanges of one kind or another conveyed the leftovers to the custody of the Burlington Northern Railroad. By and by, timberlands located in the northern Rockies and the Cascades of Washington State fell to the Seattle-based Burlington subsidiary, Plum Creek Timber Company, Inc., the nation's fifteenth largest forest products corporation. In round figures, then, Plum Creek owns about a fifth of the 300,000-acre Swan. Its sections are checkerboarded with state and private woodlands (not quite another fifth of the area) and Flathead National Forest lands. The national lands embrace about 62 percent of the valley, are administered by the Swan Lake Ranger District, are owned, at least in theory, by you and me, and are not supposed to be available for administrative giveaways, should it ever come to that. Some folks believe it already has.

Whatever the ownership, the Swan is a splendid place for trees, with all that good nutritious alluvial grit off the mountains and a measure of annual precipitation about as wet as, or wetter than, that of any other drainage in the Flathead Forest. This is mixed-stand conifer country. It is where, depending on such variables as slope, elevation, and exposure, you are likely to encounter lodgepole pine, ponderosa, Douglas fir, western larch, Engelmann spruce, grand and subalpine firs, western white pine, a few red cedar and hemlock; and, generally keeping to themselves and out of the marketplace, such deciduous interlopers as birch, aspen, and cottonwood. Lodgepole is probably the most common species. Together with the other whitewoods—spruce and the younger ponderosa, which is known as bull pine—lodgepole generally finds its way into dimensional lumber. The old-growth ponderosa—known as yellow pine—is preferred for boards. For veneer, timbermen look to the larch and the Douglas fir. And the western white pine, though not as common here as across the state line in Idaho, enjoys a lingering reputation as supplier of doors, floors, shelves, shutters, and sashes.

One of the best ways to give this Swan the once-over, short of flying the valley or climbing through springtime snow and ice to the top of a peak, is to fall in with someone like Barry Bollenbacher, the Forest Service silviculturist out of district headquarters at Bigfork, and get about five or six hundred feet above Swan Lake where a logging road swings out to a scenic vista, and then look south down the valley and hope that the clouds that have pelted us all day with rain and hail will back off just long enough to sanction the essential bird's-eye view. And suddenly they do that. We're in luck.

We're in luck to see the gray-green mid-slopes of embracing mountains, splotches of brown showing here and there where pine beetles have taken their toll in the lodgepole treetops; the head of the lake like a sheet of slate; wetlands bracketing the incoming river; the rooftops of Swan Lake Village almost straight below us, wisps of smoke above the woodstove chimneys. Behind the village the forest canopy rolls unbroken over the flanks of the Swan Front. A born-again forest, it is; for these parts, site of the government's first timber sale, I'm told by Bollenbacher; 1913 to 1919, 3,000 acres cut clear, not a stick left, the logs boomed down Swan Lake, flushed down the river, boomed again on Flathead Lake, and rafted across to the mill at Somers; then seventy years of natural regeneration to bring it to this. One of these years now, though probably later than sooner, the great-grandsons of those long-gone loggers will be back here after the second-growth. It is part of the Plan, the Flathead National Forest Land and Resource Management Plan. So much of this forest is statutory wilderness (45 percent), and so much more is soon likely to be (despite former President Ronald Reagan's veto of last year's Montana Wilderness Bill), that the Forest Service's suitable timber base roundabout is pretty much catch-as-catch-can. In the Swan district, that boils down to about 120,000 acres. But what does it boil down to in timber?

"About 1.2 billion board feet," says Bollenbacher. "That's our inventory of timber on lands suitable for production, in this district. The ASQ (Allowable Sale Quantity) is 30 million board feet a year, for the next decade."

I look down across the Swan and try to see it in the kind of calculated dimensions and sums that silvicultural thought is made of. Board feet? I prefer houses. Suddenly I imagine all those board feet out there camouflaged under the gray-green canopy and I see houses. There is a simple conversion factor: 15,000 board feet of timber equals one brand-new average American house. If that's the case, and the forest-products industry says it is, than I am looking out upon a standing volume of 80,000 brand-new average American houses. Right here in the little Swan, on lands suitable for timber production, I am looking at housing starts sufficient to shelter a quarter of a million people, a brand-new St. Paul, Minnesota, if you will; a Fresno, California; a Corpus Christi, Texas. That's if you take it all at once, liquidate the entire inventory; but of course you can't, because this isn't the Market; this is the federal woods. So you take the Swan district's ASQ of 30 million board feet a year and convert *that* into 2,000 homes, and inside of ten years you've got more than enough housing to tear down the city of Billings, Montana's largest, and build it up all over again. Just from what's planned and "suitable" for the little Swan, which is only one part of the Flathead National Forest, which is only one slice of the Inland Empire.

Among those who see the forest for its trees rather than its timber, there is a counterpart to the Inland Empire. It is known, though not very widely, as the Crown of the Continent. Unlike the Empire, which connotes a place of material wealth and exploitation, the Crown is perceived by some as an ecosystem embracing all that high, daunting country roundabout Glacier National Park, where the park's premier booster, George Bird Grinnell, is said to have coined the phrase a century ago. Nowadays, the ecosystem might be defined as an international bio-region stretching from Canada's Waterton Lakes National Park and the provincial forests of British Columbia through Flathead Country to the Scapegoat Wilderness of Lolo and Helena National Forests, U.S.A. Perched southwesterly on the side of the Crown broods the wild Swan.

There is much besides trees for visitors to cherish on the

Crown of the Continent. There is eye-tingling scenery—visual amenity, the planners like to say—and, from peripheral roads, it is available almost everywhere beyond the windshield; everywhere, that is, except in the scratchy, shadeless squares and patches where the stuff of floors and doors and shelves and shutters has been peeled from the mountainsides.

There are these world-class parks, these lodges and campgrounds and lakeside resorts. There are these vast national forests with their networks of dirt roads and seemingly unlimited opportunities for what the planners call dispersed recreation. There is big-time downhill skiing at Whitefish, Montana; hiking in the lake-dappled Jewel Basin, up on the Swan Crest; floating the three forks of the Flathead River (219 miles designated wild or scenic). There's fly-fishing for the native westslope cut throat and that Dolly Varden trout now called the bull (1,700 miles of productive rivers and creeks in the Flathead forest alone). There's autumn hunting for elk and mule deer and whitetails. And there is moseying into uppercase Wilderness, the second largest wilderness complex (the first belongs to Idaho) in the coterminous United States—the Bob, the Great Bear, and the Scapegoat, all sitting high, wide, and handsome up there on the Crown. Trailheads surround the Bob complex on all sides, but more often than not the wilderness portal of outfitters' choice is by way of the Swan.

And finally, though few visitors to the Crown ever get to see one, there are those supreme wild creatures that can prevail only where there *is* a lot of high, wide, and handsome. Namely, the gray wolf and the grizzly bear.

The wolf does not figure as directly as the bear in the story of the Swan—not yet, anyway. The wolf, an endangered species, is making its Montana comeback up on the North and Middle forks of the Flathead, and as the critter spreads south through the Bob it surely will mark its scent on the Swan as well, if it hasn't done so already. As for griz, the great silvertip bear that is listed as threatened, now that's a different situation. Across the Crown of the Continent there are said to be some 440 to 680 grizzlies at large, occupying 5.6 million acres of habitat. More than a third of this habitat—a far larger piece of it than exists even in Glacier Park—overlies much of Flathead National Forest, including the Swan Lake Ranger District. The southern reaches of the Swan, in fact, embrace crucial habitat, in that the bears use this area as a travel corridor between the Bob and the Mission Mountains Wilderness. No one knows for certain exactly how many of the Crown's grizzlies use the Flathead forest as home range; but, based on calculations of what might constitute optimum carrying capacity, the government's Grizzly Bear Recovery Plan has set for the national forest a population goal of 207 animals. The Forest Service hopes to achieve that goal through restrictions on road use and what it construes to be habitat "improvement" techniques.

Unfortunately for those in the Service who must deal with lawsuits and appeals, for litigious greenies so favorably disposed toward griz that they would hug the bear if only it were prudent to do so, and, alas, possibly for the precious bear itself, there is a catch in all of this. The catch is that grizzly habitat in Flathead National Forest happens to overlap 70 percent of the forest's suitable timber base. And while the Service may speak of road closures and management prescriptions calculated to coddle the bear, critics speak of all the new road-building and habitat disruptions that are certain to occur in grizzly country as that suitable timber base is opened to production. This is a troublesome situation. In no time at all it seems that the grizzly bear has become, like the spotted owl of the coastal rainforest, a bio-political punching bag, a pawn of both sides in this war in the woods.

We had more or less come to that conclusion, the silviculturist Barry Bollenbacher and I, standing that afternoon above the lake and the village and looking down the long, well-timbered trough of the Swan. Earlier, I had been talking with one of Bollenbacher's colleagues, Mike Enk, the Forest Service fisheries biologist. I had asked Enk why, of all the national forests in the northern Rockies, Flathead should be the one receiving such a disproportionate share of environmental flak. "It's because of everything we have here," he said, and as he went on I couldn't be sure whether I was listening to Enk the impartial government interpreter, or to Enk the wistful environmental advocate. He said:

"Because here you have the Bob Marshall. You have Glacier Park next-door. You have grizzly bears. You have wolves coming down from Canada. If you can't make a stand and try to maximize a preservation ethic for the natural order of things *here,* then you aren't going to win anywhere. If those are your values, here's your opportunity."

I remembered Enk saying that as I gazed out over the Swan, and suddenly, under its gray-green canopy, I lost count of those 80,000 brand-new average American houses and started looking for 207 grizzly bears.

Over the years the Swan has been host to a number of notable visitors, and one of the very first was the forester Gifford Pinchot. It was early July 1896. Not yet a decade removed from the ivied towers of Yale and the French Forest School at Nancy, Pinchot had come west as secretary to the new National Forest Commission, chartered to report on the present condition and future fate of the western woodlands. There had been a few weeks in the Glacier Country, a bit of hunting with rifle and binoculars, a bighorn ram taken, a grizzly sighted from afar but—as Pinchot regretfully described it—"without getting a shot." Now, with a guide named Jack Monroe ("the best man I have ever carried my pack beside in the woods"), the young dude from Connecticut started on foot up the valley of the Swan. Years later, in his autobiography *Breaking New Ground,* Pinchot would recall a "gorgeous trip" through "a fairyland, in spite of the mosquitoes." He exulted in the pathless woods. He walked among immense western latches—his favorite of all American trees; past towering ponderosa and Douglas firs as big as the Ritz. "Green above but blackened at the base," he'd write, "they told the story of great forest fires. I was seeing this forest in about as intimate a way as it was possible to see it." Life, he went on, was good along Swan River "in them thar days." (Passing strange he felt that way about it; in them thar days that magnificent forest hadn't been put to use yet.)

Before they hurtled the low divide into the Clearwater drainage, Pinchot and Monroe were out of grub, but by and by the forester's rifle resupplied them with venison and bear meat. Alas, "my only bear," he noted without mentioning the species. No matter. Though the arduous hike chalked up but a single bruin, in time the territory surrounding Pinchot's fairyland would be declared a forest reserve (later to be gerrymandered into parts of three national forests, including the Flathead).

After the Swan, Pinchot joined his commission colleagues at Belton, Montana, and set out on another round of explorations. Among the commission's fellow travelers without portfolio was the tall and bearded Californian John Muir. Pinchot was delighted. He was a great admirer of Muir (their famous falling-out would come later). The commissioners and their entourage wandered on through the wooded West—the Bitterroot Valley, the Pend Oreille Country, the Willamette, the Klamath, the Cascades, the Sierra. Muir was a constant delight. But Pinchot was losing patience with the commission's chairman, Charles S. Sargent of Harvard and the Arnold Arboretum, the same Sargent who had helped to engineer that abominable (to Pinchot) Adirondack Forest Preserve, where practical forestry was proscribed to favor "forever wild." In fact, Pinchot found Sargent curiously deficient, in that the chairman didn't "fish or hunt or know anything about the mountains." (Of Pinchot, Sargent would comment in later life: "It is badly on my conscience that I started his career.") Toward the end of that whirlwind season in the West, Pinchot and Muir were to spend an unforgettable day together at the rim of the Grand Canyon. And when they came across a tarantula, Pinchot recalled in his autobiography, Muir wouldn't let him kill it.

Pinchot would never quite understand why the tarantula had as much right as he to prowl the rim of the Grand Canyon. Even after serving as first chief of the Forest Service and principal resource consultant to his blue-blood buddy T. R. Roosevelt, Pinchot would always believe (as he wrote in *The Fight for Conservation* in 1910) that the "first great fact about conservation is that it stands for development. There has been a fundamental misconception that conservation means nothing but the husbanding of resources for future generations. There could be no more serious mistake." Conservation, he went on, demanded "the use of the natural resources now existing on this continent for the benefit of the people who live here now. There may be just as much waste in neglecting the development and use of certain natural resources as there is in their destruction." And why not? Since, according to the gospel of Gifford Pinchot, "the first duty of the human race is to control the Earth it lives upon."

So time marched on—in the Swan, in the rise and fall and rise again of its forest, in the passing parade of notable visitors. Lucky Lindbergh flew in, in the year of his trans-Atlantic triumph. They named a lake for him. The forester Robert Marshall walked in a year later, 1928; hiked a hundred miles from the Jewel Basin to the Chinese Wall at the big divide, then out through the Swan. Marshall was a dissenter from the gospel according to Gifford Pinchot. He knew about tarantulas. They named a wilderness for him.

Pinchot died in 1946 (they named a national forest for *him*). The end of the second war to end all wars, except the war in the woods, was one year old. Smokey the Bear was one year old. He had been conceived as an advertising device to alert the public to the hazards of forest fires. America could not tolerate fires in her forests. The forests were needed to grow houses. Even the Veterans Administration got involved in the postwar need for houses; it financed many of the roads that opened the forests to logging.

Meanwhile, change was sweeping the forest-products industry. Down at the mill strange new words crept into the language: lamination, veneer, plywood, particleboard. As the machinery of processing wood grew more complex, so did the way the industry had to manage its money. Interest rates, banking policies, tax structures, conspired to topple one family business after another (though not Weyerhaeuser's), and soon the timberlands and the mills became concentrated in the hands of huge corporations: Georgia-Pacific and Boise Cascade and Crown Zellerbach and St. Regis Paper and International Paper and Champion International and, by and by, Burlington Northern's Plum Creek.

Meanwhile, too, the Forest Service was about to be caught in a great mistake. The mistake had to do with how much timber might be available, on a sustained-yield basis, in the national forests. The Service had figured on sustaining yields across virtually all of its lands. The Service had not counted on educated critics stepping forward to point out that one cannot wisely harvest timber from marginal sites, from steep slopes or thin soils or places so inaccessible that the cost of getting the logs out would exceed by tenfold the value of the fiber. So presently the Service was obliged to excise great chunks from its suitable timber base, stimulating much bad feeling among loggers and mill workers who had been led to expect that the good times were here forever.

Of course, there were still the corporate lands. And as the flow of federal logs fell off a bit, here came a surge of private logs to keep the workers busy, or at least the workers who still held jobs after high-tech mechanization. Then, it was too early to tell where the companies were heading. Then, who could have guessed how much the Japanese might be willing to pay for American logs, or how quickly some of the U.S. corporations would be eager to accelerate their harvests to the edge of liquidation?

It was too early, then. People didn't think to articulate their behavior in terms of instant gratification. But surely a few must have remembered—and, apparently, believed—the gospel according to Gifford Pinchot.

2. CUMULATIVE EFFECTS

Change a dollar bill into fifty-cent pieces in western Montana and you would do well to remember that one of them, though it looks and feels like silver, was cast somewhere in the process of growing, cutting, and manufacturing wood. That is how tall the timber economy stands on the sundown side of the Big Sky State.

To be sure, there was a slight stoop to timber's stance in the early 1980s, a deceleration of economic growth, a recessionary slump reflected in a number of basic industries throughout Montana and the entire Pacific Northwest. Then, mid-decade, things started looking up. By 1987 production of timber in Montana was greater by nearly a quarter-billion board feet than it had been ten years earlier. This reflected a 20 percent gain over the happy times of the previous decade. As production figures and corporate revenues continued to rise, one might have expected that happy times were here again. And they were—for everyone but the workers. Trouble was, even though more wood was coming out of the forest and into the mills, it was being produced with fewer hands. Specifically, Montana was looking at a quarter-billion board feet more of workable wood, and a woodworking employment base of 2,000 to 2,500 fewer jobs.

How could this possibly be? More wood but fewer jobs? Behind the layoffs and attrition lay a number of causes, but environmental regulations, wilderness "lockups," and other constraints now cited in the trenches were not among them in any significant way. By most accounts, what helped more than anything else to kill those jobs in Montana (and elsewhere in the Northwest) was that usual suspect, the increasingly efficient machine, as well as a change in the configuration of the region's timber base. In a 1987 paper on industry trends, Charles Keegan III and Paul E. Polzin of the University of Montana's Bureau of Business and Economic Research predicted that the use of labor-saving technology and rising output per worker would continue as employment to produce a given product declined. The industry, they noted, "is shifting from large-diameter, old-growth timber to small-diameter, younger timber. Specifically, this means a shift from plywood and large-log sawmills to small-log mills, such as stud mills, to structural reconstituted board plants," and to other processing facilities designed to utilize the smaller stems.

"All of these changes involve fewer workers per unit volume of timber harvested and processed," Keegan and Polzin went on. And not only in the small-log mills that lend themselves to high-tech mechanization; in the woods as well. Taking down big trees has always been a hands-on, labor-intensive proposition, and no doubt will continue to be as long as there are big trees to be taken down. For felling and delimbing, you need your sawyers out there with their chain saws; you need men scrambling through the slash to set the chokers for the skidding. But get yourself into a stand of relatively young lodgepole, as loggers must inevitably do in Montana precincts where the old-growth is long gone, and you aren't messing around anachronistically. You are in there in the cab of your feller-buncher or grapple-skidder, and you alone are doing the work of four men.

Moreover, there is this vexing question of milling capacity. How much is enough; or, as some analysts are beginning to wonder, how much is *too* much? The recession of the early 1980s nudged some Montana mills into capital improvements that not only reduced their labor costs but substantially boosted their capacity for processing logs. One University of Montana study found that lumber milling capacity in the state's nine western-most counties increased nearly 20 percent between 1981 and 1987. And now comes the crunch in supply.

"Some mills won't make it," declared an editorial in the Missoula *Missoulian*. "The industry's own expansion has worsened the supply problem." Citing the sort of trends examined earlier by Keegan and Polzin, the *Missoulian* message concluded: "With the industry's expanded horizons and increased appetite for timber, Montanans must accept the unsettling truth: The wood products industry is in the midst of industrial Darwinism, a life-and-death struggle where only the fittest will survive."

The Market looked upon Plum Creek and saw that it was good. This was in the springtime. This was after the Burlington subsidiary restructured itself as a limited partnership, Plum Creek Timber Company L.P., with substantial tax advantages accruing to it under provisions of the federal tax code and Shearson Lehman Hutton Inc. offering 12,350,000 depositary units, at twenty dollars a share, to investors on the New York Stock Exchange. Though the details of this corporate facelift are extremely complex, the idea itself is quite simple. The idea is to help Plum Creek survive industrial Darwinism in the competitive marketplace of the Pacific Northwest, in order that its shareholders might sing "Happy Days Are Here Again" all the way to their banks.

According to an investment prospectus filed with the Securities and Exchange Commission, Plum Creek is the second largest timberland owner in the Northwest, after Weyerhaeuser—a claim quietly disputed by the public relations people at Champion International, whose accounts list holdings in excess of Plum Creek's nearly 1.5 million acres in Montana, Idaho, Washington, and Oregon. No matter. Whatever its rank, Plum Creek is *big,* with more than 800,000 acres, 5.5 billion board feet of standing timber, 1,300 full-time employees, and $107 million in annual payrolls and payments to independent loggers and other contractors just in Montana alone.

At the time, Plum Creek's manufacturing arm operated five sawmills, two plywood plants, and a medium-density fiberboard plant in Montana, and a sawmill and woodchip plant in Washington State. Over the next few years it expected to invest some $47 million in what it called expansionary capital projects, including a new sawmill in Idaho or eastern Washington to manufacture products designed specifically for the Japanese export market; a new sawmill in Kalispell, Montana, just north of the Swan, to process logs too small for use in a Plum Creek plywood plant nearby; a manufacturing facility near Spokane that would produce such specialty items as laminated posts and items milled to metric specifications (the Orient market, once again), and a substantial increase in the capacity of the medium-density fiberboard plant at Columbia Falls, Flathead Country.

In 1988, Plum Creek reported $90 million in operating income on revenues of $333 million, a gain of some 27 percent over the previous year. Much of the company's good fortune flowed from a "strong demand in the Pacific Rim for export logs" in general, and, in particular, from "a continued high level of residential construction activity in Japan." Nearly half of the company's operating income comes from the sale of logs for export. Most of those logs are harvested from Plum Creek lands in the Washington Cascades; none, it is said by the company, are exported from Montana.

As for the future, Plum Creek couldn't be feeling more bullish. Its announced long-term strategy is to maintain its position in the export log market, continue expanding its manufacturing operations, "reduce harvesting of fee [company] timber as its program of accerlerated harvesting of mature and overmature timber nears completion, and increase the quantity of timber purchased from the U.S. Forest Service and other sources for use as raw material" in the company's mills. Plum Creek's prospectus reveals that such a strategy is based, in part, on the assumption that the company will somehow be able to replace its dwindling supply of fee timber with logs from the national forests and other sources.

Now wait a minute. What exactly does Plum Creek mean when it says it plans to "reduce harvesting of fee timber as its program of accelerated harvesting of mature and overmature timber nears completion"? Does that mean the company is going to end its program of old-growth liquidation because it wants to save some senior timber for a rainy day, or because sooner than later, at the rate it is being cut, there won't be any old-growth left? Before the corporate facelift, company officials liked to say their old-growth in such places as the Swan could keep loggers busy for another ten to twenty years. Now, in the partnership prospectus, we discover exactly how busy in Plum Creek's old-growth the loggers have already been. Of one million company acres in the Rocky Mountain region, only a scant 50,000, or five percent, are still stocked with trees in excess of 21 inches DBH (diameter at breast height). That represents a volume of some 584 million board feet (mbf), or barely nine percent of the company's stumpage. Most of Plum Creek's Rocky Mountain trees are classified as "small sawtimber" (11 to 20.9 inches DBH), and a full third of the volume is on the books as "poletimber." Poletimber may be described as falling more or less into the diametric range of tea saucers and cereal bowls.

And how about this assumption that the company can fill its supply line with logs from the national forests and other sources? Since 1986, on an annual average, the company has utilized 673 million board feet of timber from its own land, and an additional 140 mbf from other sources, including national forests, for an annual total of 813 mbf. Now Plum Creek says the cut from its timberlands will decline to 450 mbf by the mid-1990s. Assuming the company plans to sustain the same level of log sales and manufacturing productivity that carried it in the late 1980s (and let's not forget all those "expansionary" projects anticipating an even greater volume), Plum Creek ten years hence will have to supplement its fee timber with 363 mbf annually from other sources. So much for the demand.

On the supply side, the company says that "the U.S. Forest Service has ten-year harvest plans in the geographic area of the conversion facilities which call for the sale of 550 [mbf] annually." Plum Creek may bid on up to 250 mbf of this volume (the rest being reserved for "smaller" businesses), as well as on 350 mbf available annually from state, tribal, and private lands.

Despite Plum Creek's self-proclaimed "competitive advantage" in the Inland Empire sector of the Pacific Northwest, it would be stretching the limits of probability to assume that the company could ever corner even half of the available pool of 250 mbf of federal logs and 350 mbf from nonfederal sources. After all, Champion International operates in this arena, too; it has a voracious appetite for logs to feed its milling capacity, and its own top-grade timber has been liquidated even more heavily than Plum Creek's. Then there is Louisiana-Pacific, a big player in northern Idaho; L-P owns no timberlands whatsoever; its mills depend entirely on logs from other sources. So let's be reasonable with the Plum Creek assumption and give the company, say, a third of the available other-source logs, or about 200 mbf annually. Not enough? Of course that's not enough. The company is going to need at least 150 mbf a year more than that. Where will it come from?

One place it is unlikely to come from—unless Congress drastically redefines the Forest Service mission—is the federal woods. Though the Bush Administration (in the person of Chief Forester F. Dale Robertson) has been making noise about upping the overall cut, the Service's ten-year harvest plans, which Plum Creek cites with such bullish confidence, are probably unrealistic even as they are. But there is one constraint, one bitter and ironic deprivation, that surely must exasperate a company such as Plum Creek. It is this condition that is known to the Forest Service as *cumulative effects*. It is this sorry condition that prevails when the Service looks upon the checkerboard and sees that a planned timber sale is surrounded by corporate lands laid bare, lands already subjected to "a program of accelerated harvest." Whereupon the Service is obliged to defer or cancel the sale in order to mitigate the adverse impacts that industry has wrought on the abutting lands. Whereupon the national forest's allowable sales quantity is further reduced, there is a shortage of logs to feed the mill, and the corporation, or the limited partnership, has no one to blame but itself.

Jim Fatty II is how they call it—13 million board feet of timber sitting up there on the side of the Mission Mountains, 820 acres in blue-lined patches scattered across ten checkerboard sections, your land and mine, Swan Lake Ranger District, Flathead National Forest. No big deal about the name. Jim's one creek draining the area, Fatty's another. The 13 mbf of Jim Fatty II represents a proposed timber sale listed in an appendix to the Flathead Forest Land and Resource Management Plan. The sale was scheduled. But, alas, schedules are made to be broken. No one knows when, or if, Jim Fatty II will actually be offered for sale. No one knows because there is a strong possibility that Jim Fatty II may be canceled or indefinitely deferred in order to mitigate the cumulative effects of Plum Creek Timber Company's accelerated harvest on adjacent squares of the Swan checkerboard.

For some time now, an interdisciplinary team of Service specialists has been casting a cool eye on the geographic area of Jim Fatty II, trying to assess to what extent the proposed sale might make matters worse. The matter of greatest concern to the specialists is the security of the grizzly bear. The specialists want to know if—given the recent, heavy, extensive cuts on Plum Creek land—bears using this general area can safely afford to lose any more hiding cover. They want to know if the fourteen and a half miles of new roads that would have to be built to give Jim Fatty II proper access might at the same time give the grizzly nothing but fourteen and a half more miles of human encounters and intolerable grief. Beyond the bear, the specialists are looking into hydrological matters; they want to know if increased water yields, or runoff, might be laying irreversible waste to existing stream channels. They want to know if sedimentation is spreading an unacceptable burden into the spawning waters of the westslope cutthroat and the bull trout. There are other matters, other questions. And the likeliest outcome of all of it is that Jim Fatty II will not be sold by the Forest Service, not all 13 mbf of it, not this year, not next, not until time and regeneration have put Plum Creek's cutouts together again.

It is important to understand that timber managers and loggers on private lands in Montana are not obliged to worry about the constraints of a forest-practices act. Unlike most timber states, Montana does not have a forest-practices act. It has only what is known to the trade as BMPs, Best Management Practices, gentlemanly agreements (in principle, if not in practice) to walk softly and carry a big chain saw. BMPs have one thing in common with forest plans and timber sale schedules. They are made to be broken.

In October 1988 a series of articles, entitled "Montana Timber: Surviving the Cut," appeared in the *Missoulian* under the byline of Dick Manning, one of the Northwest's—one of the nation's—top environmental reporters. Manning had cast his net upon the 1.7 million acres owned by Plum Creek and Champion International in western Montana. His catch: that boardroom decisions were driving both companies "to liquidate their old-growth timber faster than it could grow back," that the accelerated harvest programs of the two giants would "leave a gap in the region's timber supply and cause bigger trouble for small mills," and that large clearcuts and skid trails on steep slopes were depleting topsoil, degrading stream quality, and wrecking wildlife habitat throughout the region. Random inspections, he reported, had found "some departures" from BMPs at all logging sites visited, and "major departures" at an average of one out of three. Among major departures noted in Manning's own tour-and-flyover of the area were tractor incursions on streambeds and "large clearcuts on fragile slopes" near the headwaters of Jim Creek. The response from Plum Creek was that its management prescriptions were silviculturally sound.

I had hoped to get into or over the Jim Fatty myself, but it was springtime in the Swan and there had been some late snow. The ground was unfriendly to mountain travel; the sky, un-kindly to chartered planes. So one morning I drove north past where the Fatty flows into the Swan and met a man who offered to get me into the next drainage at least, up Woodward Creek. Man named Jack Whitney from Bigfork, a founding father of the Flathead Audubon Society.

A person doesn't get too far in Flathead Country before someone's telling him to check out Jack Whitney. "He's the *authentic* old-timer," a woman down at Seeley Lake had told me. "He knows the Swan better than some of the animals do." Whitney denied that when I caught up with him, but allowed he probably had more time than most critters to get acquainted with the territory, since he'd been prowling it for more than sixty years. These woods here on the Mission side, he'd come to know in 1934. The Great Depression was rattling cages then, so Whitney packed up a blanket, a fly rod, and a pistol and came up here to live off the land. For cash to buy what he couldn't hook, shoot, or dig, he picked huckleberries and sold them, four bits a gallon, to a woman who ran a lodge down in the valley. "You wouldn't believe the size of the spruce and the fir in here then," he said. We were prowling the logging roads in his pickup, in a patchwork area where sections of Montana state forest are inter-spersed with Plum Creek lands. We saw eroded gullies, silt in the streambeds, great windrows of slash waiting to be put to the torch. We saw two elk and one whitetail deer. We stopped for lunch; I hadn't brought any, so Whitney shared his sandwich. Showed me his favorite knife, too, made to his specifications by a Laplander Finn in Bonner, the blade forged from the steel fender of a 1937 Studebaker. We drove on. Patches of forest, patches of cut. State patches, Plum Creek patches.

Presently he pulled the pickup to a stop beside a clearcut that ran up over a low ridge and down across a swale to the edge of Woodward Creek. For a Plum Creek operation, this one did not seem to be an especially large cut, not like some I had seen in aerial photos, not like the whoppers of three or four hundred acres that Dick Manning and others had observed. To my eye, it simply appeared devastated. Then Whitney rolled down the driver's-side window and said, "This was about as beautiful and pristine a forest as you've ever seen."

I suppose I'll never forget what was in his voice when he said that, or how he sat there at the wheel, staring at the cut, saying nothing. And I can't even begin to guess how long it was before Jack Whitney finally put his truck in gear and drove the silent two of us away from that place.

In December 1985 the Flathead National Forest Land and Resource Management Plan rolled off the copy machines at nearly 560 pages. The Plan had been five years in the making. It projected a menu of management directions for the forest over the next ten years. It declared that at the end of the first decade "there will have been only minimal change in the overall appearance of the Forest." The Plan was quite certain on this point, even though it went on to explain that some five hundred miles of new logging roads would be built in order that one billion board feet of timber—at the rate of 100 mbf a year—might be removed to market from some 66,000 acres scheduled for sales. Some of these sales, of course, would involve old-growth timber; but the Plan said not-to-worry, there would still be enough old-growth left in 1995 to meet the needs of old-growth critters. What's more, threatened and endangered species would be better off in 1995, their habitats having been "enhanced." And fish habitat enhanced, too, and elk; and the capacity for dispersed recreation and trails brought up to snuff; and more than 90,000 acres of roadless area proposed for wilderness, and maybe triple that acreage "planned for permanent roadless management" (though, alas, other roadless acreage would eventually be roaded "as timber growth matures"). In short, here was a forest plan with something for everyone. And right off the bat almost everyone appealed it.

There were thirty-nine appellants, both individuals and organizations. Two of the organizations represented commercial interests. They said in effect that the volume of timber proposed for sale was too small. Eight of the organizations or coalitions of organizations represented environmental or recreational interests. Some of these said in effect that the volume of timber proposed for sale was too much, insofar as its harvest would surely have an adverse impact on threatened species, roadless areas, and ancient trees. The Forest Service responded to these appeals with a paper storm. The regional forester in Missoula reviewed the arguments and posted his findings to the Chief in Washington, D.C. From Washington, the Chief ruled in favor of some appellant issues and dismissed others. Win a few, lose a few. Five of the environmental organizations were not content to lose a few. They went to court.

To the U.S. District Court in Helena came Resources Limited, Inc., of Polebridge, Montana, up on the North Fork of Flathead; Swan View Coalition of Kalispell; Friends of the Wild Swan, based at Swan Lake; Five Valleys Audubon Society of Missoula, acting independently of its sister chapter, Flathead Audubon, which is not a party to the suit, and the Sierra Club. Naming Chief F. Dale Robertson, Regional Forester John Mumma, and Flathead Forest Supervisor Edgar B. Brannon, Jr., as defendants, the plaintiffs asked the court for declaratory and injunctive relief from the Flathead National Forest Land and Resource Management Plan. The Plan, they told the court, "is a prescription for disaster." In it, they said, the Forest Service proposed to "extend its program of clearcuts and roads into fragile, steep-sloped areas," to "liquidate most of the remaining old-growth forest," and to pursue a timber sale program "that [would] result in a taking of the grizzly bear and gray wolf" in violation of the Endangered Species Act. In its request for relief, the plantiffs asked the court to remand the Flathead Plan to the

Forest Service for extensive revision and enjoin the Service from any further road construction or harvest activities in bear or wolf habitat. Last I heard, efforts at mediation had broken down and Edgar Brannon was reported to be saying that a negotiated settlement of the Flathead lawsuit no longer seemed possible.

3. SCOPING

Scoping around in the Flathead Country one day, I came to the conclusion that it is not quite true there are two sides to every story. Out here, *this* story, there are three or four or five or six. It occurred to me, listening to folks talk about the various effects that are accumulating in the forest and at the mill, and maybe, too, around the fabric of their daily lives, that I had somehow drifted onto the set of a Rocky Mountain *Rashomon*—that old Japanese tale, a classic motion picture, in which different narrators re-create, from the bias of their individual perceptions, the disputed circumstances of a phantasmagoric rape.

I had thought I might find unanimity among the loggers, at least. Sure, underneath their suspenders they tend to be an independent lot, but weren't they all pretty much in the same trench? Forget all those high-flown environmental or marketplace arguments calculated to sway the Chief or the judge or the editorial writer; weren't the loggers and their blue-collar buddies down at the mill the ones whose livelihoods were on the firing line? Didn't they all believe to the very last man and woman of them that, between the corporations overcutting their lands and the conservationists forcing the Forest Service to undersell the federal lands, the workers were out on some Godforsaken kind of breakable limb? Yes? Well, not quite. Out on a limb, yes. Lousy conservationists, yes. A roll-over Forest Service, yes. But culpable corporations, no. That was something most loggers preferred not to talk about; and understandably, too, since corporations hire them as independents to harvest their trees.

One Swan Valley logger I spoke with went a little further than most. I mean in the corporate direction. I had been told otherwise; that, with his whole family active in the business and a fortune tied up in machines, he would freely speak of his fear for the future, of his dreadful suspicion that when Plum Creek had taken all it could from the Swan there wouldn't be a future left to fear. If that indeed is the way the man once felt, it appeared he had changed his mind by the time I got to him. The bleak prospect wasn't Plum Creek's fault, or Champion's, he told me. It wasn't greed or market forces driving the companies to cut so fast and heavy. It was *the regulations*. It was the environmentalists always pushing for tougher regulations. BMPs were not good enough; now they wanted a forest-practices act. So the companies had to get what they could now, because if they waited around, why the tougher regulations would simply make it too expensive to get the wood out. The logger said he'd prefer I didn't use his name, and I promised I wouldn't. Not because I thought anything but anonymity might get him in trouble; I promised not to use his name because I had the distinct feeling that the good man didn't half-believe what he was telling me.

Then there was the renegade logger from the Crazy Mountains—renegade because he does not adhere to the commercial party line. Keith Brandemihl's the name, and he said I could use it, since he'd already blown his cover long ago. I met him one morning at Seeley Lake, just south of the Swan, and we drove up the highway to Condon, my first time into the valley, then back again, talking. Brandemihl said he did some woods work out of Seeley, winters and springtime, then jumped over the big divide to his place in the Crazies near Livingston, where he spends a lot of time trying to stop the U.S. Forest Service from developing a roadless area. Brandemihl said:

"People are blind to the facts. They hear the mill owners say that wilderness is going to cost society a lot of jobs, and they believe it. People here don't seem to want to look into their own future. I'm a sixth-generation Montanan and a third-generation logger, and there's a responsibility that comes with that. You have to be responsible for trying to keep Montana *Montana*. It bothers me that the big profits made on our resources go out of Montana to Stamford, Connecticut, for example, and Seattle, Washington. Timber is a multimillion-dollar industry in western Montana, yet most of the people who are doing the real work aren't sharing the profits. They're just barely earning a living."

Then there was the other Keith, in Kalispell. Keith Olson, executive director of the Montana Logging Association. Olson said:

"Look. Congress gave the Forest Service the National Forest Management Act, the Resource Conservation Act, the National Environmental Policy Act, the Clean Water Act, Clean Air Act, Threatened and Endangered Species Act, Wild and Scenic Rivers, ad infinitum. Each and every one of these acts produced literally hundreds of issues which the environmental community can turn around and say, 'Hey! You're in violation of this act because. . . .' I don't know that the Forest Service can ever again be a prudent steward of the land if they're going to have to follow the manual. We've taken the forester out of the forest. We've put him behind a desk with a book of rules and a computer."

Olson said: "You know, we tend to forget a simple fact. Trees grow. They're growing every day and every year. In Montana, we have the opportunity to grow a generation of trees for every generation of people. The companies might sell their lands, but they can't take them with them. The land's going to be here. Are they going to grow trees or condominiums? I don't know. But if we let them, they'll grow trees. And if we manage them, they'll grow trees in a generation."

Olson said: "Okay. The case can be made that the corporations are overharvesting their timberlands. They are managing for the bottom line. On the other side of the equation is the Forest Service, which is underharvesting its lands. They are managing for public opinion. So, if the corporations are managing the bottom line and the Forest Service is managing public opinion, the obvious question is—who the hell is managing the forest?"

If the people who live in the rural communities of the Inland Empire could choose by ballot their candidate for Man of the Year, I'd bet the winner—by a landslide in logging and mill communities—would be this hombre Bruce Vincent from Libby, Montana. Libby lies west from the Flathead a-hundred-and-some miles, but Vincent's reputation reaches easily across the distances in every direction. You want to check out King of the Log Hauls, Top Gun in the Trenches, Darling of the Dirty Hands People, just swap the Flathead for the Kootenai and get on over and visit with Bruce Vincent. He's waiting in his office.

Check him out good: the boyish looks, the curly black hair, the sorrowful blue eyes, the voice of the Regular Guy, the home-spun veneer to cloak his education. In a month of Sundays, Central Casting could not have found a better candidate to fill the part that Vincent has played upon the stage of the woods war. Of course Central Casting wasn't consulted. The role was created for Vincent by the timber industry.

Bruce Vincent is the "founder" and director of Communities for a Great Northwest, an organization that likes to be identified not with industry—heaven forbid that we blow *that* cover—but with the grass roots. The first roots appeared in Libby. And then, through a series of awareness events, they spread beyond the Inland Empire to such communities as Grants Pass and Mill City and Sweet Home, in Oregon, and Forks, out on the Olympic Peninsula of Washington State. Bruce Vincent himself is a native of Oregon and a graduate of Gonzaga University in Spokane, Washington, where he studied civil engineering and business administration, though political science was his real passion and apparently still is. He has been in Libby for only five years, he and his three brothers—"us four boys and Dad," he likes to say in his down-home style—all partners in the Vincent Logging Company, which employs thirty to thirty-five people, "most of 'em cousins." Vincent Logging builds roads and cuts timber in the Kootenai National Forest and on the corporate lands of Champion International and the limited partnership known as Plum Creek.

In his little office off Main Street in Libby, Vincent says: "There are three steps to every movement. Awareness. Education. Action. We're still working on the first. For our side to even make the press we have to put on a dog and pony show. Earth First! can put three guys outside the forest supervisor's office and get the networks to cover it. We have to send for three hundred trucks."

Last year Vincent and his backers sent for almost that many trucks to haul logs into Dillon, in the Beaverhead Country, where a local mill was said to be on the verge of shutting down for lack of timber. The Great Northwest Log Haul, they called it; and while it didn't begin to solve the timber problem, it was a huge success in cracking the media. Later, logging trucks from throughout the four-state region would roll into Missoula and Seattle and Portland and Salem and Eugene, hauling the grass-roots word to cityfolk hoodwinked by tree-hugging environmentalists.

Bruce Vincent says: "I think they really believe—the leadership of these environmental organizations—that the only way to conserve is to *preserve*. The only way they see to keep man's evil filthy stinking hands from ruining the land forever-and-ever-amen is to lock man out and put it into wilderness. Look, we want clean air, too. We want clean water. We want that stuff. We got to have it. But *they* say we only have two choices. You either lock it up, or you destroy it. That's the choice they give us every night on television, like there's no in between."

In between is where Bruce Vincent would like very much to appear to be. Unfortunately, there are problems with that. "One of the biggest problems," he says, "is what I call Capital-*I* Industry. For too long people have put us over with them, and that's misleading. The two sides that have argued these issues before the Congress have been Capital-*I* Industry [the big corporations] and the national environmental organizations. And they stand around beating each other about the head and shoulders. But we're the ones—the loggers and mill workers, their families, their rural communities—who are bleeding in the middle. We live here. Our home office isn't Stamford, Connecticut. Our home office is twelve miles south of town. We drink the water, we breathe the air, we look at the mountains, we hunt the game, fish for the fish. We're the ones in the middle, and it hurts."

Vincent's effort to distance himself and his organization from the Capital-*I* people crumbles in the light of their common goal.

The goal is to up the ante in the national forests (or at least to keep it from going down) in order that Vincent might assure a continuum of work for his constituents, who sweat for their bread, while Capital-*I* looks after the flow of dividends to its own folks, who merely clip coupons. Industry lobbyists in Washington, D.C., speak admiringly of the Montanan and recommend him as a source of regional wisdom and common sense. Moreover, Vincent has received honoraria for speaking engagements before industry groups; and, in an interview early this year with the *Missoulian* writer Dick Manning, was reported to have identified the timber industry as the source of his group's "major dollars." By the time I get to Libby, Vincent is estimating Capital-*I*'s contribution at only 10 percent of income. Membership fees (twenty dollars for the individual, fifty dollars for a business), he pegs at about 40 percent. And the rest, he says, comes from checkoffs.

It works like this: Logging contractor signs an authorization form saying that the mill where he delivers may deduct one-tenth of a percent of his payment for a truckload of logs and forward it to Bruce Vincent's Communities for a Great Northwest. According to Vincent, the piecework average is about "a buck a truck." All the administrative costs of deducting these monies from a contractor's paycheck, and then forwarding them to Vincent in Libby, are borne by the mill. Some are lowercase-*m* mills. Some are not. Some are owned by Champion and Plum Creek. Capital-*C* on the Champion, please, and a Capital-*C* on the Creek.

In his office at Libby, Vincent looks especially sorrowful as he segues suddenly from checkoffs to Earth First! He says: "Tempers are getting short. Those Earth Firsters and their war against the Dirty Hands People. No getting around *that*. That's what we are. It's the Dirty Hands People who built America, the real Americans who shed real tears and bleed real American blood. Those spikes the Earth Firsters put in trees. Those aren't aimed at Boise Cascade. They're aimed at the faces of my brothers. We are so afraid, so afraid somebody from our side is going to lash out."

In a society that might elect Bruce Vincent Man of the Year, the opposite honor, Most Wanted, would probably go to an hombre who calls himself a friend of the Wild Swan, namely Steve Kelly. Matter of fact, Steve Kelly *is* Friends of the Wild Swan, since it really isn't a membership organization we're dealing with here, but rather a cadre of financial supporters, a few close friends, a post office box in Swan Lake, a telephone wherever he can find one, a battered typewriter for rapping out the newsletters and alerts, and the man himself, who holds the greatest disdain for two of America's most venerable institutions—the U.S. Forest Service, and that segment of the national conservation community which is headquartered in big East Coast cities and which, in Kelly's view, exhibits a certain "predatory" chauvinism toward shoestring efforts such as his. On the greatest-disdain count alone, if not for other reasons, some of Kelly's grudging admirers and unabashed foes believe the man is a member of Earth First!—a notion he deflects by noting that Earth First! is not a membership organization either, though he does acknowledge writing occasional pieces for its tabloid, as well as sharing much of its institutional point of view. For example, Kelly tells me:

"Timber is all the Forest Service really thinks about. They go out to do anything and they have to start with 'How many trees are we going to cut?' Then everything else has to fit that plan, support those numbers. It's a fraud, that's what it is. They're promising things they know they can't produce."

Kelly tells me: "They [the Forest Service] like to say they support local communities. Well, that's bull. They support stock markets. When they start putting out small sales, let people bid on timber in small quantities—I mean the prime stuff, ten, twenty acres—then you'll see competitive bidding and small loggers making the investment to be small loggers. But the Forest Service won't let that happen. They claim it's cost-ineffective to set up these small sales; that with people like me bitching so much about environmental impact, they couldn't possibly do an analysis on a small sale and keep up with all the work. That's what they say. But basically all they really care about is feeding the large mills."

To feed himself, not to mention his passion for downhill skiing wintertimes, Kelly works the warmer months as a tree planter in the national forests. This would be tantamount to consorting with the enemy were it not for the fact that Kelly hires out to an independent contractor from Whitefish, and thus has the satisfaction of knowing that at least some of the Smokey Bear taint will have been laundered from his earnings.

One stormy spring day, with the help of Swan Ranger District silviculturist Barry Bollenbacher and Joe Yates, who heads up the district's reforestation operations, I tracked Steve Kelly to a planting site over near Stoner Creek, in the so-called Island Unit, south of Kalispell. A crew of six was working its way uphill through a thirty-acre clearcut, Kelly, in the lead, the point man—bending low and swinging his hoe-dad hard into the planting hole and then reaching back to take a larch or a fir seedling from the tree bags on his backside and then tamping it home, each at a ten-foot interval. I followed his progress for a spell. He said the pay was good and the work was hard, and that that was the way he liked it. Liked working with hand tools. Liked swinging the hoe-dad. Liked the spike maul better. A steel gang gauge spiker he'd been, working on the railroad. Which one, I wanted to know.

"Burlington Northern," he said. "Up at Marias Pass."

I said, "I guess you're not proud."

He said, "Just greedy. Good money. It bought me my place in the Swan."

"What'd you like so much about the spike maul?"

"Oh, I don't know. Hand-eye coordination game, I guess. If you're good at hitting the spike, they put you on the job where you hit the spike. There's some accomplishment to that. You got thirty guys on a gang, and you get to be the spiker because you're the best."

For a young man raised in the somewhat tamer precincts of the Northeast, Kelly's resumé seems to run toward the most unlikely western work. Worked in an Inland Empire mill for Louisiana-Pacific. Worked at learning the hotel and restaurant trade in Denver, only to wind up as camp cook at a Forest Service timber-cruising outpost on the North Fork Flathead, and eighteen mouths to feed.

I said, "Did you poison any of them?"

He said, "No dammit. I fed them too well."

The weather scrubbed reforestation work the following day, so Kelly and I met for coffee at Bigfork and drove on down into the Swan. He wanted to show me his place back in the woods, and I wanted to find out what it was about the Swan that had him so all-fired friendly to protect it.

"I wanted a good place to live," he said. "I spent a whole year looking, went all over Montana. I had a checklist. I was looking for trees, seclusion, and no expectation of further growth. I looked around Ennis, West Glacier, Whitefish. But I couldn't find what I was looking for. Not until I came to the Swan. The Swan was the best. It's the finest valley I've ever been in." At Swan Lake Village he turned his pickup off the highway, and we followed a dirt road east toward the Crest. "We got in here on the last bad subdivision," he said. "I mean 'bad' in the good sense—nobody in their right mind would want to move up here. There was some talk at the time of a ski development. I figured, well, even if I lose, I win, since I like to ski. But I certainly wouldn't support that now. I'd fight it. The ski business isn't into skiing anymore. It's into real estate. Scams and golf courses. Skiing is just the excuse to rip it all up a little more."

Kelly parked his truck on the crown of a small rise, and we walked the rest of the way, past a garden where his wife, Kathy Togni, an undergraduate at the university in Missoula, had started an early planting of flowers and vegetables. Beyond the garden a two-story log house rose at the edge of the forest. In a little way and it was the Flathead National Forest. The regenerated forest, I suddenly remembered, for Kelly's place sits hard by the site where the pioneer lumberjacks notched their first virgin trees in the teens of the twentieth century. "Well, it's not quite old-growth," I said, "but you found your trees."

Inside, Kelly rummaged around for some papers he wanted

to share with me—Friends of the Wild Swan broadsides, law-suit addenda pertaining to the Flathead Forest. Then he showed me some of his other homework, since he's been studying at the university in Missoula, too. Though not law; fine arts. Oil on canvas and wood sculpture. Some pieces in the primitive style; others, surreal. I was especially taken by one of the oils. It depicted the Swan Front all covered with snow, as a downhill skiier might like to see it. Or as a lover might like to see it in a dream. Across the mid-slope of the range there appeared, in the hottest of reds, a pair of detached lips parted in anticipation of a lingering kiss.

"You really don't want to see any timber harvest at all, do you?" I said, staring at the painting.

Kelly said, "That's not what I'm saying. I'm not saying the Forest Service shouldn't log where they already have roads. I'm saying I'm not going to tolerate any more pioneering into roadless areas. No more."

"Is that your bottom line?"

Kelly said, "I don't get attached to bottom lines."

Before Edgar B. Brannon, Jr., no landscape architect had ever been placed in charge of a national forest. Brannon, a Rutgers graduate, broke through the unwritten code favoring timber managers for top posts in 1984, after about fifteen years of landscape and planning work with the U.S. Forest Service, some career grooming at Harvard's Kennedy School of Government, and a tour of duty as deputy supervisor of White Mountain National Forest in New Hampshire. Now, as supervisor of the Flathead Forest, Edgar Brannon seems well pleased with what his background has wrought—an appreciation of nonutilitarian values, a respect for the necessity of tradition, and a strong conviction, despite all the appeals and complaints rattling his stand, that he has brought his forest unswervingly around to what he likes to call a "centrist position."

We are sitting in his office in the headquarters building at Kalispell. On the coffee table lies a copy of the Harvard alumni magazine. On the wall hangs a photographic portrait of a Yale man who looks suspiciously like Gifford Pinchot. It *is* Gifford Pinchot! And Edgar Brannon seems well pleased to have him aboard. "You know," he says, "Pinchot and John Muir started as friends."

Yes, I have heard about that.

"And then parted. Too bad."

Perhaps.

"The break with Muir is still with us," he says. "Preservation versus wise use. Now, Pinchot was definitely one for wise use." My eyes have left the picture and I am looking at Brannon. "Of course," he says, "we recognize that values change. And so does the Forest Service."

Perhaps.

Brannon had thought that the Flathead Plan would sail straight through without a hitch. It didn't. By his own estimate, no forest plan—and there are 156 national forests in the system—received so many appeals as the Flathead's. "The thing is," he is saying now in his office, "the people who led the appeals, almost all of them, never saw a copy of the draft plan, never saw the final, never were involved. And all of a sudden they show up with appeals." He leans back in his chair, under the unsmiling visage of Gifford Pinchot, and says:

"In my opinion, the emergence of the Swan View Coalition and Friends of the Wild Swan is reflected in many parts of the country where you find new groups that are more ideological in their viewpoints and harder-lined than the old ones. They're all various spinoffs of the Earth First!—Deep Ecology movement. And those issues are much more difficult to deal with because a part of their concern is environmental in the classical sense, a concern with impacts on the physical environment, but there's that other part that is philosophic and theologic in nature. I used to think I was real good at negotiating these things, but I've been a miserable failure in some areas because I was not prepared to deal with all the energy behind this movement, this commitment, this sense of no-compromise. I don't think we could ever go far enough with this plan to satisfy them."

Brannon says: "I read some of the stuff about me put out by

Friends of the Wild Swan and Swan View Coalition and I think, 'Hey, I must be the Prince of Darkness.' My mother shouldn't even read this stuff. It's part of the game. When I first came out here I went to all their gatherings, and they used to give me their 'secret documents' as proof of what you might call the Forest Service's crimes against nature. I was quite shocked by this stuff. But as I began to look into these things, I found the situations were quite different from what they were putting out. And over time, they could see that I wasn't one of *them*. So, I became a part of the problem."

There is another part of the problem, the timber supply. Brannon says: "It's hard to sort out. But if in fact the private lands are being cut out, then surely we'll see a major disruption of the market. There won't be enough wood to go around. It's going to close mills. It's going to create social and economic chaos. There will be political pressures accompanying the companies' desire to get some quick fix."

But what, I ask, if you could meet the sales targets in your forest plan, 100 mbf a year? Would there still be a regional timber shortfall?

Brannon says: "Yes. Of course. For a couple of reasons. First, there has been a substantial increase in the private harvest over what was anticipated in our early planning process. For that we can blame the strong market. Second, some of our assumptions about the availability of federal timber are proving to be not very accurate. The volume is there, but it's the *process* we have to go through, the litigation, the tradeoffs, and now the changing values. What was acceptable ten years ago is not so acceptable now. People don't want to look at clearcuts. The Swan Valley used to be populated by farmers and loggers. They never protested the cuts. Now the place is all mixed up with retirees, summer folk, professionals moving in—the kind of people who don't like to look at clearcuts."

One day at Columbia Falls, where the Plum Creek Timber Company maintains three mills and its headquarters staff for the Rocky Mountain Region, I called on William J. Parson, director of operations, and since I was scoping, we talked for a while of such things as supply and demand and limited partnerships and industrial Darwinism. Parson did not care to spend much time on the latter topic, possibly because I wanted to know if economic survival might include the mom-'n'-pop mill owner as well as Plum Creek. "Well," he said, "it's a competitive situation." Next question.

My next question had to do with cumulative effects as perceived from the company's point of view, in the Flathead Forest in particular.

"There are a couple of areas where we've agreed to defer some harvest of our own," Parson said. "But for the most part we think that Forest Service allegations of cumulative effects or adverse impacts on wildlife or water quality are unproven. They have not been able to demonstrate to us or to others that they have justification for deferring their harvest because of the harvest we are conducting."

Then was the Forest Service playing to the environmental community?

"Yes, partly. There is certainly outside pressure on the Forest Service to do something different than what it has traditionally done. Then there's an internal problem. They have become very specialist-oriented. Now you have your wildlife biologist, your hydrologist, your fisheries person, archeologist, landscape architect."

Like Ed Brannon?

"He's a nice guy, though. Anyway, you take all these specialists looking at a timber sale or road project, you add them all up, their individual perspectives, and what you've got are cumulative *constraints*. To the point where the Forest Service is tied up in knots."

Next question: Why was Plum Creek seemingly so insensitive to the public's aversion to clearcuts, as in the recent cut on the Holland Lake Road, all stumps and slash right up to the edge? Why no buffer?

"We have nothing to hide, no secrets. We think what we're doing is responsible, professional forest management. There's nothing here to be ashamed of. We are reforesting our lands. People ought to know where their forest products come from."

It occurred to me that William Parson was not the sort of a man who concedes many points. In fact, I caught him conceding only one. He said, "Our industry has not done a good job of telling our story to the public." I was especially glad to hear him say that, if only because I have never heard anyone even remotely connected with the timber industry say otherwise. In any event, Parson believed that storytelling help would soon be on the way in the form of a new national organization called the American Forest Resource Alliance. The Alliance would promote the idea of using forest resources instead of locking them up. Not that this message was all that *new;* the American Forest Council and the National Forest Products Association (the industry's two principal trade associations, and now the chief backers of the Alliance) had been preaching the sermon of *use* for years, though without much success in converting any appreciable number of nonbelievers. The Alliance, however, would carry the effort at least one step further. It would get into the business of building coalitions, seeking "grass roots support" in rural communities dependent on timber.

Now that was really interesting, I said, because wasn't this— on a national scale—exactly what Bruce Vincent's Communities for a Great Northwest was trying to do on a regional basis? Parson did not care to spend much time on this topic. He said that trying to link Bruce Vincent to the corporate sector of the timber industry was just blowing smoke.

Oh? But how about that checkoff system that, to a large degree, was helping Bruce Vincent build his coalitions throughout the Great Northwest? A buck a truck. The money was being collected for Vincent by Plum Creek, right here in Columbia Falls, was it not? Whereupon the director of Plum Creek's Rocky Mountain operations looked me square in the eye and said: "I am not familiar with that process. You'll have to talk to Vincent about that." Next question.

Did he think that the press had been treating the industry in general, and Plum Creek in particular, fairly?

No, he did not. He said: "The press tries to tell the story, 'Gee, if you cut the trees it's bad for wildlife, all the dirt runs down the hill and gets in the crick and the fish all die.' That's what they say. Now that Dick Manning over at the *Missoulian*. He just puts out smoke. He has a hidden agenda. He buys his ink by the barrel. He's a . . . you know . . . he's a known environmentalist."

Well, look, I said. You must see the *Missoulian's* publisher from time to time, one businessman to another. What does *he* say when you complain about Manning and his barrel of ink?

"We have had some discussions," Bill Parson said. "And I'll leave it at that."

About two months after our meeting, I telephoned Parson and asked him about those discussions he had had with the *Missoulian's* publisher. I wanted to know more, I said, because I had just heard that Dick Manning was no longer with the newspaper, having quit when informed by his editors that he would no longer be covering the natural resources beat. Parson denied that he had spoken with the publisher. He said he had been referring to two Plum Creek executives from Seattle who were "fed up" with the *Missoulian*—and with Manning in particular—and had called at the newspaper to register a complaint with the editor. The editor, Brad Hurd, told me it would be untrue and insulting for anyone to imply that Manning was to have been reassigned to a different beat because of pressure from Plum Creek, the timber industry, or the business community of Western Montana.

4 . POSTURING

The decibel level is rising in Montana. One cannot pick up a newspaper, or tune in the traveler's radio news, that there isn't another gauntlet tossed, a broadside unleashed. Here now is Keith Olson, director of the Montana Logging Association. I had found Olson, when we talked early in the spring, to be a reasonable man. What a difference a season can make. Now, if I read him correctly in the *Kalispell News,* he is full of feist and anger. Olson is saying that if preservationists really want to bring more tourists to the region (tourism being the preservationists' conventional economic substitute for timber), then they should "promote the construction of a road down the middle of the Bob Marshall [Wilderness]." Take that. He is saying that if people really want no-impact timber management, they should "quit buying the resources the forest provides." And take—"if you want to save the forest, quit buying toilet paper"—that.

Here are letters to the editor of the *Missoulian*. Here's one from a fellow down in Darby, saying that Earth First! wants to put him and his kind of people out of business. (In Montana, and elsewhere, Earth First! has become the catchall for the entire U.S. environmental community.) And who are his people? Why, they're "the hardworking, sweating, taxpaying, western Montana families that have been harvesting and planting trees for the last one hundred years" and who think "the Bitterroot Mountains look damn good for having been harvested."

Sometimes the posturing goes beyond the slogans and chest-thumping. Keith Hammer, who heads up the Swan View Coalition, has lost his mailbox to vandals three times. The first box was merely knocked down. The second and third were blown apart, presumably by cherry bombs.

Malicious mischief is getting around in all directions. Flathead Forest Supervisor Edgar Brannon awoke one morning to find "Wanted" posters tacked to the trees in front of his home. On another occasion there were reports that the trees themselves were in jeopardy: Earth First! types were said to be prescribing a clearcut for Brannon's front yard. Apparently the cut was canceled. Or perhaps it has only been deferred.

Brannon's other front yard, outside forest headquarters in Kalispell, figured in another woods-war episode a while back. The incident illustrates to what extent the mention of Earth First! can trigger a kind of reflexive paranoia among U.S. foresters. It was the anniversary of John Muir's birth, and somebody at Earth First! had put out the word nationwide that it might be fun to celebrate the occasion demonstrating in front of forest headquarters here and there. The suggestion caught the attention of Keith Hammer of the Swan View Coalition, who, like Steve Kelly of Friends of the Wild Swan, is a sometime reader of, and editorial contributor to, the Earth First! newspaper. Hammer assembled a group of about twenty people, brushed up a song-and-dance routine ("No-no-no-no-more-clearcuts da-da-da!") to be performed in front of Flathead headquarters, and arranged to retire to a city park nearby for the celebratory picnic. The group included a number of children, a woman from the Bigfork Chamber of Commerce, and Richard Kuhl, a member of Flathead Audubon and seasonal wilderness ranger for the Forest Service, among other individuals unlikely to qualify as bona fide Earth Firsters. Kuhl earlier that morning had been inside the headquarters building on another matter and had noticed three "uneasy-looking" men standing in the lobby. One of them he recognized as a law enforcement man from the regional office in Missoula. "Hey," Kuhl asked, "what's going on?" The uneasy ones replied: "There's going to be a demonstration by Earth First!" Kuhl recalls what happened next:

"All during the time we were there they were filming us. When we got through singing our songs, we went back to the park, about two hundred yards away. You looked over there and you saw these guys watching us through binoculars, and then one came out of the building with a video camera and came over and videoed us while we were eating our picnic lunch in the city park. He took direct closeups of our faces, obviously for someone's files. Well, I got so mad about this I requested a copy of that video under the Freedom of Information Act, and I got it. It's a cheap way to get a print of yourself and friends at a picnic. All you have to do is sing a song in front of a forest headquarters, and the Forest Service will make the video to put your face in somebody's file, and then you demand a copy under F.O.I. And you get it."

Yet ultimately, way out there beyond poses and threats and pranks and paranoia, lurks the meanest act of them all—the spiking of trees. This is the worst sort of eco-terrorism. It is hostage taking. The trees are hostage to the spikes. Try to free these trees, the spikers are saying in effect, and the blade of your chain saw will shatter into a thousand pieces of shrapnel; or, if we miss you in the woods, our spike will get you in the mill, turning your band saw into grape shot. (No one in Montana or Idaho has yet been killed or injured in such a fashion.)

In April 1989, officials at Clearwater National Forest headquarters in Orofino, Idaho, received a letter signed "George Hayduke." Hayduke is the fictional ringleader of Edward Abbey's *Monkey Wrench Gang*. Almost everyone at Clearwater headquarters already knew *that*. What they didn't know, until the letter arrived, was that *this* Hayduke and some pals had just spent nine days driving five hundred pounds of ten-inch spikes into the trees of a proposed timber sale along the Lochsa River. The Forest Service confirmed the spiking *in situ*. Hayduke's letter was postmarked Missoula. There has been an investigation. Indictments are pending.

Before taking leave of the Swan last time out, I poked off the highway near Condon to call on Bud and Janet Moore, proprietors of some eighty acres of forest, a couple of beaver ponds, and a house made of logs that sits on a knoll looking up at the Missions on one side, the Swans on the other. Janet Moore is a member of the Montana House of Representatives. Last session she cosponsored a bill to prohibit logging within twenty-five feet of a watercourse. The timber industry spiked it. Finito. Bud Moore is retired, forty years with the U.S. Forest Service, and the full range of it, too, from fighting fires in the Bitterroots to pushing paper in Washington, D.C. Now, with a portable sawmill and a skidder small enough to hustle short logs out of the woods without knocking everything over, Moore practices low-impact forestry on his own land and the woodlots of neighbors. Two of his neighbors, alas, have no use for low-impact forestry. Namely, Plum Creek and the U.S. Forest Service.

Bud Moore worries a good deal these days about what has been happening in the corporate forest, and in the public woods, too. He said: "In Montana in 1987 more boards came off the mills than at any other time in history. Eighty-eight was a big year, too. Well, what we've been living off here is the bounty of the old-growth, the bounty that's built up in these mountains since the last ice age. And we're coming down to the end of all that. The new forests, the managed forests, are not going to have all the good things that the old one did. And it's hard for me to believe that we're not going to whack it off for smaller stuff as it comes along. It worries me, because for some of these mills there isn't the land and the wood here. We've got a limit to what the land can sustain, and we're exceeding the limit in every imaginable way. I think there's still a kind of frontier aura—I know there is. People want to believe the bounty's still out there, but more and more they're beginning to see that it isn't. The bounty is gone. And there are mills here that are doubling capacity, and because of it some mills aren't going to make it."

We talked that day about the Montana Wilderness Bill that Ronald Reagan had scuttled—Moore had personally walked the Swan Front and the Sapphire Mountains in order to enhance his own pro-bill testimony—and then I asked him what he thought about multiple use; was it a workable concept?

"It could be," he said, "but we haven't begun to touch it. To me multiple use implies that we should be managing for multiple values, and there's also an implication that the end result, the sum, can be greater than each of the individual parts. The Flathead Forest Plan is trying to work in that direction, but it hasn't got there yet. I'd say the Plan is good. I've never seen any land-use plan in all my years that's any better, or even as good. But this one, like all the better forest plans, hasn't quite reached out and really got ahold of that multiple-use thing yet.

"For example," Moore continued, "they got to the point where they delineated ecosystems and then came up with management prescriptions for each one. They give one thing top priority in each management unit. But the shortcoming in this is that the other values are left to an arithmetical decline in importance.

"The Forest Service goes in and starts talking 'mitigation.' They say, 'We'll give this thing priority and we'll mitigate the damage to the others.' We shouldn't even be thinking that way. We should be thinking—if we are thinking about the true meaning of the Multiple-Use Act—how are we going to *maximize* all the benefits from this piece of land? It's true there are places where you have to set priorities. But to say you have to mitigate around the lesser priorities—that's a cop-out. Instead say, 'We don't dare damage the lesser priorities.' Then you're starting to get someplace."

Then I asked Moore how he felt about some of the newer preservation groups that were driving his old agency up the wall on such matters as timber sales and forest plans. He said:

"There's been a lot of mistrust between conservationists and the Forest Service. Some people just won't believe that anything good can come out of that agency. I don't happen to agree. But I'm glad we've got Friends of the Wild Swan. Because those are the people who have the guts to stand in the way of the sawyers. If we hadn't had people like that back in the sixties, when we had the battles of the Bitterroots and the Monongahela and down here, we'd be facing disaster today. We wouldn't have a National Forest Management Act. We wouldn't have forest planning. We would have been fighting it a drainage at a time. It would have been one helluva disaster. Those were the sort of people that turned it around. And yet sometimes it seems to me these people can't deal with agreement. It's interesting. Some of these people *have* to have a war."

WAR IN THE WOODS II:

WEST SIDE STORY

There are at least six ways to look at a forest, and some of the ways do not get along very well with others, especially when a forest is as valuable as this one. This one happens to be the most valuable in the United States—maybe in the entire world, for all I know. It is the west-side forest, so called because that is where it lies in relation to the crest of the Cascade Range in Washington, Oregon, and Northern California. A few people refer to it also as the Douglas fir region, after its dominant species; while others, noting the region's ability to grow trees to a venerable age, have recently taken to calling its senior and most valuable parts the Ancient Forest.

A person can enter the Ancient Forest and, standing among the columnar trunks of its massive trees, experience a flood of perceptions not unlike those evoked in the vespertine stillness of a Gothic cathedral. That is one way to look at it, and many worshipful tree-huggers do. Another person may enter to genuflect in the presence of biological diversities—the dripping mosses, the rotted snags, the spoor of the elk—all testifying to the miracle of nature at work in a pristine ecosystem. That is another way to look at the forest. And many do.

Other people enter and, while appreciating the forest's esthetics, see neither a sylvan church nor a college of nature but a stand of timber. In which case, perceptions diverge. There are those who view timber primarily as jobs—jobs here in the woods, in the sawmills, in the trucks and ships that carry the logs to their destinations. And those who see timber as a source of public revenue, as receipts to finance roads and schools that otherwise would surely be funded out of the taxpayer's own pocket. And of course there are those who, owning the timber or the right to cut it, see the Ancient Forest as so much black ink on the bottom line.

There is one last way to perceive the forest, and that is with all of the aforementioned values in harmonious balance. Not many people see it *this* way, if only because no one has yet demonstrated that such a balance is possible to achieve.

So, given all of these conflicting perceptions, is it any wonder that we have this war in the woods? Any wonder that the worst part of the war, the most intensely fought, has been occurring right here where the stakes are the highest?

The problem with the Ancient Forest, you see, is that there isn't very much of it left. Sure, some wonderful old-growth is tucked away in the region's national parks and wilderness areas, and that means full protection for the trees. That's good news for conservationists. The bad news for them is that much of the best of the rest of the old-growth stands at lower elevations, in the west side's twelve national forests, enjoying no permanent protection at all. In fact, rather than protecting these pockets of sylvan antiquity, the United States Forest Service was actually planning to sell them for sawlogs. Private industry had just about liquidated all of *its* old trees, so now it was going to be Uncle Sam's turn. Uncle was going into his twelve west-side national forests to ratchet up the allowable sales quantity by a third of a billion board feet a year, an increase of more than ten percent over historic harvest levels in the previous decade. And quite a bit of that increase was projected to come from the sale of old-growth.

Predictably, the Forest Service told its critics not to worry;

that even after the sales were consummated there would still be more old-growth standing in these forests than you could shake a stick at. Whereupon one of the critics, the Wilderness Society, conducted its own assessment of the Ancient Forest and discovered—actually *proved*—that the Forest Service's old-growth figures were vastly inflated. "Less than one-half of what we thought was there still stands," the Society announced, "and the Forest Service wants to cut more."

Then someone rediscovered the northern spotted owl, noted its affinity for old-growth habitat, and suggested that possibly there weren't as many of the birds surviving as folks once thought. At which point environmentalists decided to go to court. In a suit challenging the adequacy of Forest Service plans to safeguard the owl, the Seattle chapter of the National Audubon Society, the Oregon Natural Resources Council, and more than a dozen other plaintiffs asked Federal District Judge William Dwyer to enjoin the Service from selling the owl's old-growth home out from under it. And the judge did that, his injunction effectively tying up more than a billion and a half board feet of timber scheduled for sale from national forests in Oregon and Washington. Moreover, a second lawsuit, filed by National Audubon, compelled the U.S. Fish and Wildlife Service to show cause why the owl should not be listed as a threatened species, thereby initiating a process of review that will likely continue for several years.

Then timber industry abhors the very idea of a listed owl. Its press agents have been constructing "worst-case" scenarios in which the listed owl is costing the Pacific Northwest a quarter-million jobs and nearly ten billion dollars in local payrolls and federal timber receipts—figures even more grossly inflated than the Forest Service count on standing old-growth. By and by, rural west-side people began to hang the owl in effigy and slogans. Hate follows hyperbole. On at least two occasions in Oregon, someone shot, mutilated, and strung up a northern spotted owl for real.

And that, more or less, was where the battle lines stood when Senators Mark Hatfield of Oregon and Brock Adams of Washington unveiled their so-called "compromise" solution and folded it into an appropriations bill. Passed by Congress and signed into law by President Bush, the Hatfield-Adams amendment mooted the original lawsuit by mandating release of 1.1 billion board feet of judicially restrained timber sales even as it permitted the environmental community to choose where the rest of the contested volume, some half-billion board feet, could remain under wraps.

Of course nothing in the Hatfield-Adams measure dealt with the related issue of log exports from Oregon and Washington to the lucrative marketplace of the Far East, or what might really happen to the economy of the Pacific Northwest, not to mention the integrity of the Endangered Species Act, should the Fish and Wildlife Service find that the northern spotted owl is indeed threatened. Perhaps those are questions that must be put aside for the moment.

In any event, by the end of 1989 the first battle of the west-side forest was finished. What follows is an account of how it was fought on a couple of fronts. Given the values at stake and the tempers of certain combatants, who knows? By the time you get to the bottom of this story, the second or third battle of the west-side forest may have begun.

1. THE OLYMPIC

It was and is the sort of place that inflates an impetuous person's expectations. It seems to promise more than any place should. Look first to the names—Olympic, Olympus. What a mythic scale those words imply. A sanctuary of the gods. A temple of Zeus. A showcase for excellence. Of course, for a time, expectations ran the other way. Sailcloth rovers gazed upon this shore and found it daunting terrible. A coast of sorrows and desolation it was, and unforgiving, too. Yet, promising. In 1596 a seafaring Greek found himself in Venice, entertaining folks with tales of the North Pacific. The seaman called himself Juan de Fuca. He said he had sailed from California to a strait that led eastward across the New World. Aha! an English geographer exclaimed. This must be the fabled Strait of Anian. And for a hundred years thereafter, cartographers and kings would anticipate a debouchment of the Northwest Passage where in fact there was only a cul-de-sac to be known as Puget Sound. When pale-faces began to settle on the eastern shore of that sound, they imagined wondrous things behind the mountain ridges on the other side. One might go there and find an enchanted valley, someone supposed. Yes, and likely encounter palm trees and bubbling hot springs, too. And cannibals, said a New York newspaper. At this point sensible people began to understand that there have to be limits to every expectation, even in the shadow of a mountain named Olympus, on a peninsula called Olympic.

Mountains dominate the peninsula, one twisting ridge after another, leaping from sea level to almost eight thousand feet in the wink of an eye. Glaciers and snowfields hang on up there round the year, feeding sinuous rivers deep in their valleys below. A jumble of a place this is, a maze the size of Connecticut and Delaware combined, the second largest maritime peninsula in the Lower Forty-eight, if you throw in the vertical acres along with the flat. Eighty miles separate the Pacific Ocean from Hood Canal, an appendage of Puget Sound. Most other places, you'd zip across. The Olympic isn't most other places. You go around.

It rains a lot. Offshore, there is this rainmaker called the Japa-nese Current. It warms the air. The warm air rises in clouds. As the clouds approach the ice-topped mountains, cooling con-denses their vapors of water and the clouds are rent into cats 'n' dogs. The western slopes of the mountains are said to be wetter than any other place in the United States. Precipitation mea-surements run from 90 inches on the coast to 220 inches or more on the windward heights of Mount Olympus. Falling, the rain encounters a salubrious soil. John Muir, passing this way in 1889, described it as soil "ploughed and rolled by the mighty glaciers from the mountains and sifted and mellowed and out-spread in beds hundreds of feet in depth." No ground anywhere, wrote Muir, had been "better tilled for the growth of trees."

The one Olympic expectation in which almost everyone would have to concur is that the trees of this peninsula probably constitute the finest example of rainforest remaining in North America. This particular type of forest stretches along the coast from the Alaska Panhandle into Northern California, so there is plenty of competition. Of course the coastal forest is not intact the entire way, and the Olympic forest is anything but intact, as we shall presently see. Still, the patches that are left are wonders to behold—this verdant understory of horsetail and foam flower, of hedge nettle and sword fern, bracken and clubmoss feeding on the detritus of fallen trees, and the standing trees so tall that the rays of the noonday sun arrive at the ground filtered, as one writer put it, like light in deep water. Some of the tallest trees, the girthiest, maybe the oldest, too, are queued up along the west-running valleys of the Hoh, Queets, and Quinault rivers.

Heaven only knows what the score was in Muir's day, but nowadays the Olympic holds the gold medal for growing more world-champion conifers than any comparable area in the country. Up the Queets, it has the world's largest Douglas fir, 225 feet tall, more than a thousand years old. Down near the mouth of the Hoh stands the world-champ western red cedar, 21 feet in diameter, breast-high. Over the Quinault looms the co-champion western hemlock. Here is the biggest Alaska cedar (bigger even than any in Alaska), the biggest Pacific silver fir, the biggest grand fir, the biggest subalpine fir. Here is a magnificent gold medal co-champ Sitka spruce (the other isn't anywhere near Sitka; it's in Oregon). Why there is even a deciduous champ, the vine maple. And who knows? Given the wild dishevelment of the place, the peninsula could be hiding other winners. One cannot fully explain this splendid showing simply by citing the munificence of nature, for human intervention has nurtured the big trees, at least over the past half-century, no less than the rain and the soil. I refer to Olympic National Park, in which most of the champion trees preside. Without the park's protective presence, it is likely the champs would have been toppled, measured into board feet, and trucked off to market long ago, lest they go to waste.

Men have been saving old trees from going to waste on this

peninsula ever since William Talbot and Andrew Pope, fresh from the merchantable Maine woods, came round the Horn with the Forty-niners and, since San Francisco those days was always getting burned to the ground, set up the Puget Mill Company at Port Townsend. The idea was to ship Olympic lumber south in order that the flammable Gold Rush city might build itself up all over again. Forest industries ever since have accounted for at least half of the peninsula's wealth and employment. But nowadays, communities along the east side of the peninsula tend to be less dependent on timber, being bedrooms mostly for retired folks and ferryboat commuters to the towers of Seattle across the sound. But along the Olympic's landed hinge, on the south, from Shelton to Grays Harbor, and especially on the Pacific side, over Forks way, the timber economy and the life-styles that go with it loom as big as they can get in America. Forks, in fact, bills itself as the "Logging Capital of the World." Some folks out that way expect it always was, and want to expect it always will be.

The Olympic Penninsula occupies an area of a little more than four million acres, in round numbers. Right off the bat we can dispose of the "little more" by assigning it to towns and cities and roads and farms and lakes and beaches. That leaves everything else—the flat four million—covered with trees. Well, not *exactly* covered with trees. In many lower-elevation places you find nothing but stumps. And high in the mountains, rock and ice. The rock and ice don't take up that much space, and stay fairly constant. The stumps keep spreading. Someday the slopes they march across will be forest again. But of course, by then, some of what's forest now will be sprouting stumps.

The Olympic Peninsula can be divided into four parts: federal, state, tribal, and private. The federal part consists of Olympic National Park, at 900,000 acres, and Olympic National Forest, at about 650,000 acres. (There are other, minor federal holdings, but these do not lend themselves to round numbers.)The State of Washington's part is 365,000 acres. The tribes' part is more or less the same as the state's. And the rest, some 1,750,000 acres, is private land, of which maybe two-thirds is owned by the big timber companies, and the remainder by individuals, families, trusts, estates, pension funds, and insurance companies that are known to the timber trade as the "nonindustrials." Long ago, before most of these ownerships fell into place, when much of the peninsula was—how do you call it?— open to entry, it was expected that all of these acres sooner or later would be available for the production of timber. God and the Japanese Current had put the trees here for man's use, and by God and by Japan man was going to use them.

But for those who viewed the forest from that perspective, things just didn't turn out quite right. First there was a forest preserve, which became a national forest. Then Uncle Sam turned a big piece of that forest into a national park, whence sawyers were banished under pain of sin. Just when folks were getting used to the park, what does Uncle do but swipe almost 100,000 acres from what is left of the national forest and designate it uppercase-*W* Wilderness, again barring timbermen from the premises. And now, this. This concern for the spotted owl, and yet another reduction of the available timber base.

Behold now the unraveling mummy of Olympic National Forest, as a timberman might see it; as a Forest Service statistician might want us all to see it if only we didn't insist on these damnable round numbers. No matter. Here goes. You start with 650,000 acres. Right off the bat you take away 100,000 acres and give it directly to rock and ice and sites that cannot produce trees. Then you take away 92,000 acres and give it to wilderness. Then you go to the Draft Forest Management Plan and you take away 50,000 acres and give it to a variety of recreational and natural area research uses deemed incompatible with timber harvests. After subtracting all of these takeaways, you are left with 408,000 acres. This is your suitable timber base. This is where you can cut down trees.

But whoa, hold on now. The Draft Plan has layered a few constraints on some of these acres, too. There are scenic areas and river corridors and watersheds supplying public water systems. In these places timber production is permissible, but it must take a back seat to esthetics and water quality. So you take away 64,000 acres here and give it to the front seat. That leaves you with 344,000 acres of suitable timber base where you can maximize production. Okay?

Not okay. You forgot about the stumps. There are 171,000 acres of stumps, plantations somewhere in the long process of regeneration. These acres will be available for maximizing timber production *someday*, but not now. So take it off, take it all off. Now we've slimmed the mummy down to 173,000 acres and we're ready to cut. Right?

Not right. Because here comes that flap over the spotted owl, and here comes the chief forester from Washington, D.C., anticipating litigious troubles. He is telling Ted Stubblefield, the supervisor of Olympic National Forest, to go to the maps and draw circles around known spotted owl nesting sites. The circles are to contain three thousand acres each, are to be called SOHAS, for Spotted Owl Habitat Areas, and, though they might be deemed suitable for timber production someday, realistically they are to be withdrawn now from consideration for sales. So now the mummy is down to 103,000 acres. Ted Stubblefield looks at his maps and figures: Well, we had planned to sell about 229 million board feet of timber in Fiscal Year 1989, but the SOHAS will cut that to 120 million.

Perhaps, at this point, the timberman expects that this will be the end of it. Or perhaps by now he is conditioned to expect that, for all the legalistic opportunities to save trees from sawyers, there might never be an end to it. Whatever the expectation, a lawsuit is soon filed by environmentalists, charging that the chief forester's guidelines for SOHAS in the national forests are not adequate to assure protection for the owl. Whereupon a federal judge in Seattle issues that now-famous injunction halting some 165 timber sales throughout the owl's range in the Pacific Northwest. Whereupon Ted Stubblefield looks once more at his Olympic maps and sees that about the only timber he'll be selling in Fiscal 1989 is not the 120 million board feet that remained to be sold after SOHA withdrawals, but the mere 20 million already sold in the first few months of that year, before the filing of the lawsuit.

To be sure, there is always a backlog of timber sales already executed and in the pipeline. According to Stubblefield, on October 1, 1988, about two dozen timber purchasers on the peninsula—some of them wholly dependent on federal logs—had 400 million board feet under contract. With only 20 million feet more added to the pipeline after October, purchasers by July 1989 were barely running even with their peninsula milling capacity of about 170 million board feet a year. That's all that remained under contract. And by December, Stubblefield was predicting, the pipeline wouldn't be holding even a third of that volume.

And where would that leave the smaller mills that depend on the availability of federal logs?

"Nowhere," said Ted Stubblefield.

While SOHAs and lawsuits were causing blockages in the federal timber pipeline, it was business as usual in other parts of the peninsula forest, particularly on lands owned and managed by the state and the corporations. Here the prevailing business wasn't rounding off takeaways but following the market, the preferred market being the one that is known as Pacific Rim, a euphemism for Japan, Korea, Taiwan, the People's Republic of China. Already, the Rim had taken the corporations through most of their old-growth timber, and taken the state through much of its own as well, inasmuch as policy at Washington's Department of Natural Resources mandates that the oldest trees on state lands must be harvested first. So it wasn't likely you'd find a gold- or even a bronze-medal hemlock or fir still upright in the DNR's precincts, or in those of ITT Rayonier or the Weyerhaeuser Company, the peninsula's largest exporters of corporate logs. If there *had* been such a tree on state or company land in recent years, you could bet your bottom yen it was sayonara now, lying at rest in studs and beams and panels on some residential hillside in Rimside Japan.

For its part, the DNR was not altogether insensitive to accelerating concerns over owls and old-growth. Matter of fact, with fewer overall acres than the U.S. Forest Service, but a far greater proportion of them suitable for timber production, the state could afford to lose some ground in its harvest program. In response to requests by state wildlife officials and conservation groups, DNR tucked in its chin and agreed to reduce sales planned for Fiscal 1989, on the peninsula, from 320 million board feet to 280 million. Reductions in sales volume are not taken lightly in the Evergreen State, where long-established laws and policies compel the DNR to manage its forests for maximum dollar benefits rather than multiple use. The state forest, in effect, is a trust. Revenues from the sale of state timber are earmarked for various public purposes, mostly educational. Since 1970, state log sales have generated $1.6 billion for school, college, and institutional construction projects. A billion of these dollars have come from the sale of logs for export. Statewide, more than two-thirds of the DNR harvest winds up at dockside, bound for the Orient; from the Olympic Peninsula, the state's export volume is closer to 80 percent of its total cut. Some folks do not think it is a very good idea to send so many logs across the Pacific when local mills are hurting so badly for the timber they need to stay afloat. Enough folks in Oregon in 1989 thought it was such a bad idea for their state that they voted nine to one to ban the export of state logs. That is not likely to happen in Washington. Talk of a ban in Washington and you get the flinty stare. Ban exports and you ban more than $150 million for new schools. That's what they're saying. Spare the Rimside and spoil the child.

Besides, everyone's *doing* it. Even the nonindustrials—those smaller landowners who in the past might have eschewed the opportunity to turn their back forties into tree farms—were listening to the siren song of the Rimside market. Consider the findings of John M. Calhoun, Olympic area manager for the DNR.

In the summer of 1989, Calhoun noted that tourists were decidedly louder in registering their most common complaint: Too many clearcuts. Tourists, uneducated in matters of forest management, were coming out to this beautiful peninsula to see a great national park, and what they were seeing at the side of the road were clearcuts. For outlander disenchantment, 1989 apparently was the pits. So Calhoun took it upon himself to inventory which landowners were driving these visitors right through their windshields. He got in a car and did the tourist loop, 130 miles from Lake Crescent on the north to Hoquiam, at Grays Harbor, on the southwest. Along the way, adjacent to Highway 101, he counted seventy-eight clearcuts that had been made in the past five years. The majority of the cuts could be divided, about equally, between ITT Rayonier, the largest corporate landowner on the peninsula, and small nonindustrial landowners. Nearly half of the cuts were no older than a year, and of these the vast majority were small nonindustrial.

What's happening? I asked Calhoun at his office in Forks.

"What's happening," he said, "is that people are making a fortune, relative to what they always thought their timber was worth."

Were any of the seventy-eight roadside cuts attributable to his own agency, the State DNR? Yes. "DNR has eight of those clearcuts." But didn't Washington want to be sensitive to the expectations of windshield tourists? Yes. "But you see," he said, "one of the problems we're having with this spotted owl issue is that it has restricted the areas we can go to for timber and forced us to cut in places we'd rather not, like next to the tourist loop."

Daniel Leinan is the town clerk-treasurer of Forks, the Logging Capital of the World. He is a friendly man, scout's-honor helpful to strangers who drop out of the tourist loop wanting to know why everyone in town seems so almighty agitated over spotted owls and preservationists. Helpful, too, even after he discovers that this particular stranger is an eastern journalist skulking about on behalf of the preservation press. The occasion calls for a review of the numbers. He draws a sheet of paper from his desk drawer. In neat columns, as one might expect of a treasurer, Daniel Leinan has laid out the National Park and U.S. Forest services' ownerships in Washington State. We see the acres, and the acres converted to square miles. We see that national parks and wilderness areas occupy 6,788 square miles, or 10 percent of the entire state. We see that total park and national forest owner-ships occupy 25 percent of the entire state. We see that this is more land than Hawaii, Connecticut, Delaware, and Rhode Island combined; more than Denmark or Israel or Switzerland. "It's even worse here on the Olympic Peninsula than statewide," Leinan says. "A greater percentage of federal land that people can't use. I don't know. Sometimes it seems that *they* don't want anyone living out here." *They* is a not altogether indefinite pronoun in Forks. *They* means the preservationists. Leinan says, "They have a quarter of Washington State. A quarter of it. You'd think that that was enough, but I guess it isn't. Because they keep coming back for more."

Scratch the perceptions of most residents of the peninsula's west side—the residents of rural communities throughout the Pacific Northwest—and you will likely uncover a rage and frustration much like Dan Leinan's. You do not find many folks raging against the export of sawlogs to Japan while local mills, unable to compete in the bidding, go under. If the local mill's in trouble, that's Uncle Sam's fault. Why? Why, because he's a tightwad in releasing his own timber, which cannot be exported. And you do not find many folks lamenting the rapacious harvest rates of the corporate landowners. After all, it is better to use the wood now than to let it grow old and go to waste. If Big Timber is cutting too much too soon, well that's Uncle's fault, too, because of his tax laws and his environmental regulations. Besides, that's *private* property. Does a man not have the right to use his property as he sees fit? When things go wrong, does a man not have the right to blame it on Uncle and the preservationists?

The bad aroma attending the federal presence on the west side of Puget Sound can be traced back almost a hundred years, possibly to the day in 1897 when President Grover Cleveland designated more than two million acres—half of the peninsula—as the Olympic Forest Reserve. You can imagine the outcries of rage and frustration; flak sufficient to move Cleveland's successor, William McKinley, to return a third of the reserve a few years later to the unprotected public domain. And this was just the opening round in a long succession of tack-ons and take-aways over the years, a tug of war that frequently split Uncle's odiferous personality in half by firmly pitting his commodity-oriented foresters from the Department of Agriculture against parksters in the Department of the Interior. (Teddy Roosevelt in 1909 withdrew 600,000 acres from the national forest and set them aside as the Mount Olympus National Monument. The basic idea wasn't so much to save the trees from the sawyers as to protect Olympic elk from the Benevolent and Protective Order of Elks, whose members coveted the critter's teeth for their watch-fobs. Woodrow Wilson in 1915 sawed Teddy's monument in half, in order that prospectors might discover great lodes of much-needed manganese. The basic idea was to crank up the supply of this metal for the coming war effort. "Precious little manganese was found in the liberated portion of the monument," the peninsula writer Murray Morgan observed. "But the lumbermen mined some fine spruce and fir.")

The emergence of federal park advocates after the turn of the century, with their threats of total lockups and no logging at all, gave the backwoods gentry a good excuse to lay off cudgeling the federal foresters. Not that they needed an excuse, for the foresters were beginning to sound like regular and decent guys. There was this fellow in Washington, D.C., named Gifford Pinchot. Chief of all the foresters, he was. A man who believed in *wise use*. Who believed that parks were "sentimental." Who had advocated logging in that damnably forever wild Adirondack Park. Who defended the right of stockmen to graze their sheep in alpine meadows. Who would lobby against a Glacier National Park and bad-mouth protection for the Calaveras Big Trees in California. Who would become a star witness in support of a Hetch Hetchy reservoir in Yosemite National Park. And whose disciples over the years would continue to preach the gospel according to Gifford. In the 1920s Olympic National Forest officials refused even to acknowledge the existence of the national monument within the forest, and included much of its timber in projected harvest plans. The purpose of the Forest Service, wrote one regional forester, is "to develop the National

Forests to their highest usefulness." Continuous production, he advised, would provide "a stabilizing influence on prosperity and the upbuilding of permanent communities of forest workers."

Now *there* was an agenda that might take the stink off Uncle altogether. Production, prosperity, and permanence. Who could ask for anything more?

By the 1930s, the preservationist push to transfer Mount Olympus National Monument from the Forest Service to the Park Service, and then expand it into a full-scale park, was stronger than ever. So was the Forest Service's determination to resist the scheme. In an excellent study of the inter-service rivalry, *Organizational Values and Political Power: The Forest Service versus the Olympic National Park,* author Ben W. Twight reports that while the nation's top foresters were assailing the pro-park forces as " 'ultrasentimental and emotional,' " their regional subalterns were stirring up the Olympic gentry with talk of economic catastrophe should a park prevail. It was said that within the proposed boundaries of the park there was enough timber to employ six hundred men in the woods and six hundred working in five mills, two hundred days a year. It was that simple. You could have a park, said one regional forester, or "a total community of 1,200 families from now until Gabriel blows his horn." Franklin D. Roosevelt's signature settled that question in 1938. The peninsula got the park.

Twight notes that the basic reason the Forest Service "wished to retain jurisdiction over the entire peninsula" first emerged, in 1934, in a document from the hand of Chief Forester Ferdinand Silcox, a Pinchot party-liner if ever there was one. Apparently the cutting on private lands had been intense, with little or no effort at reforestation, and Silcox felt that it was the Service's duty to fill the expected shortfall—"the period of adjustment," he called it—with "the timber resources of the Olympic National Forest." This could be a major factor, said Silcox, "in maintaining the established [industrial] structure and the social institutions it supports."

And now, more than a half-century later, maintenance is

what folks in places like Forks still expect from the U.S. Forest Service. And I suspect they'd be getting it, too, if only it were not for these other folks in places like New York and Boston and Seattle, who seem never to know when enough is enough because they keep coming back for more.

2. FORKS

The First Annual American Loggers' Solidarity Rally came to Forks on July 1, 1989, and so did I. I came from the south, up Highway 101, up the tourist loop, escorted fore and aft by a convoy of big green logging trucks with the name Jack Buel and St. Maries, Idaho, painted on the doors of each cab. A warm rain fell out of the sky. Near the bridge on the River Hoh a bearded man with red suspenders and no hat stood in the rain by the side of the road and waved a clenched fist as the convoy rolled by. Air horns started *blaaaat*ing from the trucks at the edge of town, short solos at first, then longer and louder, and the decibels reached out to join the horns of other trucks, of hundreds of trucks coming to Forks from both directions along 101.

I parked my car and got out and walked into the center of town, past Hungry Harry's and the Chinook Pharmacy and the Tackle Box and the Vagabond and the Far West Motel. There had been predictions that more than five thousand visitors would descend on little Forks (Population: 2,900) for this premier event of the Fourth of July weekend. But the rain had cut heavily into that number, and now the sidewalks of Forks seemed more cluttered with paraphernalia than people. Yellow balloons and flags and legends. "No timber, no revenue, no schools, no jobs." Over a picture of a mechanical crane: "These birds need habitats, too." On the side of a truck: "Enough is enough!" In the hands of a child: "Don't take my daddie's job." On a sandwich board: "Our Ancient Trees Are Terminally Ill."

Smack-dab at the heart of Forks, right up against the sidewalk on the east side of Highway 101, stands the town's official centerpiece. It is a cross-section of a giant Sitka spruce, with a sign that says: "Welcome to Forks. Logging Capital of the World. This Sitka spruce log came from a tree which was 11 feet 8 inches in diameter and 256 feet tall. The tree was already 259 years old in 1776." There was more to it than that, but, at the time, I thought the legend woefully incomplete. Nowhere did it say in what year the spruce became terminally ill, or who decided to pull its plug.

By and by the logging trucks *blaaaat*ed their way through town, the decibels dropped to an acceptable level—at least out-of-doors—and folks began to head at last for the high school gymnasium. I climbed up into the bleachers, took a seat, and the show began. We heard first from a local logger, one Collin King—sincere, touching, and low-keyed. Next up to the microphone stepped a man named Falen, who wore a cowboy hat and told of all the hard times those preservationists were unloading on the cattlemen of America. To bat after Falen came Chuck Cushman, executive director of the National Inholders Association (inholders being those unlucky folks whose properties are surrounded by the government's). Cushman warned his listeners to beware the "single-purpose folks who want to lock it all up and lock us out." The good people of rural America were up against a "new paganism that worships trees and sacrifices people."

Had anyone in the audience had an opportunity to negotiate with any member of the preservationist movement? "*They* just want to be *reasonable,*" Cushman said, using the familiar pronoun for the enemy. "They just want 50 percent, and you take 50 percent. That's reasonable, right? Three years later they're back. They want 50 percent of your 50 percent. And three years after that they want 50 percent of that. Well, where is it going to stop? If things keep going the way they are, *you're* going to be the endangered species, not the spotted owl."

After Cushman we heard from a couple of more moderately disposed speakers, including U.S. Senator Slade Gorton, the transplanted New England codfish-cake heir. Then it was time to stir the pot with Perry Pendley, from the Mountain States Legal Foundation in Denver, Colorado. I don't suppose too many people in the Forks gymnasium remembered what *that* outfit was all about, though they wouldn't be wondering for very long after Pendley opened his mouth. The Foundation had figured prominently in national politics in the early 1980s when its chairman and principal angel was Joseph Coors, the Colorado brewer and contributor to such conservative causes as the John Birch Society; when its top lawyer was James Gaius Watt, the once and future secretary of the interior. And now it was Perry Pendley, looking like a brush salesman and sounding like Elmer Gantry as he called down fire and brimstone on the "liberal" tendencies of the Bush Administration, on wetlands, on the press, on Congress, on Meryl Streep (for meddling in the apple wars), on the National Park Service (for the fires and brimstones of Yellowstone Park), on the spotted owl ("this flying snail-darter"), on preservationists.

"Who are these people anyway?" Perry Pendley intoned. "Let's look at who they are. Why, I heard a nationally recognized environmentalist say the other day, 'If it came down to saving the last polar bear on Earth or the five billion human beings, I would save the last polar bear.' We are in national agony over *Roe* v. *Wade* and this man wants to save polar bears. Who are these people anyway?"

Suddenly Pendley had a book in his hand and was waving it at his audience. "The Field Guide to Monkey-Wrenching," he said it was. "Ladies and gentlemen, it is the recipe book for murder and mayhem. It is the instruction manual for the death and disfigurement of fellow human beings. These people are engaged in activities that would kill Father in the name of Mother Earth! The American people don't know who these people are. The FBI knows. They've arrested them. They have their leaders in jail. But it's not enough. Ladies and gentlemen, I am announcing today on behalf of the Mountain States Legal Foundation a campaign. We are forming a national clearinghouse in Denver, Colorado, for information regarding eco-terror in anticipation of potential civil legislation later on."

Thunderous applause.

And finally there was Bruce Vincent, the director of Communities for a Great Northwest, the coalition-building outfit from Libby, Montana, that has organized many of the "log hauls" and logger rallies throughout the region in recent years (including this one). I had already run across Vincent in Montana, had noted some of his close financial ties to the corporate sector of the timber industry, had listened to his sorrowful accounts of how "the Dirty Hands People who built America" are being deprived of their birthright by callous preservationists. Here in Forks I was treated to much of the same set speech, though this time around, Vincent was primed with stand-up jokes to ease some of the post-Pendley tension. Having done that, he promptly cranked the ratchets tight again. In the 1970s, he said, the agenda of the national environmental organizations "took a big turn to the Left." It became what he called "the Big Lie." The preservationists "began telling America, 'Look, you guys, you got two choices: We're going to set it aside as wilderness, or we're going to destroy it.' "

Now Vincent had maybe a dozen people from the audience standing with him in front of the podium. He had called them up by name—an old revivalist tactic. He had the questions, they had the answers:

Q. "Are you good stewards of the land?"
A. "Yes!"
Q. "You plant more than you harvest?"
A. "Yeah!"
Q. "Can you harvest and protect the water quality, too?"
A. "Yeah"
Q. "Do you enhance wildlife?"
A. "Yeah!"
Q. "Are you truly environmentalists?"
A. "Yeah!"
Q. "Are you true conservationists?"
A. "Yeah!"
Q. "Is reasonable right and radical wrong?"
A. "Yeah! Yeah!"
Q. "Okay. Join hands and repeat after me. We can!"
A. "WE CAN!"
Q. "We must!"

A. "WE MUST!"
Q. "We will!"
A. "WE WILL!"

"Take that home," said Vincent, "because that's our hope. Thank you."

Thunderous applause.

Mason Lumber Products is a small, family-owned sawmill specializing in high-grade Douglas fir items, such as vertical grain clears and industrial boards cut to custom dimensions and tailored to stand up to high stress. The mill and its log yard sit next to the tourist loop, northeast of Forks on 101, up where Bear Creek joins the Soleduck River near Sappho. Across the river one way, and beyond the highway a couple of miles in the other direction, toward Deadmans Hill, lie the boundaries of the Soleduck Ranger District of Olympic National Forest. Until 1989 the Soleduck District was mill owner Larry Mason's principal supplier of Dougfir logs. Nine of every ten of the logs he processed came from Uncle Sam's forest. To go for the vertical grain the way Mason does, to get that resistance to high stress the customer calls for, you need old-growth Dougfir. And most of that kind of timber—I mean the available kind—is owned nowadays by the feds in their national forest. The State of Washington and the big corporations used to have a lot of that kind of timber, too, but not anymore. Besides, even if there *were* more disposable old Dougfirs on the nonfederal lands, how could it possibly profit the state or the corporations to sell them to Larry Mason when buyers from Japan were willing to pay more for the raw logs at dockside than Larry Mason could reasonably charge *his* buyers at Sappho, after turning the same logs into finished lumber?

I had heard about Mason at the time of the loggers' rally, but missed him in the crush of people exiting the Forks gymnasium. A month or two had passed. I was back on the Evergreen road again, the tourist loop. I had followed it to Mason's prefab office, at the edge of a near-empty log yard, and he was telling me how he and his wife, Liz, had come out here from Back East eighteen years ago "to build a good life." They had started modestly, milling logs from salvage operations, and then moved on to the specialty trade. In 1987, Mason borrowed money to install a million dollars' worth of improvements at his mill.

"We did that," he said, "on assurances from the Forest Service that this district would cut eighty million board feet a year in perpetuity on a sustained-yield basis. And that promise was good enough to convince the Seattle First National Bank and the Washington Department of Community Development and the Small Business Administration of the United States government. Up till January 1989 we had forty people working here and big stacks of logs. We processed three million board feet, year before. The idea was to put the least volume in and create the most jobs out, and because we did that, we're being punished."

Mason said: "Overnight, everything stopped. The Record of Decision came out from the Chief making it three thousand acres to be set aside for each spotted owl habitat area. That would effectively have reduced the harvest in this district by 60 percent. Even then we could have remained viable. But then came the injunctions, and that stopped everything. Now we've got just fifteen people working here, and we can't keep that number on full-time. All we have to saw are some pulp logs, some salvage, off private land."

Mason said: "The big corporations are reaping windfall profits as a result of this situation. The Audubon Society probably has never had a stronger membership and a greater budget in its life. And who's getting hurt? The most creative, the most conscientious, the most responsible members of the wood-products industry are the small operators like myself, and that's who's targeted in this disaster. I don't live my life in some penthouse executive suite in some big city. I'm going to work every day, and this is what I get for it. Look, I know the rank and file of the Audubon Society are sincere. I talk to people about this. I know they're sincere about the quality of the planet. But the leadership I'm very suspicious of. Because the leadership *has* to know full well that when they create a timber shortage in the pipeline by removing the federal supply, all they've done is create a windfall market situation for the private timber companies who are the least responsible harvesters and land managers. All they've done is encourage those people, those companies, to accelerate their harvests. That's what's happening. In this state, on private lands, there are devastating environmental impacts taking place right now, and the people who are doing it are being rewarded by the Audubon Society, indirectly."

Now wait a minute, I said. *Who* is "doing it?" Who were these people anyway?

"Private landowners," Mason said. "Some are companies. Some are owned domestically. Some are owned by Japanese, Koreans, Chinese. They buy the land, take the timber out of it, and either replant it for future harvest or sell it. There are investment funds, insurance companies. These are people who play with resources the same way they would play with junk bonds. These are not people who have a sense of responsibility to community stability or to how they are affecting nature."

Would Mason include the largest private player—ITT Rayonier—in this same class of bottom-liners?

"ITT would view its forest as inventory," Mason said, "and ITT would liquidate that inventory or not liquidate it depending on how it perceives the market. I don't believe things like sustained yield even enter into their thinking."

I told Mason I could understand why his operation was dependent on federal timber rather than private logs, but that his point of view seemed to me unusual, in that most folks hurting in rainforest country appeared more inclined to bash the Forest Service than private industry.

Mason said: "As far as I'm concerned, the Forest Service is the only responsible manager out there. They manage on a ninety- to one-hundred-year cycle, whereas private timber in the state is managed on a forty- to sixty-year cycle. The reason for this is that after sixty years, the growth curve starts to flatten out. And the bottom-line mentality of corporate silviculture is that when the growth curve starts to taper off, you get rid of the timber.

And that's just shortsighted, because what you're doing is settling for low quality."

How so?

"As the growth curve flattens, that's when the tree starts to put on quality—tighter grain, and the timber drops its knots. And the value you've gained by increasing the grade of that tree more than makes up for the volume you've lost with slower growth. It's good business to grow timber right. Only difference is, it's long-term business instead of short-term business. And the private sector of our industry is not very farsighted. In this country the only way you get farsighted judgment is by legislating it. I'd think the Audubon Society would agree with me on that, because that's what they've been trying to do. Only thing is, I'm not sure that we could agree on what's *good* judgment."

We left his office then and stood in the log yard looking at a scrawny pile of second-growth fir stems. Skyward, gray clouds scudded in from the Japanese Current and punched the afternoon sunlight off Deadmans Hill. "If the federal government doesn't release some timber this year," said Mason, "I'm history." That was the thought he wanted to leave me with. That and his scenario of the way it is going to be. The scenario reveals the owl as a hoax. The scenario says there are plenty of owls. When the public perceives this, the pendulum of opinion begins to swing the other way. Away from the Audubon Society toward Big Timber. And what happens then?

"Rape and pillage happens. It's rape and pillage by the same people who have already raped their own lands, made a pile of money, and are just waiting for the opportunity to dive into the public lands. They're the only players left in the game—the big companies. The small operators, remember them? They're history."

Dispatches from behind the lines, August 1989: Bert Paul calls it the dying of a rural society. Bert Paul is manager of the Thrifty Mart in Forks and a member of the Clallam County Economic Development Council, which is headquartered at Port Angeles on the Strait of Juan de Fuca. We are in the port city now, speaking with him and Judith St. Claire, the Council's executive director, about some of the economic impacts that might be expected in Clallam County as a result of the federal timber shutdown.

Right now, Clallam in general, and Port Angeles in particular, are sitting pretty. It is summertime. And summertime is tourist time. The ferries to and from Victoria, B.C., are packed to the gunwales. The vehicle count on 101 is high as the sky. Unemployment is a scant seven percent, the lowest it has been since 1974. The motels are full. The shops and restaurants are thriving. Happy days are here again. But for how long? When summer comes, can winter be far behind? Bert Paul sees a serious downturn beginning in January, a substantial falling off in retail sales. Even if the federal logjam should come apart, a crunch is certain to follow the New Year. Timber is the biggest employer in the county. When the tourists go home, timber's direct and indirect contribution to the economy of Clallam's west side rises to ninety-five cents on the dollar. But, if there is less timber, where is the dollar?

There has been talk at the Council of encouraging the development of value-added wood-products enterprises and cottage industries. There is always talk of this sort in big-timber country, from Oregon to Maine. Alas, for reasons varying from region to region, it is always easier said than done. Still, there are a few folks in Clallam County supplementing incomes with the sale of cedar lattices and alder baskets, of ferns and mosses gathered in the forest for the green-thumb trade. There is hope for mushroom ranching. And, inevitably, there is talk of employment retraining. But that is not a popular subject here, or anywhere. People want to do what they already know how to do. Besides, retraining too often implies relocation.

"Throughout our history as a nation," says Judith St. Claire, "it has always been so: Discontent with what's happening here? Then go to the frontier. Go West. Well, this is about as West as you can get. You can't go any farther. Somebody suggested loading all the people in a bus and taking them away. But where do you take them? They're where they want to be."

Dispatch: Peter G. Larsen is a logging contractor who lives with his wife and children in a house where he wants to be, overlooking the Soleduck River, just a toot upstream from Larry Mason's sawmill. It is late afternoon, and Larsen is very tired. He has been working a chain saw all day in a canyon near Sappho, on a contract let by the Cavenham Forest Industries people. The cut calls for 2.5 million board feet. With two helpers, Larsen expects the job will take him into the fall. And then? Who knows? He has never had trouble before finding work. But now. . . . He shrugs. He is distressed by the rate at which some of the lands roundabout have been harvested. He is unhappy to see so many fine logs going for export while people like Mason are hurting to pay off their loans at the bank. Some of his friends have already packed up and pulled out. There's a fishing lodge and guide service for sale somewhere up North, *way* North. After this Cavenham job is finished, maybe he'll head up that way to check the place out. Maybe.

Dispatch: At the opposite end of the Soleduck River Valley, where it joins the Bogachiel to form the Quillayute at the edge of the sea, Phillip Kitchel lives with his wife and children and worries about a lot of the things that bother Peter Larsen, but mostly he worries about the extent to which Washington's educational system depends on state timber sales. Kitchel, a member of the board of Quillayute Valley School District #402, which serves about fifteen hundred pupils on the west side of Clallam County, worries in particular about the deteriorating infrastructure of common schools in some long-settled parts of the state, and about the lack of any permanent infrastructure whatsoever in newer communities bursting their seams with school-age children.

In Fiscal 1988 the sale of state timber earned Washington's various trust funds some $163 million in revenues. The largest of these funds is earmarked by law for common school construction; it received a bit more than half of those revenues. But that's not enough to go around. According to Kitchel and other sources, the state has a $300 million backlog of common school construction projects authorized but not yet funded. "There's pressure from the state legislature," says Kitchel. "They have this idea that you just turn on the timber faucet and out comes the money for schools. When school board people go to Olympia to lobby for more money so our kids can learn how to compete in a global economy, the legislature says, 'Well, hell. Just cut more trees.' And that's ridiculous, because by the DNR's own models, the state's projected harvest on this peninsula by the Year 2000 is going to take a nosedive. We've got to cut trees, sure. But if we want our schools to succeed, we've got to have some help from the general fund, too."

A former woods worker, Kitchel is employed by the Clallam County Public Utility District. He reads meters and, if the unhappy occasion should arise, pulls the plug on people who can't keep up with their payments. Of current timber affairs on the west side, Kitchel says: "The issue isn't whether George Weyerhaeuser is going to make nine hundred million dollars on his stock options. The issue is how many people will I have to disconnect from their power next winter."

Dispatch: Ann Goos is executive director of Washington Commercial Forest Action Committee, a lobbying group dedicated to "maintaining public commercial forest lands for Washington's citizens." Her husband is a logger. They live in Forks. Ann Goos says: "I absolutely believe, the way things are going, that very soon we're going to have Appalachia out here. Part of the problem is there's no time for the community to adapt to what's happening. I've taught school, and I know. Kids sit there and say to me, 'Why should I go on with school? I'm going to work with my dad in the woods and get top dollar.' It would be very easy for me with my little master's degree to say back to those kids, 'Think creatively!' But where do I get off saying something like that?"

I ask her how the people of Forks feel about these plans I've heard are afoot in Clallam County, plans to provide—in lieu of workable timber or new kinds of jobs—counseling services to combat the social ills that tend to tear families apart in the face of economic dislocation. "That?" says Ann Goos. "That is what helps create vigilante hysteria."

From the air, at comfortable Cessna altitudes rather than Boeing's, the landscape of western Washington is distinguished by three images seen in no other state except Oregon, and only to a lesser extent there. I refer to the cuts, the cars, and the coded logs that lie in stacks at the edge of the sea. The cuts are seen on the coastal hills and the slopes of the Cascade Range, clean-shaven cuts squared-off here and there by section lines, cuts appearing tan under sunlight or gray under cloud, cuts in sharp contrast to the darker bas-relief of the standing forest. The cars sit in huge lots at the port facilities, acres of them gleaming in the sun, fresh off the boat, waiting for their buyers to arrive, bearing the imprint of Nissan and Mazda and Toyota and Honda. And the logs? The logs have come down from those cuts in the hills and are waiting for the boats of *their* buyers to carry them across the Pacific. Unloaded and then milled into lumber on the other side of the ocean, the American logs will provide jobs for Japanese mill workers, and homes for the people who built the Nissans.

The year 1989 was another big one for log exports to Asia, and would have been even bigger if the Chinese economy hadn't taken a tumble at Tiananmen Square. In the previous year, raw logs equivalent to some five billion board feet of finished lumber went to the Pacific Rim from the West Coast and Alaska, enough to prop up a good part of Korea's industrial expansion, China's attempt to rebuild its ancient infrastructure, and Japan's phenomenal 1.68 million housing starts (more than the number of starts in the United States, which has twice the population). Washington State's contribution to this outflow of fiber was not insignificant. By some accounts nearly half of its total harvest volume—counting all logs from all categories of land ownership—was shipped overseas. In the first seven months of 1989 the Olympic Peninsula's principal log yards at Port Angeles and Grays Harbor alone shipped nearly three-quarters of a billion board feet to the Rim. As the summer advanced, the stacks of logs grew higher and higher. It was said that the mills in Japan could hardly keep up with the volume provided them.

The Japanese people are prodigiously fond of wood. The texture, the color, and the smell of certain woods run with the grain of the country's traditions. Unlike Americans, Japanese builders do not act as if they were ashamed of wood, burying two-by-four studs under sheets of plasterboard. In Japan the wood is celebrated, exposed in slats and posts and beams. A quality home, considered anything but large by U.S. standards, can call for upwards of thirty tons of lumber. Japan imports almost three-quarters of the wood it consumes, not just from North America but from the Soviet Union and Southeast Asia. There is said to be a growing interest in timber from South America and Africa, too. Once upon a time, before World War II, Japan relied on its own forests to supply the coniferous species—pine, hinoki, cypress—desired for quality construction. The war depleted much of that forest and forced the country into a replanting program, the fruits of which will not be available for harvest for another ten to fifteen years. Meantime, there is this gap, and the United States, more than any other single country, is helping to fill it.

Of course, no one seriously believes that Japan will suddenly stop importing logs when its postwar forest comes of age. The Japanese are not altogether commodity-oriented; they appreciate having trees as well as timber. Indeed, one survey not so long ago found that only one out of three Japanese views the native forest as a timber resource, while many more regard it primarily as a curb against natural disasters, a protector of watershed values, or a filter of air pollutants. If such attitudes prevail over the next two decades, then surely Japan will continue to covet substitutable American softwood species—cedars, both the Port Orford (from Oregon) and the Alaska yellow; western hemlocks and Douglas fir from the Cascade Range, where the rate of growth is slower than in the coastal rainforest and thereby produces lumber more desirable to the Japanese market, with its softer texture and tighter grain; and mixed sorts of whitewood logs from the east side of the Cascade Range—grand fir and spruce and western white and lodgepole pine.

Almost all the major U.S. forest-industry corporations operating in the Northwest export logs to Japan and its Rimside neighbors, and almost all are earning handsome profits because of it. Among the larger players in this game is Plum Creek Timber Company, a limited partnership, based in Seattle, that was recently chipped off the old block of the Burlington Northern Railroad empire. Plum Creek owns some 1.5 million acres of timberlands stretching from the Rocky Mountain precincts of Bozeman, Montana, to the sundown side of the Washington Cascades. For export, the company operates yarding facilities at the ports of Everett, Lake Washington (Seattle), and Tacoma. Last year these facilities debouched to the Pacific Rim, as raw logs, about 160 million board feet of timber.

At Tacoma the logs arrive by truck, or in rafts towed by tug from Lake Washington. They are sorted according to size and species. There are dozens of sorts—some fifteen just for Dougfir alone. Each sort has its own code, painted or chalked on the butt of each log. The only logs with no marks on their butts belong to a class that is known as the east-side sort and includes grand fir, lodgepole, spruce, larch, hemlock, and white pine running from six to eleven inches in diameter. Some of this mixed poletimber, and a few large old-growth logs as well, come from Plum Creek's checkerboard sections east of Snoqualmie Pass, and from a large, solid block of timberland wholly surrounding the town called Roslyn between Interstate 90 and the topside of Cle Elum Ridge.

Randall A. Nelson is manager of Plum Creek's export log yards. On the afternoon I happened to call on him at the yard in Tacoma, a delegation of Japanese mill owners was touring the facility. Nelson explained that the visitors were big customers of Emachu U.S.A., Inc., the Seattle-based trading company, and that Emachu in turn is one big customer of Plum Creek. Among the visitors from Japan was a man in a gray flannel blazer. Nelson introduced him as Mr. Tsuno. Mr. Tsuno was said to own a mill in Gamagori, on the coast of Honshu southeast of Nagoya. With Emachu doing the stateside buying for him, Mr. Tsuno manufactured small-dimension lumber for residential construction. The saws in his mill were said to be calibrated especially for those logs that have no marks on their butts and come from the woods on the other side of Snoqualmie Pass.

A ship, *The Green Master,* was at dockside that day. Front-end loaders carried the sorted logs to the ship's booms, and the booms swung the logs through the air and down to the holds. Seven hundred and fifty truckloads, the *Master* was going to take, eighteen-thousand tons of logs, the holds filled first, the decks stacked high. "This is all for Emachu," Nelson said as we climbed a steel ladder to the bridge. "Five days to load her up, fourteen days across to Japan."

"And what's this?" I asked, pointing from the far side of the bridge at a raft of logs in the water.

"That's Emachu's, too," Nelson said. "An east-side sort, just towed down from Seattle. They'll load it tomorrow."

It occurred to me, then, looking down at the unmarked butts in the water, that maybe these logs were from one of those big Plum Creek cuts out past Snoqualmie, or possibly even from the precincts of Roslyn. When *The Green Master* got over to Japan, would trucks then take these logs to Mr. Tsuno's sawmill at Gamagori? I wondered if Mr. Tsuno, during his visit to America, would have the time to know where his east-side sorts actually come from. I wondered if he would ever get over the pass, say, to Roslyn; and, if he should, imagined how widely he'd smile to see all that timber awaiting the sawyers on the green flanks of Cle Elum Ridge.

Roslyn is nestled in a little draw about twenty-two hundred feet above sea level, eighty miles east-southeast of Seattle. The population is a shade under a thousand. Over the hill to the south lie the Cle Elum River and Interstate 90. Up the side canyons, north, stands Cle Elum Ridge, topping out a thousand feet higher. Unlike many of the ridges running off this side of the Cascades, the visible slopes of this one, at least above Roslyn, have not yet been whacked into sorts for the Rimside trade. Some of the folks roundabout Roslyn want to keep it that way.

There is a quality about this community that people have come to call a bubble in time. It is as if the clocks had stopped somewhere back toward the turn of the century and fixed everything in its place, except for the people. The people would come and go, or die and be buried in one of those cemeteries up on the hill. And the ones who replaced them, on arrival in town, would rub their eyes in wonder. For here were almost all of the elements some writer had joyfully described three-quarters of a century ago:

"The narrow crooked streets, the little houses perched on top of rocky hills, the sidewalks upon stilts or twisting around the sides of gulches, the cosmopolitan population—all the sites compose a view so utterly unlike anything else in the Yakima Valley as to be like a section of another world accidentally dropped down."

Well, okay; the stilts are gone. But not the colors and textures of unpainted siding and cedar shakes, tin roofs, unpaved alleys with board-and-batten outbuildings, gabled washhouses and one-stall barns, coal sheds (though not many privies), and The Brick—the old company saloon, built in 1889 at the epicenter of Roslyn, First Street and Pennsylvania Avenue, complete with a bar-length spittoon.

It was not an accident, however, that dropped Roslyn into the draw they once called Smith Creek Canyon. It was coal. More coal than you could shake a tipple at, and just in time, because the Northern Pacific Railroad was coming this way, looking for the likeliest pass in the mountains. And they found that, too. Tunneled the peaks at Stampede and burrowed for coal under Smith Creek Canyon, and platted this Roslyn place in '86 as the company town. By the turn of the century there were nine hundred men working the mines, producing a million tons of coal a year. Who were these people anyway? They were Scots and Poles and Italians and Serbs and Swedes, Lithuanians and Russians and Finns, Slavs, Croatians, Czechs, Hungarians, Syrians, Germans. By 1915 there were four thousand of them, counting dependents. By and by, they were producing *two* million tons of coal a year. The company store, which still stands catty-corner—but empty—to The Brick, was said to be the largest of its kind anywhere in Washington outside Seattle. Then the days and years dwindled down to a precious few, such that locomotives no longer burned coal and the railroads were a-merging. The last of the mines shut down in 1963. This was about the time in our history when the Northern Pacific became known as the Burlington Northern, though it would yet be a while before Burlington Northern, in terms of its timberlands, became known as Plum Creek.

Maybe a bit more than a decade and a half after the demise of coal in Roslyn and its neighboring towns of Ronald and Cle Elum, the old bubble in time seemed to be getting ready to go *pfffft*. Then something happened. Younger people—younger at least than the retired miners—began to discover the residual magic of Smith Creek Canyon and a chance for a life-style that the burgeoning burghs of Puget Sound could no longer provide. For here was an affordable place with funky houses and fruit trees out back, a place for dogs with no leashes and kids safe at play in the street, and the trailhead to Alpine Lakes Wilderness yonder a piece, and rafting the river, and skiing, and, wherever you looked beyond the rooftops of Roslyn, the great, mothering forest, the cutis vera of the bubble itself.

So another wave of immigrants began drifting in, worrying the old-timers at first with their differentness but soon enough settling in and getting acquainted, just like the outlander Serbs and Swedes before them. Then something *else* happened—something that would give many of the old folks and most of the new common cause. The company, the leftover lineal descendant of the Northern Pacific, the owner of all this land around Roslyn, began burrowing into the forest, mining its trees—first in huge, sweeping cuts that denuded the flanks of Roaring Ridge, back near Snoqualmie; then more cuts, leapfrogging the checkerboard, each new swipe of the chain saw one swipe closer to Cle Elum Ridge. In the letters column of the *Seattle Times,* one angry witness swiped back:

"I applaud the efforts of the Plum Creek Timber Company to hold back the flood of tourists along the I-90 corridor. At the rate those hills are being shaved, we will soon be able to take down the barricades and have the Ever-stump State all to ourselves."

For some of the old-time coal miners, it was bad enough that they had to look at these cuts whenever they drove down the interstate. But now the company—no matter that it had a different name and corporate purpose—now the company that had abandoned *them,* forced them into early retirement, was planning to cut the scenery right out from under their rocking chairs. Okay, so it wasn't a *virgin* forest. The first-generation miners had pretty well picked that one over for boards and battens and props for the mineshafts. But the trees had renewed themselves and were now eighty years along in their second growth. And now comes Plum Creek, with one eye on the Rim and the other on Wall Street. And Plum Creek is saying that it doesn't make corporate sense to hold on to this timber any longer. Sixty million board feet, there is, just within eyeshot of Roslyn. A bubble in time? Fiddlesticks! That's one helluva lot of east-side sorts.

The Yakima Management unit of Plum Creek Timber Company is headquartered in Roslyn at the upper end of Pennsylvania Avenue. Go out the front door, start walking uphill, and by and by, after much bushwhacking, you'll be standing on top of Cle Elum Ridge. The Yakima unit embraces 250 square miles of company land, mostly within the boundaries of Wenatchee National Forest, and mostly checkerboarded with federal sections. Since the early 1980s the company has been harvesting more than 100 million board feet a year from the unit, spruces and firs and hemlocks and larches and pines and cedars, leaving about five thousand acres annually to be replanted, mostly with Douglas fir. Of the total volume of logs harvested, the Yakima unit posts about 60 percent to the company's export yards on the coast, while the remainder either goes to a Plum Creek chip plant at Cle Elum or is sold to some other regional player, such as Boise Cascade.

The manager of Plum Creek's Yakima unit is a professional forester named Hartwig H. Vatheuer. In addition to presiding over the company's land and timber here, Vatheuer must also tend to some eight hundred miles of logging roads, thirty contractors, $14 million in contractual fees and payrolls, one seed orchard, and a not-altogether-impartial press. The press was not altogether impartial toward Plum Creek because it appeared to believe, no matter what Vatheuer or his superiors in Seattle might say to the contrary, that the company was determined to clearcut Cle Elum Ridge, from its windy puckerbrush top right down to the backyard fruit trees of Roslyn's outermost house.

Granted, the press might not have noticed Roslyn sitting there under a scrim of east-side sorts if it had not been for a handful of relative newcomers to town who, apprised of Plum Creek's intentions, banded together for the common cause. There would be no posturing, no confrontational acronym to stand for their badge of courage. They would call themselves, simply and directly, RIDGE, and they would fight the good fight as best they could—which, as is so often the case with grassrooters lacking the resources of a powerful corporation, turned out to be in the press. You can just imagine how Plum Creek in general, and Hartwig Vatheuer in particular, felt about that.

One fine summer day I went over the pass at Snoqualmie and down past the clearcut hillsides to Roslyn to see what the people at RIDGE and Plum Creek's Yakima unit had to say for themselves. I started with RIDGE, with Sara McCoy, Cordy Cooke, and Susan Willis-Johnson, and we sat on the front porch of one of their homes, looking out over Smith Creek Canyon and up the long green slope of Cle Elum Ridge. Only the night before, the RIDGE people had gone to the Roslyn City Council, seeking support for *their* prescription for Plum Creek's management of the thirteen-thousand acres of timberlands adjacent to town. And can you imagine how Hartwig Vatheuer felt about *that*?

"We haven't heard yet," said Sara McCoy, who is married to a logger.

As Susan Willis-Johnson explained it, the RIDGE plan offered alternatives that could protect the long-term interests of everyone involved. "Sustainable ecology, sustainable economy"— that was their motto. Cut out the clearcuts and get into selective, uneven-aged management. Stop copping out with this talk about seed-tree and shelter-wood cuts, where you leave a variable number of standing trees per acre and then go back in and take them down in five or ten years. That's nothing but a "delayed clearcut." Adopt a hundred-year rotation cycle, and cut only ten percent of the total volume every ten years, in perpetuity. Create a low-cut or no-cut buffer to maintain the "wall of trees" around town. Stay off the ridge-top. Give first consideration for all contracts to local contractors. Give Roslyn a break.

I told the RIDGE people, then, that I was going to the other side of town to talk with Hartwig Vatheuer. Cordy Cooke said:

"That's good. You'll like Hartwig. I believe he's doing the very best that he can do, or is allowed to do. Hartwig is a professional, but he is also a company man. And you know how that is. The company always knows best."

Cordy Cooke was right. I liked Hartwig Vatheuer. And yes, after more than two decades, he was a company man. Out of forestry school and aboard the Northern Pacific to work in its woods. And all the while, the old original railroad company that had received all of this land as a nineteenth-century gift from Uncle Sam was evolving into something else; something that had less and less to do with the intent of Uncle's generous subsidy—to facilitate the transport of freight and passengers—and more and more to do with ventures far trendier on Wall Street, such as oil, natural gas, minerals, real estate, and timber. Hartwig Vatheuer did not know about trends. But he knew about timber.

We got in a company four-wheel-drive that day and drove beyond Roslyn on some of the company roads to look at the company's trees. Vatheuer said:

"I told the RIDGE people we weren't going to wipe out the scenery with clearcuts. I kind of like to look out the window at scenery, too. They wouldn't listen. The problem is, foresters traditionally operate best in the forest. But they've done a lousy job of telling the public what it is they do, and now they're paying the price for it."

And maybe, I said, part of that price was having to listen to the public tell the foresters how to do their job. Right? So how did he feel about that management prescription RIDGE had uncorked before the city council?

Vatheuer said, "I just got a copy. I haven't had time to read it through. My initial reaction is they ought to sell it to some politician so they can acquire the land." (An official response came later from Plum Creek President David D. Leland. In a letter to RIDGE, Leland offered assurances that there would be no clearcutting on the slopes behind Roslyn. Of course, he was compelled to note that pine beetles had been causing "substantial mortality" on the ridge and that, of course, Plum Creek would have to salvage these dead and dying trees. As for delayed clearcuts of seed-tree or shelterwood harvests, well—not to worry, RIDGE. No plans at present for a second entry, and when that changes, you'll be the first to know.)

As we toured the territory, Vatheuer explained the prescriptions for some of these different cuts. Seed-tree, you leave about three good trees per acre, just enough to help the natural regeneration along. Shelterwood, you try to leave, say, ten to fifteen. Depending on site, you make the second entry to get those trees in five to ten years. Clearcuts, of course, you take it all at once and then replant with 360 Dougfirs to the acre, thin them out at age twelve, harvest at eighty.

We had come to a Plum Creek clearcut on the side of a hill overlooking, at some distance, the Cle Elum River. Roslyn itself was nowhere in sight, hidden behind that "wall of trees." But what we *could* see, in addition to the river and the second-growth standing straight and tall all around the perimeter of this clearcut, was a slag heap from one of the coal mines at Ronald, and beyond it the brooding brow of Cle Elum Ridge. Our talk had shifted from silviculture to other things. Vatheuer had just been saying that once upon a time his grandfather had been a forester, too. In Silesia, it was, when Silesia had been Germany, before the war. Vatheuer seemed proud of that, proud to know that his roots ran down through the loden green, back to the very place where modern forestry began.

Then we were both looking up at the ridge. I said, "How can you possibly get at the timber up there and still keep peace with the people of Roslyn?"

He said, "We can do it," and paused to let the certainty of that statement sink in, and then went on. "Look, we own that land. There are still a lot of people who have some pretty strong feelings about land ownership. And they don't believe in interference."

Even after hearing that, I still liked Hartwig Vatheuer—not for his certainty but maybe for his openness, maybe for his loden green. And maybe I should have been more open myself, at least to share with him what I was thinking. I was thinking that there are still a lot of people whose feelings about windfalls are just as strong as other people's feelings about interference in the ownership of land. I was thinking how could anyone reasonably assume a proprietary stance about land that was a gift from the American people. I was thinking: Could Abraham Lincoln and his Congress, who granted these once-upon-a-time public lands to the Northern Pacific in perpetuity, ever have imagined in their wildest dreams that one day the same land would be growing trees in order that—peace, Hartwig Vatheuer!—a CEO named David Leland might post the logs across an ocean, to a sawmill with blades calibrated to turn the east-side sort, in a town called Gamagori, in the country of Japan?

4. RESOLUTIONS

It would be a grave disservice to the Evergreen State, which is, after all, a relatively civilized place, to leave the impression that everyone who cares about trees or timber is either down in the trenches or up on the ridges blasting away at the other side. Some folks are, and some will go on doing that no matter what happens. But some aren't.

Here and there—and this seems to be unique to Washington State—men and women are laying down their dingbats and press releases, swallowing their pride, and actually addressing the needs of their traditional adversaries in an effort to work things out. Some promising conflict-resolution strategies are emerging from these efforts. To what extent they are likely to bring a lasting peace is anyone's guess. The hardliners are having no part of it. Time will tell.

The most visible form of détente in Washington these days is a process that is known as TFW, which is shorthand for Timber/ Fish/Wildlife. And fish are what started it all—salmon and the Indian tribes that claimed the salmon as their native right to harvest. Trouble was, loggers were claiming their rights, too, harvesting trees upstream in a fashion that was not altogether impartial to the spawning habits of anadromous fish. By and by and time after time the tribes went to court, and won every time. But as TFW advocate and Weyerhaeuser executive David Mumper recalls it, although the tribes continued to win in court, "the court decisions were not producing more fish." And that's when people started sitting down at the council table.

The underlying fabric of TFW is an agreement hammered out over the course of many months by many people with diverse interests, people such as Mumper of Weyerhaeuser and Marcy Golde of the Washington Environmental Council and Billy Frank, Jr., of the Northwest Indian Fisheries Commission and Jim Waldo of the Northwest Renewable Resources Center in Seattle. The agreement seeks to replace confrontation with negotiated cooperation and loosely binds all participants to a commitment to listen carefully to the other side, to articulate opportunities rather than positions, to work toward a consensus, to eschew using the press for preemptive strikes. The last-named ground rule has been the hardest for some environmentalists to accept, and understandably, too. RIDGE, for example, dropped out of a Yakima Valley TFW situation because it felt that abandoning its access to the press would leave all the cards up Plum Creek's sleeve. Moreover, as industry and environmental types felt their temperatures rising over the owl and old-growth issue, there was a noticeable and concomitant cooling of their ardor for TFW, a renewal of distrust that could dump détente right back into the bottom of the trenches.

If there was any breakthrough at all, it may well have been wrought by the Commission on Old Growth Alternatives for Washington's Forest Trust Lands, a task force of thirty-two individuals even more discrete in points-of-view than the original TFW conveners. State Public Lands Commissioner Brian Boyle charged his appointees (including several members of the Seattle

Audubon Society) to come up with consensus recommendations on how to balance economic and environmental concerns in the future management of old-growth forests on state trust lands on the west side of the Olympic Peninsula. After a year at the council table, the commission weighed in with its final report. Among its recommendations:

—Creation by the DNR of a sustained-yield unit on the state's west-side lands, a move calculated to stabilize timber supply for the local economy and income for the trust beneficiaries, and slow the loss of old-growth habitat as well. This would involve reducing annual timber harvests through the 1990s some 28 percent below current levels.

—The deferral of harvest for fifteen years on fifteen-thousand acres of old-growth habitat identified as "most critical for spotted owls." This, in the words of the commission report, "will allow experience to be gained from management and research that will lead to wise future decisions for these areas."

—Establishment of an Olympic experimental state forest and research center. Of all the commission's recommendations, this one stands out as the most significant, in that "the intent is to recognize that the DNR lands are a commercial forest within which there is special opportunity to experiment with harvest techniques. The Commission believes that the ecological values of old-growth forests include but go beyond spotted owl habitat [and that] this recommendation may lead to entirely new models of forestry including workable alternatives which balance production with ecology."

"A kinder, gentler forestry" is how Jerry Franklin describes this new approach to silviculture. Franklin, who served on the commission and inspired it with his insights, is chief plant ecologist for the U.S. Forest Service Pacific Northwest Research Station and Bloedel professor of ecosystem analysis at the University of Washington's forest resources college. For several years now, he has been known in the press as "the guru of old-growth," a role that rankles many Forest Service bureaucrats; though not surprisingly, since many Forest Service bureaucrats still believe in the gospel according to Gifford Pinchot.

The way Franklin sees it, America can no longer afford to look at the forest as if it were a pie to be divided, so much for commodity production and so much for the preservation of ecological values, on the assumption that the two are incompatible. Now the pie must be shared, not divided. Sure, let's have our old-growth and biological diversity protected by set-aside at one extreme, and our plantations for production at the other, but that's not enough. What about the forest where we can have *both*? Let's see if we can retain or reproduce some of the values of old-growth ecosystems in the managed forest even as we proceed, with gentler practices, to extract commodities from it. Let's see whether, after all these years, we can begin to develop, in Franklin's words, "a sound ecological basis for the often-maligned concept of multiple-use forestry."

And how would this be achieved? John Calhoun, the DNR's Olympic area manager who will implement some of Franklin's ideas in the west-side experimental forest, has a long list of possibles. Rubber tires, for example, where steel treads just won't do. Cull logs and other debris left at the site—"sloppy clearcuts," some folks are calling it. Snags and seed trees left standing. Size and configuration of cuts designed to enhance natural forest functions, possibly even aggregating the cuts instead of dispersing them, in order that the uncut areas might retain more of those functions. Avoidance of slash burning and bulldozer windrowing. Natural regeneration rather than plantation stocking. Use of herbicides a last resort. Pre-commercial thinnings where the debris is left to rot on the forest floor. Management plans designed to limit the number and length of roads and to restrict their use, once established.

Some skeptics say it all sounds fine, but it won't work. Maybe on the east side of the Cascades it will work. Maybe where the trees aren't so big, so destructive as they crash to the ground. But on the west side, forget it. Of course, Franklin and Calhoun and, for that matter, everyone else with a stake in the forest cannot afford to forget it. They've tried just about every other way, though mostly Gifford Pinchot's way. That didn't work. Kind-and-gentle may be the only way left to go.

If there are any lingering doubts as to the failure of conventional forestry in America, especially insofar as it has fallen short of its most vaunted goal, sustained yield, then let the doubter hie himself to the Hood Canal Ranger District of Olympic National Forest. Point him out of Shelton and up the Skokomish Valley on National Forest Primary Route 23, up past Grisdale Hill and the campground at Brown Creek, then over past Spider Lake to the headwalls of the Satsop drainage. And there let him gaze across the naked draws and canyons of the Shelton Cooperative Sustained Yield Unit to see just how miserable a failure can be when conventional foresters put their minds to it.

The Shelton unit itself was anything but conventional when the U.S. Forest Service created it in 1946 to provide that "stabilizing influence" earlier bureaucrats had identified as the agency's top mission. (Congress never intended community stability to be the agency's top mission, but never mind that. Pinchot's disciples were agency men, and you understand how *that* is. The agency always knows best.) What happened was this: The Simpson Timber Company, biggest of the private players in the southeast quadrant of the Olympic Peninsula, had just about run out of mature timber by the end of World War II. Sure, there was some second-growth coming on, but that was years away from harvest. There was going to be one helluva gap in supply, and if something didn't happen soon, why the whole town of Shelton, and McCleary, too, would be gurgling down the drain. So the Forest Service said, "Okay, Simpson. Let's have a cooperative sustained-yield unit. You put up 159,000 acres of company land, and we'll put up 111,000 of national forest land; and while your land is growing back, you come on over and cut ours, and when our land is growing back, we'll go on over and cut yours; and you get a monopoly, Simpson, as long as you put at least 80 percent of the logs through the mills of Shelton and McCleary, and everyone will live happily. In perpetuity." The contract on perpetuity expires in December 2046, should the topsoil of the Shelton Cooperative Sustained Yield Unit be so lucky to last that long.

Though no one has had to convince *me* of the failures of forestry, not recently anyway, the least I could do one day when I happened to be in the precincts of Shelton was to climb in a truck with Chuck Sisco and let him use me for practice. Sisco was the National Audubon Society's issues specialist in the Pacific Northwest, having served time with the U.S. Forest Service in Kentucky, Montana, and California. He was working now to complete a master's thesis on the life and times of the spotted owl. On our way up the Skokomish out of Shelton, he promised we'd poke into some old-growth, up above the cooperative clearcuts, and see if maybe we couldn't hoot up an owl or two. But first we had to have a look at this thing the Forest Service was calling "sustained yield."

I have seen large clearcuts up close in five or six states, in all kinds of country conditions, including the erodible siltstone conditions of Redwood country in Northern California. I had always held the Redwood cuts to be the worst of the worst—until Sisco showed me the view from the Satsop headslopes, here in Olympic Dougfir country. These weren't cuts. These were landslides. Battlefields and moonscapes, Scylla and Charybdis, the far flanks of hell. Not yesterday's harvests, either. We're talking harvests that are five, ten, or fifteen years old, maybe, and most places hardly sprouting a weed. "This is what the Forest Service calls sustained yield," said Sisco. "You want to sell gravel, this would make a fine quarry. Don't you think?"

"Well, at least quarries beat subdivisions."

"Barely," said Chuck Sisco. And we headed for the owls.

As we put Uncle Sam's cooperative quarries behind us, following the South Fork Skokomish toward higher ground, the idea of subdivisions supplanting forestland, even *scalped* forestland, started turning over in my mind. It was a problem that seemed to be much dismissed from the agendas of many conservationists. It was as if the huggers didn't want to confuse the one issue that had them in thrall, namely protecting the bio-diversity of the old-growth forest. Or possibly they just didn't want to trade in their favorite adversary, the slavering timber beast, for a buttoned-down developer. No matter that beast and button-down were becoming all of a piece. No matter that Weyerhaeuser, the

"Tree Growing" company, was now billing itself as a "major residential and commercial real estate developer," with its two-thousand-acre Snoqualmie Ridge project the barest tip of the iceberg. No matter that private nonindustrial landowners in western Washington were skinning their lands to cash in on the market, then converting the slash piles into five-acre lots. Or that state and county planners could already predict that growth in the Puget Sound area and the Interstate-5 corridor, at the rate it was going, would gobble up a quarter-million acres of forest before the Year 2000. Or that the conversion of these lands and the permanent loss of their productivity would likely leave a dent in the timber supply greater than all the set-asides in Washington resulting from the Wilderness Act of 1964. I mean even a Scylla and Charybdis landslide might grow trees *someday*, if you leave it alone long enough. But condos are forever.

At the end of the South Fork Skokomish road, Sisco parked his truck and we got out and started on foot up the trail to Sundown Pass. We wouldn't get anywhere near that far. It was four miles up to the boundary, where the national forest ends and Olympic National Park begins, and then maybe another three to the pass. That kind of walking, this time of day—well, Sisco could practice that on somebody else. So we poked up the trail just far enough to get a sense of the place, to see some big trees, and to feel relatively certain that when Sisco started hooting up his owl, some timber beast wouldn't hop out of his pickup back at the roadhead and start pumping birdshot in our direction.

The trees were big, all right. Dougfirs, mostly, some hemlock and cedar, each looking big enough to feed a month of sawmills, or rich enough to fertilize this entire Skokomish hillside with the chemistry of its own salubrious death and decay. Take your pick. Sisco was saying that the Simpson Timber people wanted to pick the month of sawmills, wanted to save these old trees from going to waste even though this is an important back-country route into the national park, a corridor offering primitive recreation, according to the national forest's proposed land-and-resource-management plan. You'd think Simpson would back off, but then why should it? Don't forget that contract that the Forest Service signed in 1946. While your land is growing back, come on over and cut ours. Remember?

The trees. Not only big but ancient. At least some of them. That cedar there. Five hundred years old maybe. Merchantable even before Juan de Fuca could tell his little fib about the Strait of Anian. Old *Thuja plicata* there, terminally ill in the sixteenth century, yet still standing, still plugged in at the dawn of the twenty-first.

Ahead on the trail, Sisco stopped suddenly and made owl noise, rolling it off the roof of his mouth. He looked as if he fully expected an answer. I checked out the map. Now if only I were in better shape, and we had a week, say, we could go right up to the top of the South Fork, over Sundown Pass, cross over Six Ridge to the North Fork, duck down to the Duckabush and over the next winding ridge to the Quinault. The world co-champion western hemlock was down there somewhere along the river, just upstream from a place the map calls—so there *was* one, after all—Enchanted Valley. I'd like to see both someday. The gold-medal hemlock and the Enchanted Valley. And I'd like to hear the cry of a spotted owl, just once. Not that Sisco didn't do his damnedest to call one up for me. He called and called and called until I thought the Skokomish itself might spread its wings. Then silence. We listened. No answer.

THE TREE ARMY

The name of this place is Blackberry Crossing, probably because, once upon a time, this was where you crossed the river to get to the berries on the other side. And the time before that, the place simply took its identity from the numerical code of a company of men who camped here among the pines and the birches during the leanest years the country had ever known. The 1177th, they called it, right here on the ferny banks of the Swift River, in the White Mountain National Forest, in the Granite State of New Hampshire. All gone now, this camp of the 1177th; all gone but the stone chimneys hiding back there in the scrub, and the cement pad of the mess hall serving up weeds, and the hollows of the old latrines mulching leaves. And the lingering memories of those who, living nearby, come back to Blackberry Crossing from time to time to run their fingers through the yellowed pages of experience; who gather themselves now for a retelling of the "Cees." I mean the Tree Army. The Soil Soldiers. The CCC.

Now comes Charles F. LeBroke of Conway. "Toke," they called him then, and still do. Toke says: "The 1177th was a real good camp, maybe the best in the country. The food was good.

The people running the place were good. The work was good. The country was good. Looking back over all these years, I'd have to say we were awful lucky, just being here. Yessir! Awful lucky."

Comes also Warren Hill of Madison, saying: "It was about the best experience of my life. It saved my family. I had a mother and three sisters that had to be fed. And there was no work for a teenager. But the Cees were an out. My mother could support herself and my sisters on the twenty-five dollars I sent home every month. Hard to believe, but that's the way it was in those days. A dollar was a dollar."

There are more than a thousand places like Blackberry Crossing in America today—grown-over places lost on the maps but not forgotten. You are walking up this woods road through the forest and suddenly here is an old clearing gone scratchy with brambles and staghorn sumac; a bucket, rusted through; the rotted corner post of a barrack; a medallion of cracked concrete; a midden of bottles and cans. Artifacts of the Civilian Conservation Corps and its short-term tenure on the land. Nine years—1933–1942—was all they had to make their mark. Yet they left more than middens. They left billions of nursery trees growing in the cutover forests, and billions of mature trees untouched by fire for all the sweat off their smoke-eating brows. They left lean-to shelters and picnic tables and bridges and campgrounds in the parks. They left new parks. They secured the eroding soil with plantings and check dams. They lifted the sagging face of a national landscape gone limp from abuse and neglect.

And if every last one of the Cees were still living today, there would be three million American men with memories not unlike those of Charles LeBroke and Warren Hill, or of Ellsworth Russell of Eaton Center, who, remembering, says:

"Depression times, before the CCC, we did odd jobs—cuttin' wood, drivin' a truck. Drivin' a truck, we got thirty cents an hour. Cuttin' wood, we'd get a dollar a cord. That's cut and split and piled. And we didn't have power saws then. Anyways, I heard about this CCC deal and I looked into it and the ranger up here, he told me all about it. So I joined up and they sent us down to Fort William at Portland and they gave us our training down there and they gave us our clothes. Then they sent us up here where they were just setting up the first camp at Tamworth. That was the 117 Company, before the 1177th at Blackberry Crossing."

And now Toke puts in: "I grew up on the West Side—what they call in Conway the West Side of the Saco River. I used to walk down the railroad tracks to high school, about two miles. And I graduated in 1936. Now we survived all right. We'd stock up with a barrel of apples for the winter, a barrel of flour, you know, and we'd survive. Go out and shoot a couple of deer and some rabbits. Raise a pig. Have a garden. And coming from that, up here, why, I was better off than most of the boys just coming to camp.

"So after I graduated, my dad runs into Peale Gray, who was a ranger here, and the ranger said to my dad, 'What's your boy doin'? Workin'?' And my dad said, 'Yeah. He's pickin' corn for Harry Smith up here for a dollar a day.' Well, the ranger said, 'We have an opening up at the 1177—the CCC camp—for a local experienced man.' Now of course I'd just come out of high school. But I'd helped my dad cut wood, so I knew something of that, and I'd helped my uncle clear trails, which he used to do a little bit for the Appalachian Mountain Club, and I'd worked on the roads, tarring, during school vacations. So they must have figured, well, if we can't get the ideal man, we'll just go ahead and take him. And they did. I took the physical and went to work the next day."

And Warren Hill says: "People nowadays can't realize the extent of the CCC program. Why, it was just like dropping a rock in the pond. The ripples spread out and out. It wasn't just us in the camp, and the work we did. It was the good it was doing with send-home money back in the cities. I honestly believe to this day that if the Cees had not been instituted at that time, there would have been—" and into the pause Ellsworth Russell interjects: "A civil war right here."

"I don't know about that, Ellsworth," says Warren Hill. "I don't know what I might have done. I do know I wasn't just going to sit there and watch my family go hungry."

The look of the country that year was reflected in the faces of the people. Everything was dry. Pinched. A desert was marching across the big plains. Hill-country Texas was blowing away in the wind. Blowing dust bloodied the sunset at Kansas City. A knock at the door brought a writ of foreclosure, then boards on the windows. Even the banks went dry; the President gave them a holiday in March. All the roaring of the preceding decade was over. The roar was replaced by a heaving sob. In Boston and Baltimore, Nashville and New York City, many of the great machines of industry stood idle. The job pool was drying up. The unemployed waited in lines on the sidewalks for bread. They waited for soup; and when it came, that was dry, too, being so thin. Only Prohibition was not dry. It was meant to be dry, but in fact it was wet. No matter. Prohibition would end in December. Now it was March. The cherry blossoms were preparing to bloom along the Potomac. There was a new man in the White House. His name was Franklin Delano Roosevelt. It was said that the President cared as much for the jobless young men waiting in bread lines as he cared for trees, and that somehow he aimed to put the two of them—the hungry lads and the thirsty land—together, in order that both these resources might be saved.

Nowadays we do not often remember Franklin Delano Roosevelt as a lover of trees, an outdoors person, a chip off the hickory block that was Uncle Teddy. We see him instead in a wheelchair, paralyzed legs under a lap robe, and he is making war talk with that potbellied Englishman smoking the fat cigar. For my own part, I prefer a different view, a different photograph. It hangs yet on a wall at the Roosevelt family retreat (now a memorial park) on Campobello Island, off the far edge of Maine. It is a young Roosevelt here, of an age, had he been born later and under less privileged circumstances, to have qualified him for enrollment in the CCC. Bare-chested, he kneels at the stern of a birchbark canoe. It's Fenimore Cooper's Hawkeye I see. It's Natty Bumppo, with the summer off from Harvard, come Down East to the fir-fringed shore. It is Franklin, acting out the Jeffersonian ideal that life is lived best in the far country, under open skies, close to nature. And it suggests—in the steady eyes and the almost too-perfect blue-blood face that in time would be twisted by private pain and public responsibility— that the out-of-doors would always loom large among his priorities, wherever the goal, whatever his mission.

One of his first missions was to fix things up on the home-base estate at Hyde Park, New York, overlooking the Hudson River. He did that by putting the place to work growing trees, by curbing the Hudson's appetite for riverbank soil. He ran successfully for the New York State Senate. As chairman of its Fish and Game Committee, he harried the game hogs and the good ol' boys with his calls for reform. Hitching his star to the presidential aspirations of James M. Cox, he ran for the vice-presidency in 1920 and lost. No matter. Possibly for the first time in American politics, conservation had been treated as a major issue. He became governor of New York in 1929. Within three years he had wheedled and cajoled the state into accepting a $20 million program to reforest a million acres of cutover marginal land. Within four, he had taken 10,000 jobless New Yorkers off the streets and put them together with the forest to implement that program.

So where had he come by this crazy notion that trees and men could be made to save each other? Some political analysts calculated that Roosevelt had simply borrowed a page from the philosophical pragmatist William James, among whose many high-minded ideas was this singular one known to James as "the moral equivalent of war." Now James, though of Harvard, had never knelt in the stern of a birchbark canoe. Thus, *his* war would require an army enlisted against nature rather than with it. "To coal and iron mines," essayed the great thinker, "to freight trains, to fishing fleets in December . . . to foundries and stokeholes and to the frames of skyscrapers would our gilded youths be drafted off, according to their choice, to get the childishness knocked out of them, and to come back into society with healthier sympathies and soberer ideas."

Perhaps it was all a bit much, even for William James. Even for 1912, when he first espoused it. According to historian John

Salmond, whose work, *The Civilian Conservation Corps: 1933–1942*, is probably the best of the Corps accounts, Roosevelt could not remember ever having read James's essay on the moral equivalent of war, and "certainly denied ever consciously connecting it" with any of his relief programs. By 1932, Roosevelt was probably influenced sufficiently by his own inclinations, if not by the example of actual precedents at home and abroad—the subsistence work camps set up by state and county officials in the public forests of Washington and California, and the forest-labor programs already established by the federal governments of Norway, Sweden, Denmark, Austria, and the German Republic.

In August of that year, Roosevelt proceeded to lay the foundations of the ccc. Accepting the Democratic presidential nomination, he said that "economic foresight and immediate employment march hand in hand in the call for the reforestation of vast areas" of the American land. As President-elect in November, he promptly dispatched the agriculturalist Henry Wallace and the economics advisor Rexford Tugwell to the office of Chief Forester Robert Stuart. The visitors instructed Stuart to prepare a plan to employ 25,000 jobless men in the national forests. Stuart was a protégé of the grandpappy forester Gifford Pinchot. He was delighted. He proceeded to draft the plan. Yet barely a month later, Stuart was told by the incoming team to scratch that scenario and work up another. It was simply a matter of scale. Not 25,000 men. Now it was to be a quarter of a million.

By today's standards, the speed with which Roosevelt created his Tree Army was breathtaking. Sworn into office on the fourth of March, he had a bill on his desk, passed by both houses of Congress and ready for signature, by the thirty-first. They called it the Emergency Conservation Work Act (though some Republicans called it other things, including "Communism"). The act provided for the relief of an "acute condition of widespread distress and unemployment . . . existing in the United States," and for "the restoration of the nation's depleted natural resources." In order to accomplish these tasks, the President was granted broad discretionary powers, one of the few conditions imposed on him being that "in employing citizens for the purposes of this act, no discrimination shall be made on account of race, color, or creed"—an amendment, and a novel one for those days, secured in the waning hours of floor debate by Republican Representative Oscar De Priest of Illinois, then the nation's one and only black congressman.

And by today's standards of management and organization, it was a can of worms. On a blank piece of paper, Roosevelt drew a square and called it Fechner, after the man he had appointed to serve as program director. From Fechner's square, lines radiated all over the page to other squares—to the Department of Labor, which would select the junior enrollees (all single men, eighteen to twenty-five years of age) and the "local experienced woodsmen" (men of whatever age and marital status, who would function afield as the straw-bosses); to the War Department, the U.S. Army, which would construct a thousand camps throughout the country, and fill them with a quarter-million men, and clothe and feed those men, and make sure that each one got out of his sack in the morning; to the Department of Agriculture, the U.S. Forest Service, which would supervise the work projects in the national and state forests; and to the Department of the Interior, National Park Service, Office of Indian Affairs, General Land Office, Bureau of Reclamation, Soil Erosion Service, each responsible for technical supervision of conservation work on lands under its respective control.

Roosevelt insisted on action that hardly seemed possible. His deadline was July 1. Three months from the ink drying on the enabling act, and everything—the camps, the men, the projects—was to be in place. Already he was upping the ante again. A quarter-million junior enrollees *plus* 24,000 local experienced men. Not 1,000 camps now, but 1,300, and distributed to every state in the Union except Delaware. To meet these goals, the Army would have to build and equip camps at the rate of twenty-six a day. The Labor Department would have to achieve and maintain an enrollment rate of 8,540 men each day—a rate greater even than that attained by the military services at the height of mobilization during World War I. But they did it. By the first of July, all those dangling squares on Roosevelt's piece of paper were across their deadlines, everything in place.

Purchase records of the program's first year show that the Cees were an army indeed: 7,000,000 tent pins, 400,000 brooms, 2,097,000 blue denim jumpers, 180,000 bags of cement, 2,000,000 linear feet of water pipe. By the end of the second year other commodities had been tallied, such as 1,406,000 hogs and 187,500 steers. Considering the exact nature of the nation's "widespread distress," and given that part of the anatomy that armies always travel on, I'd have to guess that somehow the pork and the beef were of greater importance to the Cees than the brooms and the tent pins.

More than anything else, these veterans of the Cees seem to remember the food. Their stories keep running out through the mess hall and into the kitchen. Chocolate pudding, brewed in a fifty-five gallon drum. The smell of morning coffee (brewed, some say, from surplus beans left over from World War I). Always plenty of potatoes and too much bologna. Never enough beef. Remembering the spike camp at Willey Slide, Ellsworth Russell says:

"The cook and I used to walk down to Carrigan Station to pick up the mail. Well, I had a .32-caliber pistol hidden away in my footlocker and we'd take that down there with us and go up in what they call the Frankenstein Ledges at night. We'd go up there and there were a lot of hedgehogs. Porcupines. So we'd shoot a couple of 'em and we'd dress 'em out right there in the woods and take the meat back to camp. We'd cook it up in a stew. The fellas, they didn't know the difference. Meat was meat. With a mess of onions and some carrots and hedgehog, well, you could cook you up a pretty good stew.

"Now our boss up there—he stayed in a camp down below, fella the name of McKenzie—one day he decided he'd just stay over at our place for dinner. So the cook called me out to the kitchen and he said, 'What are we goin' to do? We got two of those hedgehogs in the stew fixed up for dinner.' I said, 'Feed it to him. He's here. Nothing we can do about it. Maybe he'll like it.' Well, he did like it. He ate it right up. And afterwards, McKenzie came out in the kitchen and we were sittin' there talkin' and he said, 'By the way, where'd you get the wild meat?' 'No,' we said. 'We don't have no wild meat.'

" 'Well, where'd you get that meat we had for dinner?'

" 'Oh,' we said. 'That's just somethin' they sent on up from the main camp.'

"McKenzie, he thought about that for a while and he said, 'No, you can't push that down my throat. I've tasted wild meat before. That didn't come from the main camp.'

"So the cook looked at me and I looked at him and we thought—What the hell, there's no sense lyin'. So we told him. 'It's hedgehog.'

"He said, 'Didn't taste too bad. But how come you're feedin' the boys hedgehog?'

"We said, 'That's all we got. They send up twelve pounds of meat to last twelve of us the week, and we eat it all up in one meal. We got to have somethin' for the rest of the week.'

"He said, 'Well, we'll change that. How'd you catch 'em?'

" 'Shot 'em.'

" 'Well,' he said, 'who's got the arms?'

"I told him I had a revolver. See, we weren't meant to have any firearms. It went against the rules.

"So McKenzie says, 'You bring it on down to my camp and leave it and if you need it any time you come there and get it. But don't go shootin' any more wild meat.' Well, he took a trip down to the main camp in a day or so and after that we got plenty of meat. They fed us good."

Most of them were city boys. To the 117th at Tamworth, and later to the offshoot 1177th at Blackberry Crossing, they came skinny and scared out of Boston and Worcester, New Bedford and Springfield and Woburn and Lowell. There were Ahearn and Brodzinski and Dolan and Eagan and LaFreniere and Mancini and Quirk, Souto, Surko, and Zdonek. And there was Warren Hill. He was from Lawrence, the textiles city. He had never before been to the big woods. Few of them had. One day Hill, in street clothes, was standing at the depot in Lawrence, waiting for the Boston & Maine to carry him north. Eighteen hours later, in denim, he was bouncing in the back of an Army truck, through the white clapboard hamlet of Tamworth and up the Fowlers Mill Road to the 117th. Warren Hill got out of the truck and stared at the evergreen wall all around him. He gazed with puzzlement upon the unfamiliar tools of his newfound trade, mattocks and cant-hooks and crosscut saws. He ran a hand over his assigned cot; the mattress was filled with straw ticking. Suddenly Hill sat down on his cot and wished that he were home again in Lawrence. By payday, he had changed his mind. By payday, even the pines seemed friendlier. The tools were a cinch. The ticking felt softer than down. And twenty-five dollars—he got only thirty dollars a month—was on its way home to his mother. Let the money go south to Lawrence. Warren Hill would be staying up here, north, in the big woods.

The daily routine at Tamworth or Blackberry Crossing was pretty much the same as in any of the CCC camps. First call at 5:45 A.M., Reveille at 6:00. Roll out and into your denim fatigues, breakfast at 6:30, work call at 7:00, an hour for lunch (brown-bag bologna out in the woods), quit work at 4:00 P.M., dinner at 5:30, Taps at 10:00. For the most part, Regular and Army Reserve officers in charge of the camps were under strict orders from their civilian commander-in-chief to avoid the imposition of military discipline. Weekend passes were freely distributed to the men, and carousers sneaking back to their cots after Taps got winks rather than reprimands—unless they failed to turn out for the next day's work. There was one concession to the Army way: an inspection at 5:00 P.M., with the enrollees spruced up in their scratchy woolen olive-drab "dress" uniforms (another recycled surplus item from World War I).

From Tamworth they rolled out to White Lake Park and built a bathhouse and fixed up the beach. They staked out a road up Great Hill and raised a fire tower a the top. They hacked ski trails into the mountains, opened scenic vistas, planted trees, and stalked the incorrigible gooseberry bush that was spreading a blister-rust devil through the north country's pines. In June—it was 1935 now—Lieutenant Philip S. Robbins took Warren Hill and twenty-one other men of the 117th to a new site on the Swift River and put them to work setting up camp for the 1177th. For the first three days, they worked in the rain. When the rain stopped, they worked in a storm of mosquitoes and blackflies. Recruits arrived in August. They were up from the cities, first time ever. Warren Hill, who had re-enrolled, was among the woods-wise veterans who helped break the greenhorns in. Then Hill skedaddled to a firewatch tower in Middle Sister Mountain, down Chocorua way. Two weeks up, two days down. A city boy could learn to become an agreeable hermit this way. And so could a country boy, like Charles LeBroke, Warren's relief man:

"I was Warren's backup," Toke now recalls. "Rest of the time I did other jobs. Finally got into what they called the trail crew. Everyone wanted to be in that, and I'll tell you why. Even in those times there were some rich people who were spending hundreds of dollars just to come up to the mountains to go hiking. And that's what we got to do in the trail crew. Got to go hiking. And got paid for it, too."

On the theory that all work and no play might make an enrollee a dull fellow—or perhaps a deserter—the program planners of the CCC provided the camps with a generous franchise for fun and games. And the fun wasn't limited to compulsory hiking. There were intramural softball and baseball teams, basketball at some camps, hockey at others. Boxing was the main event, and if another camp happened to be nearby, the extramural sparring could get knock-down competitive. Warren Hill remembers a ring being set up in "downtown" Conway, and the soil soldiers slugging it out to the cheers of the local crowd.

"People came to watch from all over this area," he is saying here in the woods at Blackberry Crossing. "And that was important—building a good relationship with the community—because, you see, there was some tension at first with the CCC camps. People up here sort of resented the government bringing up two hundred men from the cities. They probably figured us all for ex-convicts. People thinking: 'They're armed. They're going to knife us to death. Lock your daughter and the cows up!' You know. Well, we had to overcome that. So we had the boxing, and we got out a little theater and put on shows for the kids from town. And we pitched in wherever we were needed. A couple of floods, a kid lost in the woods. Emergencies like that. We did all we could. And after a while, things began to change. The people and the Cees. It got to be an excellent relationship."

And every six months, a fresh contingent of urban greenhorns came north to fill the places of the men whose hitches were up. For many a recruit, the problems of adjustment were often severe. The nights were too dark. The winter was too cold. The woods were too silent. Camp leaders and work superintendents were constantly challenged to make the new enrollees feel more at home. "When rookies are received in camp," read one official advisory, "they should be inducted into the atmosphere, routine, and work of the camp in a manner that will create no wrong attitudes and impressions. They may become homesick and feel they are in a strange, unfriendly environment. This should be overcome by good orientation procedure. In some camps, certain persons act as 'big brother' to the recruits until they are oriented. Sometimes new enrollees are taken on field trips soon after their arrival. . . ."

But what might be considered a good orientation procedure in one camp might not necessarily seem desirable or appropriate in another. For example, consider that hellzapoppin' hedgehog-eating spike camp up to Willey Slide, in the Notch. Listen now. It's Ellsworth Russell talking:

"Well, they brought us a batch of recruits from the main camp and we showed 'em around and told 'em the names of things. And I said to the man who had brought 'em up, 'Well, when can they start to work?' And he said, 'Why, any time.' And I said, 'Well then, we can put 'em on duty tonight.' 'Course there was no night duty, you know, but we didn't tell them that.

"So that night we took a lantern and dumped out the kerosene and filled it with water. And we took one fella and gave him that lantern and a handful of matches and told him to go up on the side of the mountain—we showed him just where, big rock up there—and told him to sit on that rock and watch for landslides. That was his job for the night. Watch for landslides. So we sent him up there. Another guy we took down the brook to where we were building a bridge and told him to look for high water, 'cause over the radio they say we're liable to have a big flood. 'Course the radio hadn't said any such thing, but we didn't tell him that. We just said, 'Now, if the water comes up over this bridge, we have to get everyone out of the valley.' 'Course there was nobody in the valley but us. So we fixed him up the same way, with a lantern full of water and a handful of matches. And we give 'em both a sandwich. A man's got to eat.

"Well, soon as the sun gets down, I guess those two begin to shiver and shake and they go lightin' their lanterns to get warm, you know. And water don't burn. And about nine o'clock it gets to be real dark and we begin to hear these caterwaulin' hollerins and schreechins, and we had to get flashlights and go out and get 'em 'cause we were afraid they'd break a leg or run off and get lost in the woods."

Before long, everyone was in love with the Cees. Even the Republicans were lavish with their praise. The press was ecstatic. The obdurate anti-New Deal *Chicago Tribune* called it "one of the best projects" of an administration otherwise known to *Trib* readers as a "poisonous dictatorship." The Roosevelt-baiting *New York Herald-Tribune* cheered the Cees for conserving natural resources while stimulating the economy of thousands of small communities across the country. The *Detroit News* allowed as how all the early Corps critics had been silenced by the program's "prompt and unmistakable dividends." The *San Francisco Chronicle*, branding Roosevelt's Civil Works Administration a "scandal," noted in the same editorial that the Cees had won the nation's "golden opinion." In the ccc, said the *Chronicle*, there had been "not more than one-tenth of one percent of politics"—and it added that even this microscopic flaw had been effectively neutralized by the Army and the U.S. Forest Service. And, as a matter of fact, though the name went unmentioned, by Fechner.

Robert Fechner, director of the Civilian Conservation Corps, 1933–42. Fechner, the Georgian railway machinist and coal miner, the union leader, the labor negotiator, the Harvard lecturer. From that square called Fechner on Roosevelt's seminal slip of paper, the lines went out in every direction—to Labor and Agriculture and Interior and War. From start to finish, for better or for worse, Fechner was the glue that held it all together. Still, there are some hindsight accounts (and John Salmond's is among them) that portray Fechner's role in the CCC as a bit less than perfect. It is said, for example, that the director was not always swift enough with decisions, that perhaps he was too much in thrall to the virtues of conciliation. It is suggested that, rather than telling the Army how to run its part of the CCC bargain, he allowed the Army to tell him how to run his.

Whatever the facts of that matter, there can be little doubt that from the very beginning the Army devoutly wished to exercise greater control over the Cees, and all the more so as the war clouds gathered darkly over western Europe. Army Corps area commanders, who supervised the staffing and operation of the camps in their precincts, periodically called for heavier doses of spit and polish, and several of them went so far as to advocate total militarization of the CCC. So did Assistant Secretary of War Harry Woodring, who, in a article for *Liberty* magazine, exhibited uncommon insensitivity to America's growing distaste for the buzz words of Nazism by calling the Cees "economic storm troopers." The slip all but cost Woodring his job; he saved it with a public apology. Then Army Chief of Staff General Douglas MacArthur got into the act. He told a committee of Congress that it would be a dandy idea to turn the Cees into the nucleus of an enlisted reserve force. MacArthur thought the Cees were wonderful. The only thing he didn't like about them, apart from the fact that he would have liked them better as real soldiers, was that the CCC enrollee was paid all of thirty dollars a month, while an Army private earned only eighteen. No matter. A Carolina congressman favored MacArthur's idea and drew up a bill to tack on to the CCC hitch two months for soldierly training. The bill died in committee, but only after strong protest from such notable pacifists as Reinhold Niebuhr and John Dewey, and, as John Salmond describes it, "hundreds of ordinary citizens" adding "their private protests in letters to representatives, to senators, to Fechner, and to the President himself."

But this was two- and three-star general stuff. In the field, in the camps, among the captains and lieutenants who winked at the late carousers after Taps, there was an altogether different outlook on the Cees. Most of the camp commanders after the program's start-up year were Reserve officers rather than Regulars—citizen soldiers with a measure of flexibility in their otherwise olive-drab rule-book points-of-view. Their sympathies, writes John Salmond, "often lay more with the enrollees than with their superior officers," and thereby "effectively muted the harsher aspects of Army discipline and control."

And here is Colonel Philip S. Robbins, U.S. Army Reserve, retired now to a farmhouse in Center Sandwich, right down the road and over the hills from Tamworth, or under the mountains coming the bushwacker's roundabout way from Blackberry Crossing. Behind the house are beds of day lilies, thousands of them in a hundred varieties, then a bit of field, and then the green forest rolling on toward the heights of the Diamond Ledge. We sit in the Colonel's sun room and talk of the Cees.

"Of course I remember them," he is saying. "They were good lads. Good lads! I don't believe there were more than a couple of occasions when I had to speak to a man for not doing his job. They were a tough bunch, though. A third of them had reformatory or prison records. But in all those years, we never had much trouble."

"Were they afraid of you?"

"No," says the Colonel. "They were hungry."

He was a lieutenant then. An ROTC graduate of the University of Vermont, Class of 1930. On active duty with the Cees. Served as mess officer and transportation chief at Tamworth. Served as commanding officer at Blackberry Crossing.

He says: "To a lot of us officers then, there weren't any problems. There were only adventures. It was a challenge. It was the best of all possible training for a young squirt like me. Now, Roosevelt—well, I was no fan of his. I'm a conservative hang-on-to-the-nickel Republican. But in the CCC, Roosevelt really had something good going."

I ask the Colonel about proposals pending in Congress to resurrect the CCC idea in these current hard times of high unemployment.

"Yes," he says. "I'd like to see the CCC again. But it would have to be a rigorous, well-disciplined program. You'd have to turn it over to the Army."

"You would?"

"Yes. And if you did that, you know what would happen? Those Greenpeace folks would wet their diapers."

And then came a time—circa 1940—when everyone was *not* in love with the Cees. There was this growing suspicion that the program had outlived its purpose. There was this perception that jobs were no longer so scarce. People were speaking not of bread lines and the Dust Bowl but of mobilization and the specter of war. In the cities, downwind from the smokestacks of industry, the air smelled malodorously of work once again. In the country, farmers were calling for extra hands to bring in their crops. Under such circumstances, the Cees appeared not only extraneous but competitive. And the Corps was beginning to show its age.

Cracks in the otherwise flawless image of the CCC had appeared as early as 1937. That year, the desertion rate among enrollees shot from 11 percent to 20. One in five of the Cees was going over the hill, more often than not in his first week at camp. In a few camps, men mutinied, refusing to work or to be curfewed or to be reassigned to distant locations. In others, the boxing gloves were replaced with bare knuckles as men brawled along ethnic or regional lines. The press wagged its finger. The Army asked for stricter controls. The public lost interest. By April 1942, Gallup pollsters were encountering stiff resistance to the idea of prolonging the life of the CCC. Many Americans—a majority of Americans—believed that the time had come at last to abolish the program. The House of Representatives concurred. The Senate did not. The matter was referred to a conference committee. On June 30, 1942, the Senate reconsidered. There was a voice vote. And that was the end of the CCC.

Whereupon the Soil Soldiers were mustered into a world in which young men had no scant opportunity whatsoever for doing things and going places. Go now, pay later. So off they went—to Guadalcanal and Buna and Anzio and Omaha Beach and the Ardennes and Okinawa, among other ports-of-call the names of which stick to the ribs of nostalgia a bit more persistently than Tamworth or Blackberry Crossing.

By then, Ellsworth Russell had long since left his spike camp up at Willey Slide. Mustered out of the Cees in 1934 to accept a better position, Russell went on to work for the U.S. Forest Service.

From Blackberry Crossing, Charles LeBroke transferred to a CCC camp at Palisade, Colorado. Mustered out in 1939, he joined the Navy to see the world. And what did he see? He saw the war through gunsights aboard a destroyer. And stayed in the Navy for twenty years.

Philip S. Robbins, U.S. Army Reserve, also left service with the Cees in the late thirties. He was an Air Corps supply officer at Wheeler Field, not far from Pearl Harbor, that singular morning when the sun rose over Oahu on Mitsubishi wings.

And Warren Hill? But for the war, Warren Hill today might have been a retired colonel too. But for the war.

At Tamworth and Blackberry Crossing, the officers and the straw-bosses had been watching this quiet young man from the textiles city. And they liked what they saw. So they built a kind of ladder for Warren Hill and encouraged him to climb it. One rung as mess steward, the next rung as cook. Assistant leader, senior leader. One day in 1938 an Army colonel tapped Hill on the shoulder and offered him a commission. He would be what they called a "subaltern" of the Cees, with the privileges and responsibilities of a first lieutenant. He would be reassigned to camps at Poultney and St. Albans, Vermont. He would command camps at Haddam and Higganum, Connecticut. "And then," Hill recalls, "the war broke out."

He was pegged for a desk job in Washington, and with the

desk went the twin silver bars of an Army captain. But as much as Warren Hill might have wanted the bars, he did not want a desk. He was young and headstrong and feisty for action. He wanted to be overseas. So he resigned his commission and enlisted as a private. They sent him to France, a U.S. Ranger with the Third Division. He was one of a patrol of six sent in to reconnoiter this town where there might or might not be Germans waiting. There were Germans all right. And cannon and machine guns. Hit. Hit in the leg, the hand, the arm, and the shoulder. Somehow the medics managed to put Warren Hill back together again. He has walked with a steel hip ever since.

Now, at Blackberry Crossing, wearing the khaki-and-green uniform of the U.S. Forest Service, Warren Hill says: "I was one of the lucky ones." But he is not referring to that hamlet in France. He is speaking of this place, and the luck of the Cees.

For nine straight years, then, the luck of the Cees was, through their works, the luck of the land as well. To be sure, some observers today could dispute that appraisal. They could cite the Corps' zealous compulsion to fix things up, to pour concrete where wood chips might have served as well, to build roads into roadless areas, to prettify places that might have been better left scratchy and wild. No doubt there was this tendency to indulge in a kind of structural overkill. But to dwell on such practices, to utter regrets in this golden year, would not only be peevish; it would ignore the salient fact that what America needed in the 1930s—needed no less than erosion control and reforestation—was access and accommodation in its forests and parks. Especially in the subsequent decade, in the unrationed postwar years of motorcar leisure, Americans needed a way to get out of their cities and rediscover that lost heritage called the out-of-doors. And by then there *was* a way. The Cees had built it.

By 1938, in national, state, county, and municipal parks, the Cees had built 3,000 bridges, 1,000 sewage and water systems, 18,000 campground facilities, and enough tables and benches and fireplaces to appoint some 16,000 acres of picnicking ground. That was the scorecard for parks only. In state and national forests, the CCC's contribution to the recreational infrastructure was even greater. In fact, in some national forests—and White Mountain leaps foremost to mind—outdoor recreation might never have attained its current preeminence over timber management if the Cees had not been there in the thirties with their shovels and picks, plugging the gap in the much-vaunted concept of multiple use.

And as the structures multiplied, the land base grew to receive them. Before the CCC was three years old, Congress had added five million acres to the national forests in twenty-two states, and substantial add-on acreage was authorized for Great Smoky Mountains, Shenandoah, and Mammoth Cave national parks. Seven states established their first state parks with CCC assistance, while thirty-seven states acquired a half-million acres to round out park systems already existing.

So much for statistics. As for the intangible benefits of the program—they are now beyond measuring, and no doubt were immeasurable even then. How does one calculate the growth of human confidence and hope? Across the span of half a century, a man cannot easily articulate to what extent a hitch with the Cees might have altered his life. There are not enough memories of that sort to go around. There are only scraps of impressions. The writer John Salmond found one. In his definitive work on the Corps, he quotes an undated letter from a California enrollee to Robert Fechner, the Corps director. It went like this:

"The mornings of sunlight, the evening dusk, and shaded sun when the stars are so close to the Earth one could almost reach out and touch them, these are glorious days that shall never be forgotten. Each night I face the setting sun that floods the peaks of the distant mountains with crimson grandeur, and with me is the song of the hills. . . ."

U. P.

On maps it is shown as the Upper Peninsula, but folks in Michigan like to shave that down to "U.P." A little name for a lot of country. From Ironwood on the Wisconsin border, it stretches east more than three hundred miles to Potagannissing Bay. Only one freshwater peninsula in North America is larger, and that is Michigan's lower append-age, a place some northern people disdainfully refer to as Down Below, as though it were hell. These same pilgrims like to say, and not without satisfaction, that there are more miles between Ironwood and Detroit than between Detroit and New York. For true measure of distance, they are short by some fifty miles. No matter. The U.P. is a place apart. Its shoreline, edging three of the Great Lakes, is almost as long as Florida's. Its forest could swallow southern New England whole. Its rock yields a third of the nation's iron ore, or did, when they were mining it. Its win-ters set records for snow and windchill sufficient to rattle the bones of an Eskimo. The U.P. is a hard place. A person has to want to hurt a lot to live there.

It is a handsome place, too, such that thousands of people who do not tolerate much hurting go there every summer to splash in its pristine waters and sip its salubrious boreal air. From nether places Down Below and on toward Dixie, they stream across the Mackinac Bridge to play on the U.P.'s piney hills and pebbly beaches; and, for the most part, they prefer things the way they are rather than the way some local folks would like to see them now and in the hurtful years ahead. It is the same in Machiasport, Maine, and Mountain Village, Alaska, as in Munising, U.P. Hawking souvenirs to tourists and granola bars to bog-trotters hardly enhances the native pride.

And it is an edgy place. I mean in the sense that it still hangs on out there like a rawhide flap of the old frontier, outposted from the swirl of mainstream America. There aren't many such places left: the aforementioned forty-ninth state for certain, the Dogpatches and Skunk Hollows of downunder Appalachia, the Big Cypress, the slickrock canyon country of Utah, the sagebrush boondocks of Nevada. The U.P. Just a handful of places where the line is drawn tight between the textures of nature and the demands inevitably made of nature by people living closest to it, or not close enough. By and large, the local folks stand on one side of this line, the visitors on the other; and personal feelings do get heated, especial when there is some tough hombre to stir things up. Once, in the Big Cypress, I met a ranching man who stirred things up just wondering why anyone should worry if there would be any water for wood storks, after Holsteins and humans had taken their fill. "Horsefeathers," said the rancher, an avowed ecological agnostic. "The good Lord takes care of things like that." Much like the gentleman who ran unsuccessfully for the governorship of Alaska, saying that the timber wolf no longer served any useful purpose in God's scheme of things, and, by the way, "to hell with the Forty-eight," meaning meddlers from Outside (Outside being Alaska's Down Below). And the county commissioner in southeast Utah who told the Sierra Club to go home because, without coal-burning powerplants, his region had nothing to export except empty pop bottles and its own jobless children. And the state senator from Ironwood, U.P., who tells me:

My people were the first to propose a Porcupine Mountains park. They wanted it to be like the Black Forest in Germany. There were going to be interior campgrounds. There were going to be access roads. It was going to be a place for tourists from the city. And it was to be managed by expert foresters. And you know what we got in the end? They designated the thing as a wilderness park, with the only access by paths, so that older people will never see the interior of the park. And the timber! The timber's dying. The timber's rotting on the ground. The game leaves the area. There's nothing to eat. In the end, they spoiled the finest stand of timber in the whole Midwest. What is wilderness? God gave man an intelligence to make the world a better place to live in—to make the most good for the most people. When I see timber going to waste, I say that's sinful. When a tree reaches maturity—a tree worth three or four hundred dollars—and you let it rot, that's not what the Creator gave us these trees for.

In the summer of 1980, I drove across the Upper Peninsula of Michigan, from Ironwood to St. Ignace and back again, the south-shore way, to Escanaba. Actually, the driver was David Plowden, the photographer, and I just rode shotgun beside him, watching the country through the window, and scribbling notes when he stopped to catch the shadows that sometimes play along the edges of things. We did not see all of it; missed Cedarville and Caribou Lake, Rock, Sands, Helps, Hardwood, Northland, Ahmeek, and Little Girls Point. Still, we brushed through a number of places most outlanders skip, and some they can't skip; saw the Porcupine Mountains and the Pictured Rocks, the Two-Hearted River and the Grand Sable Banks, the forest near Baraga and the mines near Marquette, the pastie shops and totem villages vacuuming the tourists off the north end of the Mackinac Bridge. At Ironwood, with a full itinerary of stops ahead, we looked at empty railroad sidings only and then pushed on to Ontonagon and the Porcupine Mountains.

There is a legend: that from camps long ago at the mouth of the Ontonagon River, Chippewa Indians could look down the curving shore of Gitche Gumee, toward the sunset, and make out the shape of a porcupine crouching beside the lake. Thus did some blue-eyed surveyor find a name for these hills, though flat-lander maps would inflate them to "mountains." But they are steep enough in places, with broken declivities tumbling down into sandstone creeks; hills unsuited for skidding big logs to the lake. All around the Porcupines, after the Chippewas moved from the river, after the first call for shingles and clapboards, the tall trees came tumbling down. Yet double-bit loggers turned back at the edge of the Porkies, cursing the lack of good access. Thus did the State of Michigan in 1944 acquire these fifty-eight thousand acres for what is now known as Porcupine Mountains Wilderness State Park.

And what a magnificent park it is. Twenty miles of roadless Superior shore, eighty-five miles of trail winding through what is said to be the "largest virgin stand of hemlock-hardwood tim-ber remaining in the United States." Lakes and ponds and wa-terfalls aplenty, and the Presque Isle River carving amber pot-holes in the bedrock as it rushes to the lake. The air smells of resin and leaf mold. The perfume of wilderness. The tonic of earth, sun, and sky.

The forest is everywhere. It covers 90 percent of the peninsula. A person could walk through forest 250 miles from the edge of Ironwood to the suburbs of the Soo and, if he chose the route carefully and anti-socially, would cross a paved road no more than a dozen times the entire way. It would be hard going, though. Through spruce bogs and tamarack swamps, deadfalls and puckerbrush, aspen thickets and jackpine jungles. Lovely country for wilderness, fair to excellent for pulp, but overall marginal at present for lumber. No matter. Forest products—mostly pulp for paper and chips for reconstituted boards—are the region's greatest extractable asset, after ore, and potentially the base of its most dependable year-round employment. Not bad for a stretch of woods that, by most accounts, is among the most underutilized forests in accessible North America.

So why—I found myself wondering as we drove east through the forest toward L'Anse—why all this fuss over wilderness? Was there truly a shortage of timber up here? Did fifty thousand protected acres in the Porcupines really withdraw that much timber from the available supply? Would another fifty thousand acres of wilderness in the U.P.'s national forests—Ottawa in the west, and Hiawatha, east—drive industry over the border into Wisconsin? Good grief, no. There are nine million acres of commercial forest land up here; billions of cubic feet on the stump. The state's chief forester, Henry Webster, has data showing that the allowable cut is twice the current harvest. The people at Champion International Corporation, one of the U.P.'s major pulp operators, tell me they have studies showing that annual growth exceeds the harvest by a factor of three. Champion is so bullish about the supply outlook that it is building a new $500 million mill at Quinnesec, near Iron Mountain. Mead, the paper company, is expanding at Escanaba. Champion and Mead don't need those old-growth hemlocks in the Porkies. They need aspen and maple and basswood and birch. They need spruce. For chips. And with or without wilderness, they are managing quite well. The peninsula's forest is a chippable feast.

True, much of the private, nonindustrial land is unproductive. There are these small landowners, maybe thirty thousand of them, holding a third of the U.P. forest, and most of them never lifting a finger to manage their woods; no thinning, no harvest. A consulting firm from Finland, Jaakko Pöyry, has recommended to the Michigan Department of Natural Resources that forest cooperatives be set up in the U.P. Let there be a union between landowners and the state, Jaakko Pöyry suggested. Let the professional foresters into these woodlots. Let some economists check out new markets. Let there be loans for equipment to harvest the cull. After all, why not? It works in Finland. Why not the U.P? Well, it is somewhat conservative, the U.P. There's a fondness for Finns, to be sure. But their homeland? Their homeland is socialist. Jaakko Pöyry's solution therefore must be a socialist solution. And that is no good for the U.P. Or so it is said among some of the folks who would chain-saw the wilderness while, for want of thinning, their own trees grow scrawny and die on the stump.

Notes on a hard place. In Ontonagon, we came to a crossroads. At the corner stood a pole with two signs, one above the other. One sign said Zinc St., the other said Iron. Two blocks away we came to another signpost. One part said Tin St., the other said Brass. A resident stopped to chat with the photographer. He said that many of the village streets are like these, named after natural resources. Hearing this, I wondered why we had seen no street named Sunshine. And imagined the answer: It's not a resource if it can't be mined.

The village of L'Anse sits at the foot of Keweenaw Bay. L'Anse is a French name. Across the bay is the village of Baraga, which is a Viennese name, after one Frederic Baraga. Frederic Baraga was not a natural resource. He was a nineteenth-century bishop who beseeched the Indians to trust in the Christian God.

The two villages share a common telephone directory. The French and the Viennese are gravely outnumbered by Finns. Jarvinen, Jaukkurri, Jokela, Jokipii, Juntunen, Jukkala, Jurmu, Jurva. Kaarlela and Kyro. Lampinen and Lyyski. Still, the mayor of Baraga is a Pole. It is all the same to the Finns. The Finns grow bigger strawberries. In L'Anse and Baraga, there are many blonds and saunas. The blonds have blue eyes. The saunas have potbelly stoves. Everyone works hard and pays taxes. No loafing allowed.

Heading over this way, I met a man from Georgia at the paper mill in Ontonagon. He had been working there for a year, turning wood chips into corrugated paper, the stuff of which cardboard boxes are made. It was a good job, he said, and a good town; and though the snow that first winter had taken some getting used to, he and his wife were as pleased as Punch to be part of the U.P. community. Now they were looking for some land at the edge of the lake, where they hoped someday to build a place of their own with a view of the sunset. It wouldn't be easy, though. It would all depend on the paycheck.

"You got three hundred thousand people living up here in this wonderful country," he said. "And we sure want to keep it that way. Trouble is—" and here he paused to run a hand through his thinning hair—"the three hundred thousand got to make a living just like everyone else. Some people here say they don't want the town to grow, but they want everyone in it to have a job. Then these same people say they do want the mill to grow, but they don't want any environmental problems. People are funny."

Later I discovered that the paper mill would be shutting down for a week. No work, no paychecks. Not because the wood wasn't there to be chipped. Not because there was too much wilderness. Not because of the eco-extremist radicals who were rocking the economic boat. Because of inflation and recession. Because, in hard times, who needs cardboard boxes?

And some notes on hard times: The artifacts of failure crowd the edge of the highway. Ramshackle barns and derelict tractors, hayrigs rusting in tangles of wild grass, sun-bleached porches with blistered paint, aspen invading the orchards, windows without glass—the eye sockets of foreclosure.

The U.P. is not the worst place in America to be a farmer, nor is it the best. Some years, the growing season seems to be over the day after it begins. Some places, the soil has too much of one thing, or not enough of another. Not all of it is marginal. Over toward the Soo, farmers tend a kind of hay so splendid it is the pick of racehorse stables a thousand miles away. And here and there dairymen report a profit from cows, though not much. The land is best suited to growing trees.

Years ago, in country much like this a few miles down below the Straits of Mackinac, I stood at the edge of a sand road. There was a clearing in the forest. In the center of the clearing stood an empty house. It was the summer of 1938, I think; and the nasty whiplash tail of the Great Depression had been toppling Great Lakes subsistence farmers right and left. Here was the evidence. The house had no door. It had fallen from its hinges. Through the opening we could see a room. Sunlight fell in fluted shafts through a perforated roof. In the middle of the room was a table set for four—four plates, glasses, knives, forks, spoons. A chipped enamel pitcher. An oval platter bearing the petrified relics of some meal, uneaten. And four chairs; three of them upright, the fourth, flat on its back on the floor. Spiderwebs and dust. On the far wall, beyond the table in a shaft of light, hung an object in a thin wooden frame. Askew on the wall. Embroidered letters: *In God We Trust*.

Landmarks of peninsular history. Jacques Marquette wintered at the Soo in 1668. Baron L'Houtant that year discovered a boulder of copper near Keweenaw Bay. In 1721, Pierre François Xavier de Charlevoix paddled west toward a land called the Mississippi. Pontiac's Conspiracy failed. The Empire English went on the warpath. The Chippewas sat by the shore and conjured up slumbering beasts. Blue-eyed surveyors grew burdened with gadgets. At Negaunee in 1844, or rather at a place that would soon bear the name, surveyors William Burt and Jacob Houghton were thrashing around in the bushes one day when they saw their gadget's magnetic needle moving in strange ways. The incident was duly reported. Men came with shovels. They dug through the sands and the glacial till and the calcium dust in the graves of the fossil beasts. Then the shovels came to rest at the top of a cherty plate. The plate seemed to run off in every direction. Someone sent for a geologist. The geologist looked at the rock and pronounced it to be banded in some places and disseminated in others, and fine-grained, with a splendid castic horizon, and all of it hematitic for certain. Someone begged the geologist to speak up in plain English. The good man said he would try. He said that the rock was a ferrous ore. "This donkey means iron," someone shouted. And that was the start of it.

In time, they drilled the shafts into the bowels of Negaunee and Ishpeming; and the towns grew up around them. Miners came from Ohio and Pennsylvania and Tuscany and the Alsace-Lorraine. There was a French Town and a Finn Alley. The immigrant Italians knew little of mines; in their spare time, which wasn't much or often, they planted small vineyards and danced on the grapes. From Land's End, in England, the Cornish came over with underground tin-mining roots running back to the reign of the Caesars. They imported the pastie, the miner's meat pie. Miners still eat them, though not underground.

At full capacity, the cherty plate of the Marquette Range

serves up one of every three iron-ore pellets produced in the United States. Cleveland-Cliffs Iron Company is the principal operator, and has been almost from the beginning. One of its open-pit mines here is named after a founding father, Samuel J. Tilden of New York. This was the same Tilden who, in 1876, won the keys to the White House by popular vote, only to see them turned over to Rutherford B. Hayes by larcenists from the Electoral College. Perhaps with that lesson in mind—that one should never shave a contest too close to the edge—Cleveland-Cliffs over the years has managed to acquire a commanding lead in the business of extracting natural resources from the U.P. In addition to two other principal mines, at Republic and Palmer, the company controls 400,000 acres of U.P. timber, a private holding exceeded only by Champion's and Mead's.

Cleveland-Cliffs' regional headquarters are located in Ishpeming at 504 Spruce Street. The photographer and I stopped there, heading east, and called on Don Ryan, the man one sees about matters of public information. This particular day, Don Ryan was a sad-looking man. He handed me a press release:

"The Cleveland-Cliffs Iron Company today announced plans to reduce iron ore production at two mining operations managed by the company on the Marquette Range." The decision reflects "the severe drop in steel production nationally." Initially, "2,000 employees will be affected by this action. . . . These employees will be laid off at the end of operations on June 28." Then, a statement by Senior Vice-President E. B. Johnson: "While we are looking at some very difficult times during the remainder of 1980, I'm confident that the future is bright for Cliffs on the Marquette Range. We plan to resume operations at the earliest possible time."

Jacques Marquette found his own difficult time toward the end of that winter three centuries ago at the Soo. The Indians brought him dried fish. He nibbled. Beneath the heavy robes, Marquette discovered his rib cage. Outside, snow as white as a surplice covered the ground. Night was a requiem cassock. When will it end, Marquette repeatedly asked of the village sachems. The sachems replied it would end either at the earliest possible time, or when there no longer was too much wilderness. Whichever came sooner.

Harvey, Skandia, Dukes, Sundell, Rumely, Eben Junction, and Slapneck. The little hollow circles that you see on the map. And when you look up, half a town's gone, it passes so quickly. Woodsheds and water pumps. Post office hiding in the general store. Long front porches with light-blue ceilings. Sunflowers drowsing over backyard fences. Hound-dogs drowsing by the rocking chairs. Onward. Across the next river and into the trees.

To my way of thinking, rivers—trout streams—are the leitmotif of the Upper Peninsula, and of the best of its literature, too. The finest fiction ever written about this country was Ernest Hemingway's story "Big Two-Hearted River," Parts I and II. And the best fact, by John D. Voelker, alias Robert Traver, the fly-fishing district attorney and judge from the Iron Country. Traver is best remembered for his novel *Anatomy of a Murder*, set in Big Bay; but he is probably better loved for his personal narratives of the magic and madness of fishing for trout in the Middle Escanaba and Yellow Dog rivers, U.P. In fairness, I should qualify the use of the word "fact." Fact is, there is no such thing as a factural fishing story. Fishermen—especially fly fishermen—are by necessity if not by nature extravagant liars. Traver confessed as much himself. And Hemingway, unconfessed, was a treacherous liar, at least in the matter of catching trout on the Two-Hearted River.

It is a fact, much ignored by the literati, though not by anglers, that Hemingway deliberately misguided his readers to the Two-Hearted in order to save the productive pools of the Fox, nearby, for himself. The photographer and I crossed the West Branch of the Fox on our way to Seney. A slow-moving, deep-bellied stream, it flows out of the fat pine plains of Schoolcraft County along the edge of a sand ridge. We stopped to pay our respects. Somewhere out there to the north, beyond the farthest tufted tree line, Hemingway, in the guise of his alter-ego, Nick Adams, had taken lunker trout on grasshoppers. And Seney, down the road a piece, is where Nick got off the train from St.

Ignace and saw "nothing but the rails and the burned-over country," the town with its thirteen loggers' saloons wiped away by a forest or slash fire, such that "even the surface had been burned off the ground." Now, Seney was whole again, though somewhat short of both loggers and saloons, so we continued on to the Two-Hearted country and stopped on an open hillside above that river. Devil's paintbrush and wild asters were in bloom on the slope, and a forest of pine and cedar and birch leaned over the rushing water on the other side.

Perhaps the Fox is still better for trout than the Two-Hearted; at least, that's what the locals say. No matter. Perhaps the Two-Hearted is better for scenery. It is protected now under Michigan's Natural River Act. One hundred and fifteen miles of main stem and tributary are zoned for protection. One-hundred-foot set-backs, do-not-disturb, on either side. One-hundred-yard buffers against mining, either side. Papa Hemingway would have been delighted. Onward. Out of the trees to St. Ignace.

St. Ignace is the tourist capital of the U.P. It is a summer place for people who like to spend Saturday nights looking at doo-dads and souvenir birchbark canoes. There is a Frontier Museum and an Indian Village. This is the frosting on the cake. How thin it seems.

One Saturday night in St. Ignace, the photographer and I went browsing. At the Indian Village we saw a souvenir dessert plate inscribed with a heart-warming message: "Good mother makes happy home." On the bottom of the plate was another message: "Not for food use. Plate may poison food. Made in Korea." Down the aisle we passed purple cows, schmoos, stag-horn salt-and-pepper sets, black-bear candle holders (made in Hong Kong), St. Ignace T-shirts (made in Miami), Budweiser T-shirts (made in Pakistan), American Indian pen-and-pencil sets (made in Japan), and hand-woven American Indian baskets (made in Taiwan). Having found nothing that appeared to have been made in Michigan, much less the U.P., we headed empty-handed for the checkout counter. The sign on the cash register announced: "We understand there is going to be a Depression. We have decided not to participate." So did we.

In the morning, westbound along the Lake Michigan shore toward Naubinway and Manistique, we stopped at an historical marker by the roadside at Pointe Aux Chenes. The marker said that the Treaty of 1836 granted three square miles at this point to Chief Ance and his band of Chippewa-Ottawas. And that was how the place became known as the "last resort" of the St. Ignace Indians. I looked around for survivors. Only two were in sight, a man and a woman seated on a bench beside the door of a low, frame building. A sign behind them pointed the way to "Totem Village." I took a few steps closer. Then I saw that the seated Indians were made of wood.

PAPA COUNTRY

I n the summers of those early years he lived in a white clapboard cottage that looked across a wide sand beach to the
lake. Birch and cedar grew along the edge of the beach,
and maple, pine, and hemlock on the slopes of the backside hills.
On sunlit days, the lake was a pastel blue. Woodburning
steamers sailed past the cottage, tooting their whistles, and,
going the landward way, a one-lane track for horse-and-wagon
threaded the woods over the hills to the village of Petoskey on
Little Traverse Bay. Wild blackberries hung in thick patches in
the roadside clearings. There were bass in the lake in front of the
cottage and trout in the streams cross-country toward Wolverine, and grouse in the aspen thickets of the cutover lands the
double-bit loggers had long since passed through. Indians still
lived in the shanties of the lumber camp back in the woods. It
was good country, then. It was his kind of country. In time, he
would turn away from it to France and Spain and Africa and
Cuba and Key West and Ketchum. In going where he had to go,
and doing what he had to do, and seeing what he had to see, he
would find a few more places that were his kind of country. But
no matter where he went or what he did or saw, the boyhood

sights and sounds and smells of northern Michigan would be the ones against which Ernest Hemingway would have to measure all the countries of his sensory world.

Nowadays, the lakes and woods of Michigan somehow seem apart from the mainstream of the Nobel winner's life. We tend to memorialize him in bolder, more romantic settings, and almost always the strong round face is framed by the impeccable white beard of the elder Papa. It is that, or the broad-brimmed Kilimanjaro hunter in safari cloth, the sun-bronzed Gulf Stream skipper, the wine-bottle war correspondent, the portrait of the artist with hairy arms poised above the portable typewriter. Those are the images in sharpest focus. The other ones, of a young beardless man with a packsack and a fishing rod in Michigan, seem faded and remote, and possibly, some might think, beyond the depth-of-field of his works. After all, what did Michigan contribute but a handful of very short stories, most of them dismissed as unimportant by the snootier critics, and one short, satiric, throwaway novel called *The Torrents of Spring*, set in Petoskey, dashed off in Paris, and widely regarded as Hemingway's most forgettable book?

All right, but word counts and critical notices are beside the point. The point is that Michigan was where Hemingway made his first contact with the out-of-doors. As Carlos Baker accounts for it in the opening lines of his biography: "As soon as it was safe for the boy to travel, they bore him away to the northern woods." That was in early September 1899. They were Dr. Clarence Edmonds Hemingway and his wife, Grace, of Oak Park, Illinois. The boy, Ernest, was all of seven weeks old. It was his first season at Bear Lake (soon to be renamed Walloon). Before he would be finished with Michigan, of lakeside summers there would be twenty more.

And probably, in the early to middle range of those summer seasons, young Hemingway found what comes to many people who are exposed to an idyllic natural environment in the cusp of the so-called formative years. In northern Michigan, on the blue water and in the green woods and under the expert tutelage of a hook-and-bullet, uphill-tramping outdoor dad, he found his center of perceptual gravity, his continuity with nature, his sense of place. The flash-card impressions would be lasting ones—red sunsets, water lapping under plank docks, narrow streams with pebbled bottoms, steep sand bluffs, driftwood campfires, fishing worms in snuff cans, grasshoppers in dew-wet fields, splitting wood, hauling cook-water, the texture of pine needles underfoot, the spatter of Crisco under frypan trout, citronella and cheesecloth vs. pesky mosquito, the sweetgrass smell of that Indian girl Prudy, morning fog off the big lake. Michigan. Country.

Gone at last from Michigan yet still under the influence of its stimuli, Hemingway would proclaim his allegiance to country in his earliest stories and the first keeper novel, *The Sun Also Rises*. *Sun* narrator Jake and his buddy Bill are trout fishing high in the mountains of Basque Spain. Their creels are full; the wine, springwater-chilled. Toward the bottom of the first bottle, Bill offers a blessing. " 'Let no man be ashamed,' " he says, " 'to kneel here in the great out-of-doors. Remember the woods were God's first temples.' "

It is easy, if making words is how you earn your living, to be envious of Ernest Hemingway. He made them so damned well, made the whole writing process seem so pure and simple you were stunned to discover, if you tried, that it wasn't that way at all. No one spawned more imitators than he did. I mean imitators—Bless me, Papa, for I have sinned; it has been two paragraphs since my last confession—of his prose style. His other styles, of bluff and swagger and monumental pride, even his greatest admirers would rather eschew. But the words. The productivity of the man—to write hard every morning in order that each afternoon might be spent in the temples of the out-of-doors. That is something to envy.

For my part, I have another reason to be envious of Ernest Hemingway, a reason that has more to do with country than with words. I envy him his score of summer seasons up in Michigan, including the formative ones. My time up there ran out at seven, when I was just warming up.

It was not the same as Hemingway's, our piece of Michigan.

Ours was north, maybe fifteen miles, beyond the deep-watered Little Traverse Bay, at a place called Seven Mile Point, on Lake Michigan. My first season was the summer of 1932. I was all of six months old. Hemingway hadn't been in Michigan for a decade. He was out West that summer, in the Yellowstone Country, killing trout. Our summers there, we lived in a log cabin that looked out through a hole in the woods at the big lake. On a clear day, from the bluff where the cabin stood, you could see Beaver Island like a smudge on the far horizon. Ore boats sailed by, high on the ends and low in the middle. Behind the cabin was an icehouse surrounded by ferns and shaded by sugar maples. Beyond that, a gravel road leveled out though a sumac thicket. Going north, the road took you all the way to Cross Village, where Ojibway and Ottawa Indians made baskets of sweetgrass with porcupine-quill decorations. Going south, you came to the village of Harbor Springs, where the fancy white yachts of tycoons from Chicago and Cleveland and Cincinnati were moored side-by-side with the flaky gray, fish-smelling boats of commercial gill-netters from Brutus and Alanson.

So it was a different piece of country, though not by much, and a different era, though only by a generation; and the rest of it, pretty much the same: blue water, green forest. There were cousins in the cabin next-door, and of sufficient number to mix up two good sides of hide-and-go-seek and capture-the-flag, and even if you happened to be the youngest, as I was, the twilight games in time taught you an important lesson. Hiding or seeking, you learned not to be afraid of the woods. And then there was the wide yellow beach beyond which stretched a hundred miles of open, westerly-fanned water where you learned, if not to be afraid of Lake Michigan, at least to respect it.

Best of all was the hike from our place down to Five Mile Creek, along the beach. We whooped through the sea rocket and beach grass at the edge of the dunes and splashed through the long, still pools of standing water trapped in shallow sloughs behind the drift zone, and the slime in the pools felt good between the toes. Wading in Five Mile Creek where it tumbled out of the cedar woods across the beach felt even better. The creek flowed clear and cold. From its cobbled mouth, a path led upstream to a staircase of pools with undercut banks. We would lie on our bellies, still as Indians, watching the pools for speckled trout, and would see two or three big ones almost every time. It was a good break for the trout that we were not yet wise to the ways of fly-rod angling. The cabin proprietors, our Old Man and our Uncle John, were bait-casting boat fishermen, and I recall that our most common quarry was probably not trout but rather the succulent walleyed pike of Burt Lake, a splendid body of water not unlike Hemingway's Walloon, only bigger. Always it seemed to rain as soon as our boat arrived at the choicest fishing grounds of Burt Lake, and always the biggest walleyes seemed to strike under the shower's first drops.

There were seven summers like that. They ended in 1938 for reasons I was too young then to understand and which may now be explained by the fact that it took that long for the Great Depression to catch up with my Old Man. Thus was I sentenced to what I feared would be a lifetime of long, hot lakeless summers in southern Ohio. In southern Ohio I learned to fish in streams and how to use an axe and pitch a tent and hit a mark, or a squirrel, with a gun—in short, all the things I would rather have learned in northern Michigan. I dreamed of Michigan. Through all the homebound years my sleep was filled by blue water and green forest and the cabin on the bluff and the smudge of island out where whitecaps float like feathers across the floor of the sky.

Presently I outgrew those dreams and discovered the writings of Ernest Hemingway. First for me was *The First Forty-nine Stories*. Some of the titles caught my attention. "Up in Michigan," for example. "Indian Camp," for another. The last story in this collection was "Fathers and Sons." And that one made me wonder about Hemingway and *his* Michigan, especially when I got to the part where the son says to the father, " 'What was it like, Papa, when you were a little boy and used to hunt with the Indians?' "

The end of something had come and gone when Hemingway was a boy hunting black squirrels with his Ojibway friends, up in

Michigan. It was more than the end of the white-pine lumber boom, the sound of the big saws rasping in the mills and then, suddenly, no more logs, the second-growth sprouting in sawdust and silence. It was much bigger than that. It was the end of the American frontier. The frontier had galloped across the white pine country to the plains, the mountains, and the deserts, and then it had collapsed, all stitched up with barbed wire and homestead claims, even in Oklahoma, which was supposed to have been Indian Country but wasn't, just as it was once supposed, before statehood, that Michigan would be Indian Country, too. Sure, and the Hemingways might still ride over the hills to Petoskey in a horse-drawn wagon, but each summer there were always a few more motorcars parked along Main Street, and a lot fewer authentic Michigan Indians.

As soon as he was old enough to hike and camp and fish alone, or with a couple of friends, and could be trusted not to waste his daily allotment of shotgun shells (three), Hemingway turned eagerly from the knee-pants beach at Walloon Lake to the woods roundabout, which, though no longer virginal, were still substantial and wild. He was afraid of nothing, except, perhaps, that he had somehow just missed the best of times in the best of all possible country.

But there were still good times to be had. Instead of traveling to northern Michigan in the customary familial mode—by lake steamer from Chicago to Harbor Springs—twice in his teenage years Ernest contrived to jump ship at a more southerly port-of-call and to hike the last hundred miles or so cross-country, fishing such rivers as the Manistee, the Boardman, and the Rapid along the way. Occasionally, Ernest and his companion, Lew Clarahan, would hitch a ride in a passing farm wagon, or hop a freight on the Pere Marquette line. "They did not walk much of the way," noted Mama Grace Hemingway in one of her albums. "That is bunk," countered Ernest in a marginal note. "We walked 130 miles."

By all accounts, Mrs. Hemingway did not share her menfolk's love of the outdoors. She was a woman of frustrated artistic ambitions, and, if you read between the lines of her son's biographers, she was likely the cause of much domestic friction at Walloon Lake. Young Ernest kept his distance by camping out—in a tent behind the lakeside cottage, or down at Murphy's Point, or across Walloon at a small farm the Hemingways had acquired for acreage and summer provender. Later, he would distance himself even farther by hanging out with friends at Horton Bay, four miles west of Walloon on the shore of Lake Charlevoix.

And waiting to swallow him, always, was the green forest, the overgrown logging roads reaching out toward Indian River, the slash piles covered with fireweed, the balsam thickets where he could cut fresh boughs to cushion his bedroll. He would not have missed it for anything—well, almost. He would miss it for the war and the ambulance service and the fighting along the Piave in northern Italy in the summer of 1918, and he would come home with a sharpnel-tattered leg and an ache in his heart for that night nurse, Agnes, who had thrown him over for a handsome lieutenant from Naples. There was a place to take the cure: up in Michigan.

As soon as his legs were strong again, he was hobbling off to the pine barrens of the Pigeon River Country—"five days," by biographer Baker's account, "without seeing a house or even a clearing—'wild as the devil,' said Ernest," emerging with a scruffy beard and "smelling of fish, citronella, and woodsmoke." That was the summer of 1919. Before it was over, he was off again, fishing the Black River over toward Onaway; and then to the Upper Peninsula, to the burned-out lumber town of Seney, to fish the Fox.

There was another season, 1920, most of it spent at Horton Bay rather than Walloon, and then a final one the following year, at which time and in which place—Horton's Bay, Hemingway called it, adding the possessive, in his stories—he married his first wife, Hadley Richardson. And that was all of it. After that Ernest Hemingway always seemed to be somewhere else, in another country.

He returned to northern Michigan only once, in 1947, but not to summer beside the blue water; to say hello to his sister Sunny (Madelaine Hemingway Miller), who had taken over the cottage at Walloon, and to his old friend, Dutch Pailthorp, in Petoskey; hardly a visit at all, a mere pass on his way west to Idaho. It was not quite true that one couldn't go home again, as Thomas Wolfe had claimed; the going just got less likely (as Wallace Stegner would note years later). Throughout his life, Hemingway would test the likeliness of going home again. He would return to Paris and to East Africa and to Spain, playing hide-and-seek with the memories, and usually coming out of it the worse for wear. And once he would even return to the Piave, looking for traces of the crater made by the Austrian shell that had shattered his leg. But, except for the one-time pass in 1947, he would never return to northern Michigan. It was too civilized now, he is said to have told his friend Pailthorp. It was less than likely that he could spend any length of time in Michigan ever again.

"A country was made to be as we found it," he had written a decade earlier in *The Green Hills of Africa*. "We are the intruders and after we are dead we may have ruined it but it will still be there and we don't know what the next changes will be." Hemingway knew a good country when he saw one. Africa, or Michigan. It was all the same. "Here there was game, plenty of birds, and I liked the natives. Here I could shoot and fish. That, and writing, and reading, and seeing pictures was all I cared about doing. And I could remember all the pictures."

In the summer of 1974, I managed to get back again to northern Michigan for a couple of weeks, renting a small cabin on a pond in the woods east of Cross Village, which was about as close as I could afford to be to the old familial blufftop place at Seven Mile Point. I had been through this country once or twice in the early fifties, but not really in it, not seeing it, not noting the changes, not taking the time to remember the pictures from my Michigan dreams; so that, in effect, this seventies-time-around was almost like coming into the country cold after an absence of thirty-five years.

There were plenty of changes, all right. Not so much in the back-country. That was still scratchy and wild, though some of the roads had been paved, including the one past our old place, from Harbor Springs north to Cross Village. Paved, and with a stripe down its center just for good measure. There had been a dairy farm on the road to Harbor Springs. Now it was growing mortgages on vacation estates. The long beach where we had whooped down the shore to Five Mile Creek was no longer so lonely; a new generation had raised its sundecked castles in the dunes. The creek was fished out. The beach was posted. The litter cans were full. The village of Harbor Springs had become a town. White yachts still hunkered at dockside; the gill-net trawlers were gone. Ferns hung in baskets from the ceilings of waterfront saloons; small print on the baskets read *Made in Korea*. The town of Petoskey had become a city. Not that the in-town, year-round population had changed all that much. It was the out-of-town population, and the cheese shops and the boutiques and the designer labels in the windows, and each day there were always a few more motorcars looking for parking spaces on Main Street. And it didn't take an ethnologist's eye to see that the blood of intruders now ran a generation thicker in the veins of the lingering Indians.

There was, and is, one change of which Ernest Hemingway might have approved, or at least noted with passing interest, for he was much enamored of downhill skiing. There was no such thing in northern Michigan in his time or mine. His slopes were in the Rockies, or the Alps. Now, Papa Country has become the Ski Center of the Midwest. There is Boyne Mountain in his old backyard, Nubs Nob in mine; and a dozen more such places sprinkled across the sand hills of the region. Skiing here has made tourism a booming year-round industry in this extreme northwest corner of the Lower Peninsula, and Petoskey is its capital city. So perhaps Hemingway would not have approved after all. The skiing, yes. But tourism? Not very likely.

Over the past decade, the business of making words has taken me back to northern Michigan a number of times. Once, traveling north toward Petoskey on U.S. 131, a sudden fancy to meander down a county road brought me along the east shore of Lake Charlevoix to Horton Bay. And sure enough, there was the general store and post office with its high false front, just as Hemingway had described it in his story "Up in Michigan." It was late, so I did not stop.

And once, traveling east from Petoskey on the backroad to Wolverine, I saw a young man crossing a field with a small pack on his back and a rifle or shotgun snugged in the crook of his arm. It was the season for taking rabbits, and squirrels, too, I suppose; and for a moment I imagined the youth to be Ernest Hemingway, setting out on one of his cross-country trips. And then I wondered who the young man really was, and what he thought and felt about the country he was hunting through. It must have been his kind of country. It had to be, though it was different from mine, and from Hemingway's. Yes. It was just as Hemingway had figured. A country was made to be as we found it. But if it could not be that way—well, with any kind of luck, with this young man's kind of luck, it would still be there.

UNFINISHED

REDWOOD

Almost from the start of it all, there was this urge to make the park more than it could ever be. That was the tree's fault. The tree made people think big. The tree was so impressive that some people could not help but think big—not just in terms of how many thousands of acres the park might embrace (in fact, the first thought wasn't big enough), or how many millions of dollars should be appropriated to procure it, but also as to how it might serve as the five-star quintessential park of them all. Even men opposed to this park, who measured the tree by its capacity to render board feet rather than inspiration—even these had to go for broke, though in the opposite direction, for it was their apocalyptic duty to predict socioeconomic catastrophe should the park come to pass.

Yet it did come to pass, in 1968, when the United States Congress approved the establishment of a Redwood National Park in Humboldt and Del Norte counties, hard by the headlands of California's North Coast. And it did come to pass once again when, ten years later, a wiser Congress enlarged the park in order to save its old-growth stands, including the world's tallest trees, from clearcut loggers honing their saws along the original boundaries of the national park. Still, for all the great and perhaps unreasonable expectations, Redwood National Park somehow seems a little bit less than it might have been, or could be. Inexplicably, it has the aura of a forgotten park. For certain, it remains an unfinished one.

The three pre-existing state parks that were to have become integral units of Redwood National Park—Prairie Creek, Del Norte Coast, and Jedediah Smith—still remain outside the jurisdiction of the National Park Service, and consolidation of management responsibilities under the federal Smokey Bear hat seems less likely today than it did twenty years ago.

Erosion and sedimentation from logging operations upstream continue to threaten the old-growth of Redwood Creek, including the Tall Trees Grove, even as the Park Service spends more than a third of its annual Redwood budget on a program to heal the chain-saw scars of yesteryear.

Purist and Philistine still grapple over the best and highest use of the park, the one seeking to be inspired by the forest, the other, to be entertained by the acquisition of gift-shop souvenirs.

And despite a generous federal effort to mitigate economic losses in local communities, the prevailing public mood of Del Norte County remains rancorous and decidedly anti-park. Old allies, meanwhile, have turned to other causes. The constituency is spread thin. No more the redwood-rallying cry that former Secretary of the Interior Stewart Udall once called "the best understood and most honorable" of all the slogans of the conservation movement. No more the Sierra Club posters and the full-page ads, the clip-out coupons, the letters to Congress, the four-color books, the multimedia blitz that, for a time, turned this singular botanical species into a symbol more powerful even than the image of Spaceship Earth. *Save the Redwoods?* Now? After more than twenty years—after nearly seventy, if you take the Redwood National Park idea back to the real beginning—it would seem that most Americans likely to care have put saving the redwoods behind them. Alas, in the nitrous nineties, tree-huggers are more inclined to be thinking big about saving themselves.

No one who has stood at the base of a mature coast redwood will ever forget it—the deeply fluted bark, the columnar bole tapering through a chiaroscuro of shadow and sunlight, two hundred, three hundred and more feet to the top of the canopy, the rings of annual growth unseen beneath the cambium layer, one thousand, possibly two thousand rings running back to the very core of the heartwood; and the puny visitor knowing that ancestors of this tree flourished in dinosaur times across two continents, before changes in climate restricted its range to this narrow last stand at the edge of the world's widest sea. No wonder, then, less than a century after Anglo-Americans arrived in these precincts in appreciable numbers, that someone would propose the idea of creating a Redwood National Park.

Already there was a state park, at Big Basin south of San Francisco, in 1902, and a national monument, at Muir Woods northside of the Golden Gate, in 1908. But that wasn't good enough for California Congressman William Kent, who had donated the monument lands to the federal government and now, in 1913, resolved that there might be a grander U.S. park among the groves of giants farther north. A world war intervened. By the time it was over, tree lovers in and out of California were beginning to hear about a new organization called Save-the-Redwoods League, whose founding fathers included such influential men as the Old Guard patrician Madison Grant, Henry Fairfield Osborn of New York's Museum of Natural History, the Berkeley paleontologist John Campbell Merriam, and Stephen Mather, descendant of those flinty Puritans, Cotton and Increase, and, more to the point, the first director of the National Park Service. Mather had his eye on some splendid groves along the lower reaches of the Klamath River, and, since the big trees were in private ownership, proposed that some public-spirited citizens might cough up the purchase price for Uncle Sam. Those days, Uncle did not buy parks; he only accepted them from philanthropists, or carved them, at no cost at all, from the public domain. But the public spirit was no match for the price of the land, and before you could yell "Timber!" the tall trees of the lower Klamath came tumbling down.

Save-the-Redwoods League meanwhile was pressing ahead on other projects. For its executive secretary, it had hired the Bay Area adman Newton Drury, already well known for his talents at public relations and fund-raising. Drury's mission was to carry the League's cause to the entire nation. Drury was to be the ambassador. For architect, to target the redwood groves most worthy of preservation, the League brought in Frederick Law Olmsted II, son of the nineteenth-century park-maker. Olmsted focused on four relatively accessible forest units, all with high marks for botanical quality and esthetic visibility. In Humboldt County, Olmsted favored the giants along Bull Creek for one park, and the groves between Prairie Creek and the beach at Gold Bluffs, for another. In Del Norte, he saw merit in the magnificent stands on the flats of the Smith River and Mill Creek, and along the fog-wreathed coastal hills south of Crescent City. In time, all four would be acquired and brought into the California state park system; the latter three eventually residing, in theory if not in practice, within the confines of Redwood National Park.

And yes, as early as 1930 the Purists and the Philistines were already having a go at it. The League tended toward purism. The National Park Service, under the direction of Mather's successor, Horace Albright, was beginning to lean the other way. "The greatest good for the greatest number," Albright was heard to say, "has to have a small place even in the national park administration." To the Purist, so utilitarian a view simply served to confirm a suspicion that the Park Service was heading fast to become, as Drury called it, "a glorified playground commission." As if to underscore the disenchantment, the League in 1930 amended its bylaws to delete as an objective the creation of a Redwood National Park. (Drury himself went on, ten years later, to inherit the Mather-Albright job. Historian Susan R. Schrepfer, in her definitive book *The Fight to Save the Redwoods*, reports that Drury, as Park Service director in the Roosevelt and Truman administrations, did his damndest to hold the recreational Babbitts at bay, opposing the "fire-fall" of burning brush at Yosemite and the Yellowstone circus of garbage-fed bears.)

For a time, then, saving the redwoods became not a matter of going for broke with a national park but of putting together, with League donations and state matching funds, a string of memorial groves so fine that even Drury could claim that the crown jewels of the redwood forest were at last in safe hands, namely California's. But were they? Even as Drury spoke, America was in an orgy of homebuilding, and many Americans, especially in the West, were keen to have their orgy with redwood siding. On the privately owned lands above the Rockefeller Forest at Bull Creek, for example, industry was busy rendering the surrounding woods into board feet, the slopes into naked gullies. Suddenly, to the Purist eye, it was beginning to look as if the artillery duels of Flanders Fields had just been replayed in the hills of Humboldt County.

And it looked even worse after the drenching winter rains of 1955. With nothing to hold back the runoff, flash floods surged over the flats at Bull Creek and toppled more than five hundred of the best trees in the Rockefeller Forest. Whereupon some of the redwood saviors began once again to think big, especially in the war rooms of the Sierra Club where, as Susan Schrepfer would describe it, one could detect a new and "apocalyptic" vision. The way Club archdruid David Brower saw it: "What we save in the next few years is all that will ever be saved."

Redwood Creek gathers its headwaters at an elevation of some five thousand feet in the Coast Range, then tumbles northwest for fifty-five miles to the ocean at Orick. It is a small stream when measured against the Mad or the Klamath, but what it lacks in volume of flow is of little consequence when one measures the size of the trees that sprout from its banks. Going back a generation or two of tree-hugging, the watershed was briefly considered a candidate for national park status, but was soon dismissed out of hand. The creek, some said, was inaccessible; and besides, its groves, however commendable, fell outside the Olmstedian crown-jewels view.

Yet one of the very factors that failed to inspire League interest in Redwood Creek gave the Sierra Club something to think about. *Sunset* magazine editor Martin Litton, a director of the Club as well as a counselor to the League, saw the watershed as having the best park potential precisely because it *was* off the beaten path of U.S. Highway 101, the so-called Avenue of the Giants. David Brower and other Club leaders such as Edgar and Peggy Wayburn agreed, and soon Litton, in his private plane, was flying payloads of federal decision-makers over the winding canyon of Redwood Creek.

Three events in 1964 figured prominently in advancing the national park idea. The first, in June, was a White House Conference on Natural Beauty; President Lyndon Johnson took the occasion to direct Interior Secretary Udall to prepare a redwood proposal for Congress. The second, in July, was an announcement by the National Geographic Society that it had discovered at a horseshoe bend of Redwood Creek the "Mount Everest of All Living Things," a tree 67.8 feet taller than a football field is long. And the third, in September, was passage of a measure authorizing the Land and Water Conservation Fund, which, for the first time in history, assured the nation's park-makers that they could think big without breaking the bank.

That was the good news. The bad, unfolding over the next few years, was how difficult it became at times to tell which fight-to-save-the-redwoods was more bitterly intense—the one between conservationists and timbermen, or that other conflict, the internecine one pitting Redwood Creek advocates against proponents of a national park centered on the Mill Creek watershed in Del Norte County. Some conservationists not of a mind to think big even argued that what had already been saved by the League, in state parks, was all that need ever be saved. That only brought a riposte from Edgar and Peggy Wayburn in their introduction to the Club's *The Last Redwoods and the Parkland of Redwood Creek*. While praising the League for its "tremendous job" in saving primeval groves, the Wayburns characterized some of the state parks as "see-through roadside strips" and others as being "almost as tall as they were wide." And when, in 1967, the

Johnson Administration suddenly took its support from the Club-backed Redwood Creek plan and shifted it to the more modest Mill Creek proposal, Brower took out full-page ads in six metropolitan dailies under the headline: "Mr. President: There is one great forest of redwoods left on Earth; but the one you are trying to save isn't it. . . . Meanwhile they are cutting down both of them." In fact, while the advocates lobbied and the White House waffled and the Congress put its finger to the wind, some four thousand acres of old-growth redwood in proposed parklands fell to the chain saws of industry.

At last, in 1968, the parties arrived at a compromise. There would be a national park, but of 58,000 acres only—and half of that was already preserved in the three state parks. It took in only a minor piece of the Mill Creek watershed, which was bad news for the League; and not even half of what the Club·had proposed for Redwood Creek. In the stretch of that creek that brackets the Tallest Trees, for example, the new park was barely a half-mile wide. To some people it appeared as a shadow of those "see-through" strips the Wayburns had lamented. To Susan Schrepfer's hindsight it resembled "the results of a taffy pull." Still, for all its shortcomings, the new park was going to cost the government nearly $200 million, and that was more acquisition money than it had ever spent before, in any one place.

If anyone thought that the fight to save the redwoods was finally won by *this* national park, he was badly mistaken. Even as a phalanx of dignitaries (including President Richard Nixon, former President Lyndon Johnson, and future President but then Governor Ronald Reagan) gathered in the Lady Bird Johnson Grove near Orick to dedicate the new park, this being August 1969, logging trucks were bouncing over the ridgetops nearby, chain-saws were *brrrrrrapping* along the private side of the taffy pull at Redwood Creek, and a plug of eroded sediment was working its way downstream toward the Tall Trees. Part of the impending impact might have been mitigated had Governor Reagan's forest-practices bureaucracy been of a mind to regulate the timber companies. Instead, the regulators either looked the other way or actively sanctioned some of the most destructive practices, including huge clearcuts on the steep, unacquired slopes above Redwood Creek.

Throughout the early and mid-seventies, the fight focused on establishing some kind of buffer around the alluvial groves—if not by industry agreement, which would not be forthcoming, then by an enlargement of the park, which would be. It would take almost another ten years, another round of lawsuits, confrontations, appeals, studies, challenges, oversights, and enforcements. It would take big-thinking California Congressman Phil Burton's oversize plan for a 74,000-acre addition to Redwood National Park, and small thinking by the National Park Service for a 21,500-acre addition, to bring about, in 1978, the Carter Administration's compromise expansion of some 48,000 acres. The new park boundaries would, perforce, embrace much land already cut over. But they would also extend protection to the hydrologic divides on the ridgelines above Redwood Creek. In addition, the 1978 legislation established a 30,000-acre Park Protection Zone upstream, in which the Park Service would have some power to review logging activities. There would be unprecedented measures to mitigate local economic impacts, including employment losses. And there would be $33 million in additional funds authorized for rehabilitating the battered slopes of Redwood Creek. The Park Service, in effect, was going to get all the king's horses and all the king's men to put the whole watershed together again.

In the spring of 1967, at the height of the conservationists' civil war and the apogee of the timbermen's hubris, the editors at *Newsweek* in New York, where I was working at the time, decided to post me to California to separate fact from opinion in the redwood forests of Humboldt and Del Norte counties. It was hard work to detach yourself from opinion in redwood country, those days. Hard, if you cared about wild things as much as you cared about journalistic integrity; hard, if you listened to the assurances of the foresters at Arcata Redwood Company and Georgia-Pacific and then got in a car with Lucille Vinyard or Dave Van de Mark of the Sierra Club and followed a back-country track to the tractor clearcuts the foresters did not want you to see; hard, if you took up a paddle in a borrowed canoe, bow stroke to Club troubleshooter Gary Soucie's stern, and rode the spring freshets down Redwood Creek to that holy place where the Tallest Tree in the world was born. Somehow I managed the separation. Or perhaps my editors managed it for me, so that—at least on the copydesks of Madison Avenue if not in the boardrooms of Arcata and Georgia-Pacific—a measure of journalistic integrity appeared to survive my experience, even as many of the wild mid-slope redwoods we had passed on the way downstream would survive not at all. Years later, after all the park-making and remaking was legislatively over, what I would remember most vividly of that first time in redwood country was the carnage that could not then dispassionately be described— the rutted skid trails, the slash and the silt in the streambeds, the stumps on the battered slopes. And the slick propaganda. "It takes big equipment to move the heavy logs over steep country," explained Arcata Redwood, then a subsidiary of the Weyer-haeuser Company, in one of its brochures. "The ground does get scuffed. Like a cornfield just after harvest."

In the summer of 1987 I returned to Redwood Creek to see how the national park was faring at the close of its second decade. Too many years had gone by since I had last hugged a *Sequoia sempervirens;* so I wanted to do that, and pay my respects to the Mount Everest of All Living Things, and maybe mosey up into the Lady Bird Johnson Grove, where I had not yet been. And I wanted to check out some of those left-behind Arcata and Georgia-Pacific cornfields—those Flanders Fields up the mid-slopes—to see if it was truly fact, or merely errant opinion, that the process of restoration was well under way. Not just restoration the old-fashioned way, by natural succession. I mean the National Park Service's newfangled way, supplementing the natural juices with booster shots of men and machines—ironically, some of the very same men who, with the same kinds of machines, had helped to bring in this harvest of shame in the first place.

My guide this time out was the photographer and Park Service management specialist Bob Belous. From the park's operations center at Orick, we drove up the winding Bald Hills Road ("Bald" for its high prairielands rather than the scalped woodlands, below) and followed the ridgetop divide southeast toward Schoolhouse Peak. At pulloffs along the way we could look across the valley of Redwood Creek to the tributary canyons on the other side— McArthur and Bond and Tom McDonald. And there were the old wounds all covered with scar tissue of red alder and Dougfir and, coming in last but not least—though you couldn't fact it out at such a distance—the toy *sempervirens* of rootstock second-growth. "We're lifting this place out of its tomb," said Belous at one over-look. "And its working. *Man* is it working."

And what a deep and awesome tomb it had been when the work began in 1979: thirty-thousand cutover acres, much of it scalped over the preceding decade; nearly three hundred miles of logging roads, most of the roads built with little or no con-cern for the fact that water was made to run downhill, and for ev-ery mile of road at last ten of tractor skid trails—enough to cross the country coast to coast, and then some. The prescription for at least half of the disturbed acres called for heavy machinery (in Forest Service parlance) to "disaggregate" the roads and skid trails, restore slopes to original contours, and excavate debris from stream crossings, in order that the natural watercourses might rise from the dead.

Some acres only time can heal. Off the west side access, in the Bond Creek drainage other side of the valley, Belous pulled us to a stop where some alders were beginning to choke one of the logging roads destined for "disaggregation." We got out of the vehicle and followed the road through the alders for about a hundred yards, and suddenly we were standing at the lip of a yawning abyss, a great slide where the road and everything sup-porting it had said good-bye to the hillside and skedaddled for down below. How do you fix *this*? I asked Belous. "You don't," he said. "When we discovered this, we couldn't find enough money to pour into it. So we live with it. You can't bring back what was here. It's all down there—in Redwood Creek."

Possibly no other terrain in North America is less suited to large-scale tractor logging than the hills of California's North Coast. Slope, to be sure, is a large constraint in any hill country; but it isn't just any hill country that is cursed, as the hills of Redwood Creek are, with the Franciscan assemblage, which sounds like the name of a Roman Catholic choir but in fact is a complex association of sedimentary materials described by Belous as ranging from fine alluvial grit to "stones the size of bowling balls." And all of it is highly susceptible to the forces of erosion. Take, for example, that missing stretch of logging road, and all the hundreds of other slumps and slides in the watershed, and you have what Belous apocalyptically describes as a "great glut of gravel associated with years of logging outwash that is now trying to work its way down Redwood Creek in annual rain-driven pulses."

Next stop: Bridge Creek, a Redwood tributary selectively logged in the early fifties, then clearcut in the seventies before the park's expansion. Up a steep and winding logging road, near the creek's headwaters, we found Louise Johnson, a Park Service geologist, supervising the work of two bulldozers and a hydraulic backhoe. The backhoe was yanking big redwood butts from the channel of a feeder stream. "A Humboldt crossing," said Johnson. "From sometime in the fifties." To get a haul road or a skid trail across a stream in those days, timbermen couldn't be bothered with culverts; they simply piled a number of parallel logs in the channel, then surfaced the crossing with gravel. Inevitably, the spaces between the logs would fill up with sediment, whereupon, come the next winter flood, that gravel glut in Redwood Creek would grow even greater. Johnson explained that after the hoe and the dozers finished restoring the crossing area to its original configuration—and they'd have to hurry, for the rainy season was on its way—the raw soil would be mulched with straw to prepare it for the planting of redwood seedlings. I asked Johnson how, after almost eight years, she liked working twelve-hour shifts up here in the dust and the mud of hardhat country. A big California sunshine smile broke through. "I wouldn't trade it for anything," she said. "It's great work, helping nature get back to the way it ought to be."

If Bring-'Em-Back-Alive folks like Louise Johnson and her straw mulch and the backhoes-for-our-side were the park's best news this time around, the worst was that great glut of gravel abuilding in the streambed of Redwood Creek. So our final stop that day was at the end of a downslope logging road, and Belous and I got out of his vehicle and hiked the last quarter-mile where the forest was getting back to how it ought to be, and then there was an opening ahead and the glare of afternoon sunlight on waterslick stones. We were down and out in the mainstem canyon. The streambed was wide here, but the creek itself, in dry-down summertime volume, needed but a tenth of the vernal channel I'd floated with Soucie two decades ago. Crossing to the other side on a footbridge, Belous and I followed a trail round the horseshoe bend to the Tallest Tree. We paid our respects in silence. Then we turned toward the streambed to address the glut in Redwood Creek.

There were, as I interpreted Belous and would read in official reports later on, a number of problems. There was this unchanging fact about water; alas, after twenty years, it was *still* made to run downhill. And then there was the untuneful Franciscan assemblage. Those were the natural basics, and without any help whatsoever from loggers, they accounted for a measure of sedimentation all by themselves. Then there were the historical basics, such as the fact that men had been logging the upstream watershed for many years before and after the park and its expansion; and the fact that upstream, in the so-called Park Protection Zone and beyond, there were no Louise Johnsons or backhoes-for-our-side to put Mother Nature together again. There were only these gentlemen who measure profit or loss in running lengths of board feet, never in tons of runaway soil.

Consider CFIP, the California Forest Improvement Program. CFIP offers private landowners an opportunity to improve their forest resources at public expense. CFIP picks up seventy-five cents of every dollar spent on an approved project in thinning, brush control, wildlife-habitat improvement, fisheries restoration, tree planting, and erosion control. One need not be a pedigreed forester to understand that, in the upper watershed of

Redwood Creek, any project involving revegetation or erosion control would greatly benefit the national park by reducing the accretion of sediment downstream, in the park. Yet what is the response from the logging folks of the upper basin, and there are plenty of them. Practically zilch. According to one Park Service report, no CFIP projects were undertaken in the basin in 1985, and only two were completed in 1986—both totaling a mere $12,500, for release thinning, a form of brush control calculated to hasten standing timber toward the marketplace.

Then there was—there *is*—this problem of timber-harvest reviews in the upper basin of Redwood Creek. It was the understanding of Congress, during deliberations on expanding the park in 1978, that timber operations throughout the entire watershed would be regulated by the State of California while the National Park Service played an ex-officio role in reviewing all harvest plans, not only in the Park Protection Zone but in the upper basin beyond it as well. And that's the way it worked as long as Governor Edmund Brown, Jr., sat in the statehouse at Sacramento. Not that the Park Service got around to reviewing *all* the upper basin harvests. But at least it was batting .500. Then George Deukmejian moved into the statehouse. That was in 1983. That's when the rules changed. Then, instead of routinely offering the Park Service access to inspect proposed cuts in the upper basin, or to monitor plan conformance after the harvest, Deukmajian's Department of Forestry said that the feds must independently secure the landowner's permission to visit the site for inspection, which—given the typical landowner's aversion to inspectors—was tantamount to slamming the door. Since 1983, according to Park Service figures, federal inspectors have been batting about .130 in the upper basin of Redwood Creek.

If the California Department of Forestry were an adequate batter itself, perhaps there would be no need for a federal inspector at the plate. But by all accounts except the State of California's, the department's performance in the North Coast region since 1983 has been one long hitless inning.

"The state's forest practices look good on paper," says long-time redwood watchdog Lucille Vinyard of Moonstone Beach, "but they're not working on the ground."

"Our biggest problem," says Redwood Park Superintendent Douglas Warnock, "the prime sources of sedimentation, are the logging roads upstream. That's where you have the failures, the plugged culverts, the diversions, the washouts. The state makes its final inspection of a road three years after construction, but that's just about the time the failures begin to occur. And since we are denied access, we can't determine where all the new sediment is coming from. There are a lot of boards in this boat of a park, and a lot of water's getting between them."

"Certain ongoing practices on [Park Protection Zone] lands," says a Park Service report to the United States Congress, "also comprise a risk for large-scale erosion and sedimentation problems during the next major storm event. . . ." Among the recommended solutions, which only California can implement, if it will, are "tighter controls for road location," "altered road-building practices at stream-crossing sites," and mandatory "long-term maintenance of logging roads."

"Although the persistent cumulative effects [of sedimentation] measured in Redwood Creek are a direct result of land-use practices conducted during a period of little land-use regulation," write the Park Service researchers Danny K. Hagans, William E. Weaver, and Mary Ann Madej in a 1986 technical paper, "current timber harvest and road construction regulations still largely ignore the potential for stream diversions—the principal cause of gully erosion in the Redwood Creek basin. The results of both earlier and ongoing practices continue to significantly affect fluvial erosion rates . . . and the volume and residence time of stored sediment."

The California Department of Forestry appears inured to such criticisms. It responds—at least to me, and from its North Coast regional office in Santa Rosa—that the state's forest practices are indeed working on the ground, and very well at that; that the regulations are being enforced; that it would not be "appropriate" for the department to grant feds access to regulatory matters that should remain strictly between the state and the private landowner; that long-term maintenance of logging roads is soon to be implemented under new regulations. That, in short, there is nothing to worry about in the woods of the North Coast in general, and of Redwood Creek in particular.

But no-sweat wasn't the way Bob Belous saw it the afternoon we stood in the Tall Trees Grove, looking out across a gravel bar as big as the Ritz. It had all been underwater when I canoed the creek in '67. "And half of it wasn't even here yet," said Belous. "It was still up there, in the hills." The surface of the gravel bar, he figured, of this one and all the others downstream, was five, maybe six, feet above the level of pre-logging days.

So, I said, what difference did that make? These tall trees here were still five or six feet above the gravel bar.

Yes, but gravel displaces water in flood times, said Belous. You get hydrostatic pressure pushing the water up into the tall trees' root systems.

"And then?"

"And then the trees die. Or get undercut and topple in a truly big flood. It can happen. Remember Bull Creek."

But if the rate of sedimentation could be reduced—if all the loose practices in the upper basin could somehow be made tight, if the state would play ball again, if the roads were properly maintained—then what?

"Then," he said, "with the scouring effects of winter storms, this awful plug of stuff here would work its way to the sea."

And how long would that take?

"With nothing added but the sediment from natural erosion? That could take a decade. Or a century."

Crescent City is a community of some 3,400 people tucked between the Pacific Ocean and the green hills of Del Norte County, about an hour's drive north on U.S. 101 from the bridge, at Orick, that takes you over the gravelly waters of Redwood Creek. Crescent City had one brief fling with notoriety in 1964 when a tidal wave rolled into town and swept many of its buildings and some of its residents out to sea. Since then the town, and the county of which it is the seat, have experienced one wrenching dislocation after another—a glut on the timber market, a closing of mills, a fishing industry increasingly at the mercy of zealous regulations, a commercial crop of Easter lilies that bloom, alas, only in July. Given such a thin gruel of economic indices, you'd think that Crescent City would be delighted to have a national park at its door. But that's not the way the city fathers saw it when I talked to them. The way they told it, the park was a millstone, a broken promise, such that Crescent City would be far better off with a max-security prison, the largest penal unit in all of California.

Pique and loathing for all things federal appear to be endemic in Del Norte County, as they are in most rural places nationwide. But Del Norte folk have this extra twist to their discontent: Most of the county was already owned by the federal government, in Six Rivers National Forest, when it reached out to grab these other lands, these *private* lands, for its national park. That was what hurt in the beginning. What hurts now, they were saying in Crescent City, is that Redwood National Park just hasn't delivered the punch that was promised by Congress two decades ago.

"They promised us everything," said Mayor C. Ray Smith when I called on him at City Hall. "They talked about tourism and all these visitor days boosting the economy. And it just never materialized. When you look at dollars and cents, the contribution that park makes to the community doesn't add up to much of anything."

Though Mayor Smith declined to define what might constitute "much of anything" in his book, in my book the park's contribution in dollars and cents, wholly apart from tourism, has been great indeed. The park expansion act of 1978, in fact, mandated a huge contribution of dollars and cents to offset the expected economic impacts of removing forty-eight thousand acres from the marketplace. Of course most of those acres are in Humboldt County, and to Humboldt have flowed most of the dollars. But Del Norte County has shared in the federal largess as well. Over the past decade in the two counties, several thousand laid-off woods and mill workers have received more than

$100 million in benefits and severance pay, relocation allowances, and job retraining grants—regardless of whether or not the layoffs were directly related to park expansion, and most were not. The park itself, which is headquartered at Crescent City, has an annual payroll approaching $3 million, and most of those dollars change hands in Del Norte and Humboldt counties. Another million is spent locally in the park's purchase of goods and services, including the leasing of heavy equipment.

Beyond these infusions of money, the feds have offered to sweeten the North Coast pot with public works projects and revolving funds for loans to small businesses. Ask, said Uncle, and you shall receive. Humboldt County asked, and it received more than $10 million. And Del Norte, where the mayor of the county seat wondered aloud why the feds "can't do anything right"? Del Norte hasn't even bothered to ask. According to a recent Park Service report, not one governmental agency in that county applied for funding under the economic mitigation sections of the Redwood National Park Expansion Act of 1978. When asked why not, Del Norte assessor Gerald Cochran, who also serves as the county's chief lobbyist and grantsman, professed puzzlement. "*What* sections?" he wanted to know.

Del Norte's disenchantment on the tourism issue is a different matter, and it is complicated somewhat by geography and by local perceptions of what the national park experience should rightfully be. The North Coast region is, in a word, remote. Some 350 miles separate Crescent City from San Francisco in one direction, from Portland, Oregon, in the other. There are not a whole lot of people who live and play in between. Strangers to the territory tend to be passing through. Several years ago a survey of Redwood park visitors found that for nine out of ten the park was not the primary destination of their trip; that, in fact, the same proportion planned to spend fewer than eight hours in the region. (I mean, when you've seen one redwood, you've seen 'em all. Right?) Perhaps more telling is the estimate—albeit by unofficial count—that more people visit the Trees of Mystery, near Klamath, than the Redwood Creek unit of the national park. The Trees, a commercial roadside venture that a Walt Disney might have dreamed up, with Phineas Barnum as site-planner, promotes itself as an "American Experience." The experience begins with a forty-nine-foot-tall Paul Bunyan (misplaced from the Minnesota woods) and ends somewhere on the "Trail of Tall Tales."

For their part, the feds were off base in the visitor numbers they first projected ("deliberately inflated" is how one Del Nortean recalls it). And some folks still feel they were wrongfully led to believe that the park would be developed intensively. "They told us we were going to have it just like Yosemite," said Bob Berkowitz, owner-manager of Radio KCRE in Crescent City. "They said once they got the land they'd just pour all kinds of money into it. And what did they do? They left it alone."

Kathy Catton is executive director of the Crescent City-Del Norte County Chamber of Commerce. Before that she was a ranger, for seven years, at Redwood National Park. Catton's chief complaint about her former employer, Uncle, is that he doesn't know or care anything about promotion. "Who promotes Grand Teton and Yosemite?" she says. "Not the Park Service. The concessionaires. But the legislation creating Redwood National Park prohibits concessions. They've got to be outside the park, and that's part of the reason there aren't any. There are only these same old small motels."

But look, I say. Redwood isn't supposed to be a romper room, or a lawn-chair resort.

"I'll tell you," says Catton, "except for walking some trails, there's not much to do at this park. There aren't enough campground facilities. There's nothing to show the folks back home that you've been here. People go to a national park, they expect to come out with junk stuff. You know, the mugs from the concession shops, the T-shirts. But Redwood? It's not here. So the people go home with souvenirs that say Crescent City."

Possibly one day soon some people can go home from the North Coast with souvenirs that say Del Norte State Prison, for that seems to be the only economic glimmer in Crescent City's future. Now under construction a few miles north of town, the 2,200-bed max-security facility is expected to have an annual payroll of more than $40 million and employ upward of 1,200 people, almost half of whom would be hired locally. As one newspaper pundit put it, embracing a state prison elsewhere would be "the municipal equivalent of trying to catch herpes." But not in down-and-out Del Norte. As a measure of the prison's acceptability in the community—and possibly of the North Coast sense of humor—State Senator Barry Keene launched a contest to find the institution a proper name. Among the suggestions: Crescent City Incarcerary, St. Dismos State (Dismos being the patron saint of prisoners), Camp Runamok, Dungeness Dungeon, Slammer-by-the-Sea, and Big Trees Big House. The Senator himself had wanted to call the place Prison of the Redwoods but, alas, found that for some curious reason the name had almost a universal lack of support.

There is a certain matter of unfinished business pending at Redwood National Park. It is this matter of jurisdiction, of United States apples and California oranges, of state parks doing their own things and going their own ways within the federal park, and in some situations, not even acknowledging that they are a part of it. Visitors can hardly keep it all straight—what Bob Berkowitz calls "this bungling confusion" of state and federal boundaries. "So you end up," he says, "with a national park that has no substance. It's on the map, but when you get there you can't even find it. It reminds me of the little kid piping up from the back seat, 'Hey, Pop, are we *there* yet?' Well, we're not there yet."

It had seemed such a simple thing to accomplish ten years ago. The 1978 legislation had provided for transfer by donation to the National Park Service of Prairie Creek, Del Norte Coast, and Jedediah Smith state redwood parks. A year later, California executed an agreement to transfer management (as distinct from title), but the Park Service declined to sign it. And there the matter rested until 1985, when Park Service Director William Penn Mott, Jr., a former California parks chief, renewed the effort to consolidate management of state and federal holdings. Then the seen-one-seen-'em-all Reagan Administration threw gags and manacles around the office of William Mott, and not much has been heard since of bringing this schizoid situation to its proper end.

"It doesn't make sense," says Redwood Park superintendent Douglas Warnock. "The public's paying for everything twice." It has been estimated, for example, that management of the parks as a consolidated unit might trim upward of half a million dollars a year off state operating budgets; the savings would come through elimination of duplication in services, personnel, and capital equipment. Roads and trails crossing park boundaries could be maintained to a uniform standard. Fire control, public safety, and fish and wildlife management, now under three separate agencies in the state parks, would fall under one, the National Park Service. Moreover, there have been reports that the California state park system is experiencing financial woes greater even than those of the federal establishment. The California system is huge and, given adequate funds, efficiently managed. But, as Douglas Warnock notes, "money runs to where the people are, and in California they're at the other end of the state."

For these reasons, or others, the conservation establishment favors the idea of transferring management of the three state parks to the feds. One of the other reasons: The Park Service has consistently used fragmented jurisdiction as an excuse for not fulfilling some of the goals in its management plan. A few friendly critics, for example, are disturbed in particular by Smokey's failure to develop more back-country features, such as hiking trails, and by what might be construed as a lack of imagination in interpreting the park to visitors in a meaningful way.

Some of the calls for consolidation, however, are hitched to qualifications. Save-the-Redwoods League, for example, would have the state at this time relinquish management of Prairie Creek only, partly because of that park's proximity to the major federal holdings along Redwood Creek, but also because of the League's displeasure with the state for "permitting vehicles to drive onto Gold Bluffs Beach" and allowing some of Prairie Creek's trails to get run down. As for transfer of the other two state parks, the League stands by a policy dating to 1978. As re-defined later in a letter from the League's executive director, John B. Dewitt, to William Mott, "None of us favor transfer of Jedediah Smith or Del Norte Coast to the National Park Service unless [it] will complete the acquisition of the entire 17,000-acre Mill Creek watershed for protection of these two park gems." Aye, and there's *that* creek again. Echoes of the inter-necine wars of the 1960s.

The League's long-time love affair with the Mill Creek basin has lately turned into a passion for a larger watershed, namely the Smith River, of which the creek is a principal tributary; and that, in turn, has spawned a big and intriguing idea that could truly provide protection to the redwood gems of Del Norte County. The idea is to take the entire 610-square-mile Smith wa-tershed, from the high divide of the Siskiyou Mountains almost to the corporate limits of Crescent City, and turn it all into a Smith Wild River National Park. The federal government al-ready owns about 85 percent of the land, mostly in Six Rivers National Forest. The private lands, for the most part, embrace those 17,000 coveted acres along Mill Creek.

That the watershed as a whole is of national park quality is be-yond question. It encompasses: two existing wilderness areas, the Siskiyou in the southeast and the Kalmiopsis to the north, over the border in Oregon; miles of existing trails; a mainstem river already designated "wild and scenic" under both state and federal river-preservation systems; world-class sportfisheries (for salmon and steelhead); superb whitewater rafting and ca-noeing year-round. Proponents point out that the new park could be administered jointly, and cost-effectively, with Red-wood National, out of the Park Service headquarters at Crescent City. No doubt it all sounds like a nightmare to the good people of Crescent City, and probably to the U.S. Forest Service, too, which has measured its Six Rivers unit down to the last board foot and would rather *cut* it down to the last board foot than let the greenies have it. At stake on the Smith are some 1,500 acres of old-growth redwoods. "If the Forest Service continues to ap-prove big clearcuts for Six Rivers," says Dewitt of the League, "the entire Smith, not just those redwoods, will be whacked to death."

On my last afternoon in redwood country I went up an unpaved road off Highway 101 to a place in the national park that is known as Lost Man Creek. I had never been there but had heard about it when it was the focus of some concern during the park-expansion wars of the seventies, and I was intrigued by the romance of its poignant name. Going either way on 101, you can easily miss the road to Lost Man, for there is no sign along the highway to slow you down for the turn, only a small Park Service legend that is practically invisible until, on a hunch, you *do* make the turn and it happens to be the right one. The park's on the map, Bob Berkowitz had been saying in Crescent City, but when you get there you can't even find it. And that reminded me of something Sierra Club Chairman Michael McCloskey once told me about his own perceptions of this park he had lobbied and labored for so many years to create. "At last we get this billion-dollar national park," McCloskey said, "and sometimes the Park Service acts as if it were *embarrassed* by it."

At the Lost Man picnic area, where the unpaved road turns into a trail, I followed the creek upstream for a few hundred yards through the shadow of forest giants, redwoods mostly, western hemlock with gnarled branches, Dougfir festooned with green-gray moss. And there it occurred to me that the park, after these twenty years, is still like that nameless man-up-the-creek, lost in its own unfinishedness. People tend not to like that sort of thing. People abhor loose threads. I mean, who wants to be told: "Hey, it's not ready yet; come back in a hundred years"? If the park is to last that long, there are some things that will *have* to get finished fast. Like bringing the discrete parts into the organic whole by consolidating state and federal management responsibilities. Like forcing the timber industry and the State of California to clean up their act in the upper watersheds.

On the other hand, there are some things that cannot be rushed. That great plug of gravel by the Tall Trees Grove is going to take its own sweet time slipping down to the sea, and there are still all those healing scars up on the mid-slopes, and the bandages of straw at the Humboldt crossings, and the grudging alder giving way to the fir, and fir ever so slowly to redwood, and the russet rings of growth in widening circles under the cambium layers. Okay, so give it time. Give the park time to tie its loose ends together for those "generations yet unborn"—those posterity people we ecofreaks like to invoke to make our actions, now, appear selfless and noble. Then, after one of those generations has actually been around for a while, maybe Redwood will be finished at last, our first national park raised from the dead. Then let there be big signs by the side of the road. Not too big, mind you, but big enough to proclaim that here is a park. A park that is all it could ever be.

LORD OF

THE EASTERN

FORESTS

In all likelihood, they were the first North American trees to catch the European eye. Were, if you write the Vikings out of the Book of Records, since spruce were probably their first trees, and replace the Norse with zip-lipped Basque and Breton cod-men who dipped nets off down-west Maine long before Columbus Day and didn't bother to write home about it. At least not about the pines. The white pines. The gangling, sky-thrusting conifers that poked their crowns above the canopy of green; scarecrows above the forest stubble; sentinels at sunup. A half-mile out, our first-time fisherman peered through the dissipating mists and spied a tassel, a mere speck of evergreen, catching dawn light above the dark and shrouded shore. Here was no palm atilt in the doldrums of Christopher's Tropic of Cancer, or Leif's stunted spruce on a Labrador ledge. Here was the great white pine of the fairweather country, and a whole new world lay at its feet.

It is so noble a tree, this *Pinus strobus,* this lord of the eastern forests, that, to sing its praise, one is tempted to trespass into the precincts of hyperbole. And that could be dangerous, for despite the white pine's superior loft among eastern trees (it can lift itself higher even than the tulip poplar), among conifers at-large and worldwide *P. strobus* is a relative runt, written out of the Book of Records by some of the firs, a few of the spruces (the Sitka and the Sikkim), at least one western cousin (the Jeffrey pine), and of course the giant sequoias and redwoods of California.

To the aficionado, all of that is so much apples and oranges. The true test of any tree is not its size but its character, its essence. Yet in the case of Strobus, no single word seems to sum it all up. *Elegant* is okay for openers, just as *scruffy* might begin to parse the pitch pine. *Sober,* yes. *Practical,* oh heavens, yes— used to be the most practical tree in the eastern forests. Why, there's hardly a third-generation native-born American nowadays who can't claim kinship to some ancestor born in a house made of white pine boards, baptized in a pine church, and consigned to the worms of the great beyond in a straight pine box. Betwixt the boards and the box, Old Forebear probably fingered white pine barrels, buckets, butter paddles, and bridge timbers, too.

For all its practical uses, the most inexplicable characteristic of this tree is its ability to bring out the anthropomorphic in us. I confess to having stooped to such improper thoughts myself, though not since I was a child with a Scout knife, cutting through the thin gray bark of a young pine in sap time and then pulling back, aghast that a pine could bleed. Or weep. I wasn't sure, for the sap was clear. How venial, this, compared to the mortal and romantic notion of a certain H. D. Thoreau of Concord, Massachusetts, who, on the last day of autumn 1851, ascended Fair Haven Hill to perceive "a clump of white pines far westward over the shrub-oak plain." It was a soft feathery grove, Thoreau reported, "with their gray stems indistinctly seen, like human beings come to their cabin door." It was as if the trees had—hearts. Wrote Thoreau: "[The pines] impress me as human. . . . Nothing stands up more free from blame in this world than a pine-tree."

And of the lords of the Maine woods, Thoreau would have this to say: "But the pine is no more lumber than man is, and to be made into boards and houses is no more its truest and highest use than the truest use of man is to be cut down and made into manure."

Aye, what elegant sentiments from the man who, not even a decade earlier, "borrowed an axe and went down to the woods by Walden Pond, nearest to where [he] intended to build [his] house, and began to cut down some tall arrowy white pines, still in their youth, for timber." Singing as he worked, Thoreau hewed his main timbers six inches square, his studs on two sides only, and the rafters and floor timbers on one side, leaving the rest of the bark on. He carried a "dinner of bread and butter, and read the newspaper in which it was wrapped, at noon, sitting amid the green pine boughs which [he] had cut off, and to [his] bread was imparted some of their fragrance, for [his] hands were covered with a thick coat of pitch." Young H.D.T. could rationalize anything, of course. Like many of the loggers who had preceded and would follow him to the stump, he could claim to be more the friend than the foe of the pine tree. And how was that? Why because, having used it, he had become "better acquainted with it."

No other pine east of the Mississippi is so widely distributed as the white, though the range of the shortleaf yellow pine in the South runs a close second. From the Maritime Provinces and Maine westward across the Lake States to Minnesota and down the Appalachian spine into northern Georgia, Strobus tolerates most any soil but seems to fare best on well-drained sites, less often in pure stands than in association with other species such as oak, ash, and hemlock. In pristine virginal times, some whoppers may have attained heights of well over two hundred feet and annual growth rings approaching four hundred. No more. Nowadays the healthier trees top out at about a hundred feet, and longevity is harder to come by, no thanks to the pine weevil and the white pine blister rust, a fungus wind-borne off currant and gooseberry bushes. (A related species, *P. monticola,* the western white pine, shares Strobus's, susceptibility to blister rust as well as its overall appearance, though perhaps not its lordliness, for the westerner's posture is compromised in association with the baronial Douglas fir and the regal redcedar.)

One of the white pine's most notable tendencies is its ability to colonize abandoned farmland, often to the exclusion of other successional pioneer species. Sun-loving and fast-growing, young Strobus hits the ground at a full run and soon shades out its competitors. Within the span of a single human generation, an old pasture thus becomes a budding pine grove. Strobus moreover is prodigious at reproduction. At ten to fifteen years of age, it begins bearing seeds—bumper crops of seeds every three to five years thereafter, upwards of a million seeds per acre in a pure, unencumbered old-field stand. With these feats in mind, one comes to an understanding of how the white pine almost took over central New England and parts of upstate New York and Pennsylvania in the mid-Nineteenth Century. Here, behind the sugar maples and the stone walls, were all these forlorn pastures and corn patches, their proprietors fetched west by the promise of Manifest Destiny. And here were all these pine seeds, floating on the wind. Inevitably, most of the old-field stands were logged off after the turn of the century, whereupon the insurgents, the long-suppressed hardwoods, were suddenly free to replace them.

Gifford Pinchot, America's premier forester, was a great admirer of the white pine. No doubt what he admired most was its multiple usefulness—much like H. D. Thoreau, friend of the useful pine at Walden Pond, his hands dripping blood, pitch, and newsprint. Pinchot in 1896 put his name to a little monograph entitled *The White Pine, A Study*. The study was mostly of pines in Pennsylvania. Pinchot was greatly encouraged. Not to worry, he wrote. If left to its own devices, the white pine "will at length resume possession of practically all the situations it occupied in the virgin forest." Alas, the good man knew full well that, short of wilderness (something Pinchot could hardly have understood), nothing in nature is ever left to its own devices. In any event, Pinchot was elevated to Lord High Forester, from which lofty height he proceeded to promulgate the myth of sustained yield.

For may own part, I have led a dreary life of white-pine deprivation. There were none of a wild kind in the haunts of my Ohio youth (the victim of my Scout-knife slashing being nursery stock, a neighbor's ornamental). But then riverine Ohio wasn't even in Strobus's range. Our own familial pines were Scots, I think, and also ornamental, and rough-barked, and scruffy. In the three or four eastern places I have since lived, there were always a few white pines on somebody's turf, but never on mine; at least not until I imported two from the wilds of New Hampshire to the silvicultural zoo of my Staten Island yard. Gone from that place for more than a decade, I am instructed by former neighbors, though perhaps inaccurately, that the pines are doing well and will soon be lording it over the nearby towers of the Verrazano Bridge. As for my here and now, which happens to be southern Connecticut, the occurrence of white pine is sparse. Old fields roundabout tend to give themselves over to eastern redcedar (a scratchy species). Of course, I could always whack down some hardwoods, let in the sun, and plant a few pines from the wilds of New Hampshire. The chickadees would be eternally grateful, but then so would the too-many deer, which would soon consign the young pines to the worms of the great beyond.

It is likelier that I shall leave the pines where they are happiest to be, and visit them in their own backyards from time to time. And where might that be? New Hampshire, of course. When I close my eyes and think on it, I see Strobus in New Hampshire, but spruces in Vermont. I see the pines along the Connecticut River near Cornish, and on the shoulder of Sunday Mountain back of Orfordville, and beside the road into Tamworth and along the old logging trails of the Pemigewasset. Westward from the Granite State, I remember the crisp bouquet of pine needles in the August heat of an Adirondack afternoon. And in Michigan? O, in Michigan: the leaning pines on the lakeside bluffs at Seven Mile Point, the virgins of Hartwick at Grayling, and a splendid grove not far from Midland, shown me by a native son in return for my pledge to divulge the location to no one. And so am I obliged.

Last but not least, we must lay on a word for Massachusetts, which put the white pine to its first real test and, by colonial extension, roped frontier Maine into the bargain as well. And what did Maine become when at last it divorced itself from the Bay State? Why, Maine became the Pine Tree State, and out of all the fifty, it's the only one that we have.

The first test for Strobus was perpendicular to that other main, the bounding briny one. It seems that after a hundred years of ruling the seas, and the hundred before that just scrabbling to get to the top, Old Britannia was coming up short in its supply of naval stores. From the pines of Scotland to the oaks of Sussex, by the 1690s the Admiralty was sorely hurting for wood. And what hurt the most was a severe shortage of the kind of tall and limber boles needed for masts. And that's where Strobus came in.

In 1691 there was inserted in a new Massachusetts Bay Colony charter a certain clause reserving to the Admiralty all white pines "of the diameter of twenty-four inches and upwards at twelve inches from the ground." The King's men ranged through the forest giving royal whoppers three whacks with a hatchet. They called it the mark of the Broad Arrow, but by all accounts the brand more closely resembled the track of a crow. And woe to the colonist caught with a log or board of illegal width. Enforcement, to be sure, left much to be desired, though not nearly so much as compliance. "To the eastward at York, Wells, Saco, Scarborough, Casco Bay, Kennebec, and Pemaquid," came one Down East complaint, the pine poachers "cut and saw at pleasure and send them where they please."

To head off the poachers, the Crown in 1722 extended Broad Arrow protection to *all* white pines in the colonies, of whatever size. By 1775 the ports of New England had shipped some 4,500 pines to the Royal Navy's mast sheds in England. That is much mast indeed, but barely a fraction of one percent of the large pines then standing and accounted for in the forests of New England. Nonetheless, Broad Arrow was finished. It has been said that interdiction of the mast trade by American colonists after 1775 had more than a little to do with the poor performance of the Royal Navy in several subsequent high-seas adventures.

With all those big pines still extant, and all those powerful rivers plunging out of the interior to spin the sawmills or carry the logs down to the sea, Maine was perfectly suited at the dawn of the nineteenth century to become the nation's top producer of pinewood products, not only for naval stores but for housing America's burgeoning crowd. The Frenchman F. André Michaux, touring the northern states in 1800, marveled at the ubiquity of white pine as a construction material and estimated that there were no fewer than half a million houses here made of it entirely, not counting the nails. Michaux may have been skirting the edge of hyperbole, for at the time—and it was a time of large families—that many pine houses would have meant one for every ten people in the country.

For almost half a century, Maine was the center of it all: the choppers and the swampers, the barkers and the captains of the goad, the oxen on the skid roads, the handspikes and the peaveys breaking up the jams, the summer thunder of logs rolling down the Penobscot and the Kennebec, the Saco and the Dead. In the autumn of 1853, the reformed pine-slayer H. D. Thoreau stood on the deck of a steamer crossing Moosehead Lake and discoursed once more on the subject of the white pine. He had come all this way from Concord, his listerners were told, to see where grew the stuff of which houses were made, but alas, he had found it a scarce tree. Yes, Henry. And so had the choppers.

Already the choppers and the captains of the goad were heading out, following the sawdust trail across New York to the Lake States. "WANTED TO GO WEST," a Bangor advertisement read. "One first rate head Sawyer to start immediately. Also, in 3 or 4 weeks, a gang of 10 or 12 Wood Choppers, to cut Pine wood for steam Boats." And west they went. To the Michigan watersheds. To the Tittabawassee and the Thunder Bay, the Au Sable and the Black, the Muskegon and the Manistee. And at last they went across the Straits at Mackinac, to make stumps on the Manistique and the Sturgeon, to retell the tallest of Down East tales by lanternlight in logging camps on the Kingston Plains.

PARADOX IN

THE PEMI

They called it a wilderness long before anyone had much understanding of what that word was all about, and went right on calling it a wilderness after the hobnailed sawyers had hightailed it down the track with the last of its spruce logs. It was, and remains, one great roadless void on the map of New Hampshire—the Pemigewasset, 100,000 acres wall-to-wall. There isn't a blank space any larger in all the national forests of the East. So people got to calling it the Pemigewasset Wilderness. Unofficially, of course, since there was no congressional seal of approval for the uppercase *W*. Now, believing that time heals all wounds, some folks want to make an honest statutory thing of the Pemi. Others do not. Not that disagreements over wilderness are in any way unusual. We have come to expect them. Perhaps we have come to *depend* on them, the clashing perceptions all done up for us in two-tone packages of black and white. Bad guys, good guys; spoilers, saviors. Easy plots. But in the case of the Pemi, no such luck. The case of the Pemi is gray.

Gray was more or less how I perceived the place my first time out, though there may be some slight discoloration of the memory, for I am peering across the span of nearly two-score years. I was a punky kid from the flatlands of Ohio then, not a single ascent to my credit, and not much sense about mountains. My sister and I had scrambled out of the valley of Daniel Webster and the Old Man of the Mountain, and, overburdened with too many rucksacked cans of pork and beans, puffed up the trail to a lean-to shelter at Liberty Springs, hellbent for Mount Washington in four days or bust. Early the next morning we were on top of Franconia Ridge. At forty-four hundred feet, I had never been so high up. The world was all gray up there: underfoot, a monotone of granite porphyry; overhead and sidewise, a purling scrim of wet clouds; and visibility—a hundred feet.

Common sense should have turned us back. Mount Lincoln, farther north up the ridge, topped out some six hundred feet above us. The guidebook warned: "Do not continue farther in unfavorable weather, as there are places near Mount Lincoln where the ridge is a dangerous knife-edge with sheer slopes on both sides." Ah, my flatland acrophobia. Yet the guidebook added: "The trail is in the open with magnificent views." We pressed on.

Somewhere near or on the serrated knife-edge between Little Haystack and Mount Lincoln, the clouds began to lift in shreds and tatters. To our right, beyond the edge of the abyss, a great bowl appeared, its sides and bottom warped by low ridges and pinched valleys. It was the Pemi. It was Owls Head and Thirteen Falls and Bondcliff and Stillwater and Carrigan and Galehead and Guyot, and Whitewall and Willey yonder on the shrouded shoulder of Crawford Notch. Rocks and trees. I had never seen so many trees, or such a formidable forest. What I could *not* see was the condition of the forest, the immaturity of the individual trees, the piles of rotting slash and the tumbledown stumps beneath the canopy, the hemlock cross-ties from which, hardly five years before, the loggers' rails had been ripped for scrap— melted down and forged into bomb casings, probably, to help win the war. The uppercase War. And I could not see where, for at least another year or two, the last of the loggers would be at it yet. Then our porthole on the Pemi misted over. In came the rain and the cold and down we went, busted, along the other side to the tamer precincts of Franconia Notch.

Wounds mend fast in the humid Northeast. I returned to the edge of the Pemi in 1953 and looked down into the great bowl from mounts Garfield and Guyot. Perhaps it was only the improved light, but everything looked greener. And the loggers were gone. From the summits, under sunlight, you could see the barest traces of the relict cuts below. Still, to my eye it was wilderness. I went back in 1959 and camped at the confluence of the East Branch Pemigewasset and Franconia Brook, and in twenty-four hours saw only two other people. To me, that was wilderness. Ten years later, I was back again, wading the East Branch with a fly rod. That I caught no trout is not important. That I saw no people, is. What did I see in there? I saw wilderness.

By the 1970s, people were beginning to look at the Pemi's potential as statutory wilderness. The Pemi had missed out in the first round of picks—the Great Gulf area north of Mount Washington being, at that time, the White Mountain National Forest's only entry in the National Wilderness Preservation System—and then missed out again in 1975 when the Eastern Wilderness Act added one more New Hampshire unit to the system, the Presidential Range-Dry River area. Then came RARE II (the Forest Service's second Roadless Area Review and Evaluation), and a baker's dozen White Mountain roadless areas suddenly turned up on the Forest Service's lists of recommended wilderness areas, including some seventy-five thousand acres of the Pemi.

The Pemi had a lot going for it then. RARE II appraisers applauded its diversity (elevations ranging from twelve hundred feet to more than five thousand), its accessibility (120 miles of foot trails, including about 20 of the Appalachian Trail), and its obvious popularity among back-country hikers and ski-tourers (seventy-seven thousand visitor-days, more than in any other proposed New England unit). Even more appealing, only thirteen thousand acres were classified as commercial forestland (proportionately fewer than in any other unit). And, finally, the Wilderness Attribute Rating for the Pemi, with exceptionally high scores for such values as "solitude" and "primitive recreation," was, by the Forest Service's own reckoning, "the highest" in the entire White Mountain National Forest.

For the Pemi, the Forest Service recommended wilderness designation and comments were invited. In 1979, no doubt influenced by unfavorable comments from the New Hampshire congressional delegation, the Carter Administration withheld the big *W* from the Pemi and placed it on hold for further planning. And there it has been ever since, growing greener and wilder—and more popular—with each passing year. A final recommendation from the Forest Service is imminent. Or so it is said.

Once upon a time, in 1839, to be exact, the muse of Walden Pond, Henry David Thoreau, wandered up this way seeking the source of the Merrimack River, of which the Pemigewasset River is a major tributary. He followed the main branch into Franconia Notch, noting how *"at first it comes murmuring to itself by the base of stately and retired mountains, through moist primitive woods whose juices it receives . . . enjoying in solitude its cascades still unknown to fame."*

Thoreau was a casual tourist. He took no note of the great stone face presiding over Profile Lake, the Main Branch Pemi's fountainhead, though many years later he would scale the stately mountains of Franconia Ridge to render blessings on the higher, wilder watershed of the Pemi's East Branch—wherein, by generous hindsight proxy, the loveliest cascade in all the mountains now bears his name.

Possibly the first published notice of the wilder Pemi appeared in 1876, in Sweetser's guide to the White Mountains. Calling it "the great wilderness which surrounds the East Branch and its tributaries," the writer warned that "this inner solitude should be entered only under the guidance of experienced foresters. . . . The scenery is simply that of a primeval forest." Yet within a decade, Sweetser was woefully out-of-date. Now the man in charge of describing the scenery was one James Everell Henry, who liked to boast that he had never seen "the tree yit that didn't mean a damned sight more to me goin' under the saw than it did standin' on a mountain."

They called him the King Contractor of the Mountains, and later the Grand Duke of Lincoln; and long before he would be through with it, folks would refer to the Pemi as Henry's Woods. The Duke started from the north, from the Boston & Maine Railroad in the Ammonoosuc Valley, and carved his own rail-bed up the Zealand River into the tall trees. This was in 1884. Down went the rails and up went the logging camps. And down came the spruce and the fir, down the skids to the dugways, down the track through Zealand Notch to the smoking mills. By 1890 or so, sawyers could stand at Thoreau Falls, their backs to a wasteland, and look down the North Fork of the East Branch to an untouched forest beyond. So the Duke took all he could and pulled out and swung around to the other side, and punched in that way, up the East Branch from Lincoln. Before he was finished, there were fifty miles of track through the Pemi, reaching out to Mad River Notch and up past Owls Head to the Thirteen Falls of Franconia Brook. Down it all came, a billion board feet of virgin softwood timber.

There might have been more for the Duke to tally were it not for his profligate practices and the sparks in the sawdust, embers glowing in the throwdown slash. The fires were spectacular, starting with the great Zealand burn that seared twelve thousand acres in 1886, then flashed again in 1903, turning the soil to ash in places; and then the rains, pelting the naked ledges, and rock slides carving whitewall scars down the mountainsides. "Death Valley," one observer called the notch at Zealand. "An abomination of desolation," said another, "as lugubrious as that spoken of by Daniel the prophet."

Not that one should take all this as cause to squash a black fedora over the memory of J. E. Henry, for history may judge the Duke's hat more appropriate in a softer hue, such as gray. Perhaps, as the historian Roderick Nash once noted, a culture must lose its wilderness before wilderness preservation can truly begin. Perhaps we needed the Duke, if only to open our eyes. In his foreword to C. Francis Belcher's excellent book, *Logging Railroads of the White Mountains,* former New Hampshire Governor Sherman Adams wrote that J. E. Henry and sons "contributed more to the cause of forest conservation and wise use of resources than all their competitors put together." Smoke from the Duke's fires often hung over the nearby summer hotels, Adams wrote, and "stirred up the people in their rocking chairs on the broad porches."

So it was thanks probably to the Duke, more than to anyone else, that out of the rocking chairs in 1901 came the organizers of one of New England's premiere conservation groups, the Society for the Protection of New Hampshire Forests—for short, the Forest Society. And it was thanks in large measure to the Forest Society that, after a ten-year campaign, the Weeks Act of 1911 established a National Forest System in the East, with the White Mountain National Forest as its cornerstone. But nowadays in New Hampshire, and no doubt within the Forest Society as well, opinion is divided as to whether or not the cornerstone needs any more designated wilderness than it already has. Some people point to the scars left behind by the Duke and say, "How can you call *that* wilderness? It's already been touched by the hand of man." Which reminds me of a story that David Brower used to tell of a lecture by a forester who believed that landscapes once exploited should thereafter be up for grabs. The audience, said Brower, liked a question from the floor: "Because the lady has slipped once, must she go professional?"

Paul Bofinger, president of the Forest Society, is a different sort of forester than the straw man in Brower's yarn. Bofinger believes in timber utilization *and* uppercase wilderness—not in the same place, of course, and more wilderness, in fact, than is presently designated in the White Mountain National Forest. He speaks in favor of new wilderness for the Sandwich Range and of extending the boundary of the Presidential Range-Dry River unit. But he does not favor wilderness for the Pemi. Wilderness for the Pemi, says Bofinger, could wipe out the White Mountain National Forest's proudest tradition—broad public support for what he calls a balance of uses.

No doubt it is difficult for certain lovers of wilderness to understand how a conservationist might speak as Bofinger does.

The less enlightened might even challenge his credentials, not knowing that over the years Bofinger and his society have played a critical role in blocking construction of an interstate highway through the fragile intrastate notch at Franconia and blocking, too, a clutter of condos at Sandwich Notch; in preserving for public use such landmarks as Kinsman Notch and Gap Mountain (the Society itself owns natural areas totaling ten thousand acres); and in working—sometimes against the will of the U.S. Forest Service—to improve harvest practices throughout the Granite State's woodlands.

To understand Bofinger's position on the Pemi, I suspect one must first understand a thing or two about the White Mountain National Forest. To a greater extent than any national forest in America, the White Mountain is a recreational forest for certain; it has been managed with recreation as the primary use almost since the time of its authorization. More than a fifth of the United States' population, and a fair chunk of Canada's, too, reside within one day's striking distance. Among noncoastal vacationlands, the Whites rank number one in the Northeast, providing a rare blend of opportunities for windshield tourists as well as wilderness trekkers, for snowmobilers as well as cross-country skiers. It is not only the most heavily-used forest but also the most complete, the most thoroughly acquired, within authorized boundaries, of all the national forestlands in the East. Which may say something about New Hampshire, and about a rare blend of people who get things done by playing by the rules of common consent.

I suppose the secret is that, for all their tight-lipped Yankee ways, New Hampshire folk somehow manage to talk to one another—the skiers and the skidooers, the daisy-sniffers and the chain-saw charlies, the native and the new. Not that people in one part of the country are greatly different from those in another, though I daresay the poles of perception, at least on the issue of resources, are closer together in Franconia, New Hampshire, than in Arcata, California, or Moab, Utah. Perhaps the gap is smaller because New Hampshire has had a head start in ironing out its cultural kinks. There is this town-meeting tradition of local participation. One learns that accommodation does not always entail the selling of one's soul. After all, it was accommodation that put together this national forest in the first place, and filled its boundaries 90 percent, and got it some designated wilderness when the getting was good. And this is probably what Paul Bofinger is thinking of when he speaks of a balance of uses, including more White Mountain wilderness. But not for the Pemi.

Over the years, Bofinger's has been the voice of moderation in this matter of White Mountain wilderness. When the first round of RARE II picks was issued, recommending wilderness designation for 168,000 acres, he declared: "Withdrawal of nearly 25 percent of the White Mountain National Forest from timber harvesting and the variety of recreation uses presently available would be a political disaster. The coalition of interests who have fought for and won congressional approval for land purchases [in the forest] will be split apart." Wilderness designation, he said, was not the only, nor always the best, means of preventing such abuses as clearcutting and mining. Instead, he said, the future of the Pemi area, in particular, "may best be served by special management, with a considerable extension of the Lincoln Woods Scenic Area."

Designated by the chief of the U.S. Forest Service in 1969, Lincoln Woods occupies some eighteen thousand acres in the northeast corner of the proposed Pemigewasset Wilderness. Under the Code of Federal regulations, management of a scenic area is more flexible than it is for wilderness. Though logging, mining, and construction of permanent roads are prohibited in scenic areas, other nonwilderness uses *are* sanctioned: developed tenting sites, off-road vehicles on certain trails, erosion and flood-control measures, if necessary. There is a more fundamental difference, however. Theoretically, statutory wilderness is forever. An administrative scenic area can go down the tube at the flick of a pen.

For the most part, Bofinger's perspective on the forest in general, and the Pemi in particular, was unchanged when I called on him one day at the Forest Society's solar emporium in the hills north of Concord. We spoke first of the forest.

"Look," he said, "the Society has been fighting the Forest Service for years over even-aged management, and it has not been a cozy relationship. Clearcutting is a bureaucratic solution to a complex problem. When people see a clearcut on the hillside, they're naturally going to be upset. You add to this a public suspicion of government nowadays, and what's the reaction? 'Put it in wilderness.' That's what's been happening. Well, there ought to be more public concern for the future of good timber, too. Big trees, if you will. And if those big trees happen to be growing in the middle of a heavily used recreation area, who's to say you can't go in and take those trees selectively without making the place look like hell? If you put too much of the forest into wilderness [designation], it's just going to concentrate the demand for timber elsewhere."

And he spoke of the Pemi: "You go in there today on what is called the Wilderness Trail, and there it is—a green testament to the recuperative power of the New England climate. There's the story that should be told—that, given protection, thoughtful management, and a spirit of cooperation, you can do something with a place that looked like hell just eighty years ago."

So, I wanted to know, why not wilderness?

"Go on in there," said Bofinger, "and have a look for yourself."

The Pemi is gray, cloudy, and humid, and a mizzle of rain comes later on in the day. We go up the Duke's path, up the East Branch, following the old rail-bed—the Wilderness Trail—with its enduring cross-ties and here and there an iron bolt still impaled in the rotting wood. Straight-out, and flat-out, a beneficent grade for the golden-age gadabout, a grinding bore for his robust companions. "Some *trail*," says Susan Garvan, the photographer. "Some *wilderness*," says Jane Difley, the forester and interlocutor from the solar emporium at Concord. We lunch out of the rain at Black Brook, under the remnants of the Duke's last remaining bridge, and thank him for it, and then trudge on to an East Branch crossing where we can see the helical tracery of overgrown haul roads on the slopes of the Crystal Brook ridge.

Wilderness? Well, no; not if you measure it by the standards of Alaska, or Montana, or even Colorado. But for New England, for the wetter side of the hundredth meridian, for a place only three hours from Boston and six from New York—why not? Hadn't it all been picked over, more or less, this side of the Mississippi? Hadn't the Great Swamp Wildlife Refuge in New Jersey, one of the first additions to the wilderness system, once been used as a dump? Wasn't the Pemi like Seney Wilderness, in Michigan, nothing but burned-over country after the loggers passed through? And hadn't the Dolly Sods and Otter Creek wilderness units in West Virginia been pretty well blitzed, once upon a time? Then, why not the Pemi?

"Maybe," says Difley, "because saturation recreation isn't what wilderness is meant to be about."

She has a point there. I mean, the place *is* heavily used. There's that huge parking lot back on the Kancamagus Highway, and fairly full, too, considering the inglorious weather and this off-time in the middle of the week. Already I've seen more people on the Wilderness Trail than in all my previous visits combined. Solitude? Maybe, if we go in far enough, though too far and we'll hit the rush-hour traffic on the Appalachian Trail. And apropos of Difley's comment, I remember the U.S. Forest Service's social scientist John C. Hendee saying, "Every use has a saturation point, beyond which it becomes another kind of use." So where would they draw the line, if *this* were called wilderness? With a permit quota system, probably, and maybe new trails to disperse the multitudes allowed through the gates.

"You know," says Difley, "there's this popular notion that the primary function of wilderness is to provide backpackers with a nice place to go. Well, maybe there should be wilderness areas where *no one* goes, because the primary function would be the preservation of biological diversity."

"A good idea," I say, "but you'll never sell it to New Hampshire."

"You'll never sell it to America," says Garvan.

Canadian air arrives overnight, and in the morning the Pemi sparkles under the full range of the visible spectrum. Onward to

Thoreau Falls (a pity he missed them), to the Ethan Brook Trail, and through the notch to the hut beside Zealand Falls. The hut is maintained by the Appalachian Mountain Club and is one of three that fall within the RARE II boundaries for the proposed Pemigewasset Wilderness. To keep the wilderness designation honest, if it should come to that, the Forest Service would have to draw circles around these huts, excluding them from the designated unit. Still, for a variety of reasons, Appalachian Mountain Club leaders prefer that the Pemi be left pretty much as it is, and they throw their support toward wilderness elsewhere in the White Mountain National Forest.

From the porch of the Zealand Falls hut there is a splendid view south through the notch, past the Duke's rock-slide graffito on Whitewall Mountain, across the North Fork Pemi and Shoal Pond country to that other notch called Carrigain. It is the kind of view that puts a hard knot on the esophagus.

"So there it is," says Difley. "How do you call it?"

I know how others call it. I know that the Wilderness Society wants it all, and then some. I know that Peter Kirby, the Society's coordinator for forest-management programs, gives it top priority over all other New Hampshire wilderness proposals now under study. "The Pemi," he says, "captures the best of the White Mountain wildness, thanks to its size, its ruggedness, and its accessibility. And the price is right. Little would be given up if we preserved its stellar values forever. The area contains only a minuscule 0.33-1/3 percent of the state's commercial timberland and is simply not needed for timber production."

And I know, too, that Paul Bofinger has valid reasons to believe that wilderness for the Pemi will only tear apart a useful coalition that has been building since the Duke stirred up the gentry in their summer rocking chairs.

"So?" asks Difley.

"I'm mulling it," I say. And I'm mulling it still.

[*Author's note*: In 1984, two years after this piece was written, Congress placed forty-five thousand acres of the Pemi into the National Wilderness Preservation System.]

THE MAN WHO MARRIED

THE MOUNTAINS

Mount Colvin is a scruffy crewcut peak 4,057 feet high, and is said to be thirty-ninth in order of height in the Adirondacks. Many years ago its summit was known to local woodsmen as Sabele, after an iron-questing Indian. But that was before Verplanck Colvin of Albany came here to measure the mountains and set things straight. Higher mountains, such as Marcy and Seward, had already been named after august governors of the Empire State, even though the ancestors of Sabele had known the peaks by better names, such as Tahawus (Cleaver of the Clouds) and Oukorlah (The Great Eye). It seemed more appropriate to Colvin, however, to have among the mountains majestic monuments to those who had so often received the public trust, thus giving, as he explained it, "a peculiar and historical character" to geography. So he promptly bestowed on a triad of great summits the names of three more New York governors, and did not object when someone named a lesser peak for him. True, he was only the superintendent of the survey. But he was also the conceptual father of the Adirondack Forest Preserve. No one has yet explained what—beyond the barest scientific facts—he was seeking at these elevations. Probably, no one ever will. That is why I have come here to praise Verplanck Colvin and his peculiarities. He deserved higher loft.

Not that there is anything wrong with his *mountain*. It is a fine and venerable pile of rock beneath the evergreen scrub, with many visual surprises along the ascent from the Lower Ausable Lake. In my own Adirondack seasons, going back some twenty years, I had eschewed this mountain as being somehow beneath my—how do you call it?—dignity. Marcy, yes. Haystack and Skylight, Gothics and Giant, Nipple Top and Dix, yes indeed. First time up Dix I spied upon the center of the summit a bolt of copper in the rock. Etched faintly on the face of the bolt were the number 10, the words "Adirondack Survey," the year 1873, and the initials VC. Colvin had hoped that his copper bolts might last forever, if left undisturbed. The bolt on Dix is a rare survivor. Here, upon the granitic peak that bears the surveyor's name, the hardware is of a different design and vintage—three steel eye-bolts implanted in 1896 (one of his last seasons afield) to embrace the feet of a stan-helio reflector. A Colvin invention, the stan-helio was a thing of nickel-plated copper sheets. When hung (he explained) upon an axis so that its vibrations would be in the plane of the meridian, the stan-helio would supply "the great desideratum" in geodetical surveying—a cheap, reliable signal for long distances. I stand here now on the scant summit rock and try to picture the device vibrating in the plane of the meridian. It is not an easy image. I am distracted by the view.

So was Colvin, his first time up here in 1873. He would report that he had found "a throne that seemed the central seat of the mountain amphitheatre." Deep in the chasm at his feet was the Lower Ausable Lake, "each indentation of its shore sharply marked as on a map; beyond it the Gothic Mountains rose, carved with wild and fantastic forms on the white rock, swept clear by avalanches and decked with scanty patches of stunted evergreens. Everywhere below were lakes and mountains so different from all maps yet so immovably true." Yes, I see it. Exactly. The Adirondacks. The largest "park" outside Alaska, more than nine-thousand square miles of public and private lands, enough square miles to swallow Vermont, enough to hide twice over our girthiest non-Alaskan *national* park, Yellowstone, with room to spare for Yosemite, too. One-fifth the land area of New York State, sprawling from Lake Champlain to the Black River, from the suburbs of Glens Falls to the outliers of Potsdam and Malone. And more than 40 percent of it, some 2.6 million acres, constitutionally protected as the "forever wild" Adirondack Forest Preserve. Not that I can see it all from here—too many gubernatorial mountains get in the way. But it is enough. Enough to celebrate the Adirondack Park, the Forest Preserve, and the memory of Verplanck Colvin, hoisted here above the ancient rock, dead center among the pitted eyebolts, vibrating in the plane of its own meridian.

Points of reference: In 1837 Ebenezer Emmons, a professor of chemistry from Williams College, climbed to the top of a conical peak near the Tahawus Iron Works and named it in honor of William Learned Marcy. Emmons declared the summit to be 5,467 feet above the level of the sea, and for many years thereafter it was thought that Mount Marcy was the second-highest mountain in America, after Pikes Peak. Parochial boosters were as careless of facts then as now. Among the first to boost the Adirondack region and promulgate the fiction of Marcy's penultimate height was Joel Tyler Headley, a one-time minister who had gone to the mountains to cure what he called an attack on the brain. His book, *The Adirondack: or, Life in the Woods,* came out in 1849. Verplanck Colvin could not yet read. He was only two.

Father: Andrew James Colvin, descendent of Mayflower stock, the district attorney of Albany County. Mother: Margaret Crane Alling, sister of Andrew Colvin's first wife (deceased). Verplanck: a grand-maternal family name, Dutch Knickerbockerish, rooted in the Hudson Valley.

The boy fancied maps and the out-of-doors. Andrew and Margaret figured this, too, would pass. He would practice the law.

At the time, a frequent visitor to the North Country was Samuel H. Hammond, the editor of the *Albany State Register.* Confessing that he went to the mountains to feel like a boy again, Hammond evinced a manly vision. "Had I my way," he wrote in *Wild Northern Scenes: or, Sporting Adventures with the Rifle and the Rod*, "I would mark out a circle of a hundred miles in diameter and throw around it the protecting aegis of the constitution. I would make if a forest forever." This was in 1857. Verplanck Colvin was reading.

It was a place of magic, the Adirondacks, and the romance of it all was much in the air and upon the printed page. In 1858 the artist William James Stillman arranged a convocation of ten philosophers at Follansbee Pond, in the Adirondack lake district. The party included Louis Agassiz and James Russell Lowell and Ralph Waldo Emerson, who later wrote in his poem "The Adirondacs":

> Ten Scholars, wanted to lie warm and soft
> In well-hung chambers daintly bestowed,
> Lie here on hemlock-boughs, like Sacs and Sioux,
> And greet unanimous the joyful change. . .

It was illustrative of Emerson's great rapport with nature that the hemlock boughs were in fact spruce and balsam, with nosegays of cedar to accent the bouquet. No matter. Stillman observed that the wilderness seemed to bring out in Emerson a certain crystalline limpidity of character. News arrived, while in camp, that the Atlantic cable had finally been laid and a message sent across the bottom of the sea from America to Europe. The philosophers applauded, then tried their rifles at a mark. Thoreau of Concord had not been invited. He was in Massachusetts that summer, dreaming of the White Mountains; but would not have been invited in any event because Lowell despised him. Henry Wadsworth Longfellow, with "The Courtship of Miles Standish" in press, *was* invited. When he heard that his eminent colleague Emerson was bringing a rifle, Longfellow remembered that he had a previous engagement, adding to his regrets the warning: "Somebody will be shot!"

Then came the great war among brothers. Colvin's half-brother, James, went off with the New York Militia to fight the Grays in the Piedmont South. At his desk in Albany, young Ver-

accompanied his father on litigious trips to the Helderberg Hills downstate, where rent wars and boundary disputes were distracting public attention from the national fratricide. Young Colvin, afoot in the Helderbergs, found boundary-pacing the better part of the law.

He was eighteen now. He had an insatiable curiosity about lines. And cartographic voids. On the maps of the North were many voids. He longed to fill them. It was springtime. The big war was over. Abe Lincoln's body lay smoldering in the grave. Colvin turned north, walked north, up the Sacandaga Valley toward Speculator. The edge of the Adirondacks. The tamest fringe of the wilderness. He looked at the old patents, the lines drawn by whiskeyjack surveyors long dead. The lines overlapped. The summer passed. He returned to his studies in Albany. The law did not suit him.

On or about April Fools' Day 1869, there appeared in the bookstalls of Albany, Boston, and New York a slim volume entitled *Adventures in the Wilderness: or, Camp-Life in the Adirondacks*. The author was the popular Boston preacher William Henry Harrison Murray, who had an abiding faith in the recuperative power of balsam-scented air and a flair for fiction disguised as fact. Murray promised his readers that all manner of sporting would be "easy and romantic" in the Adirondacks. His landscapes, of course, were those of the lake district rather than the high peaks; and besides, Murray loathed hiking. In *his* Adirondacks, one did his sporting from a boat. If you wished to go out for a fish, he noted, your guide paddled you to the spot and served you while you handled the rod. "This," wrote Murray, "takes from recreation every trace of toil." The book was a sensation. It started a stampede into the wilderness.

Colvin was already there, his fifth time out. He was twenty-two now, and unlike Murray's laconic Romantics, he was staying on through December. On New Year's Eve, hunting on snowshoes near Indian River, and (as he put it) willing to "forgo the fatigue," Colvin struck the track of a large bear and pursued it for two days before slaying it. His guide and companion, one

Sturgis, declared it to be the largest bruin ever taken in Hamilton County.

September–October 1870. Once more to the mountains, and to Mount Seward in particular. In Colvin's opinion, the view was magnificent: "Wilderness everywhere, lake on lake, river on river, mountain on mountain, numberless." His report was submitted to the Board of Regents of the State of New York, published in the annual report of the state's Museum of Natural History, and widely distributed throughout the legislature. It closed with a strange and somewhat derivative plea: that the forests should be preserved for posterity, and the region set aside as a park for New York, "as is the Yosemite for California and the Pacific states."

May 15, 1872. Approved by the legislature, Chapter 733: for Verplanck Colvin of Albany, New York, ten hundred dollars to aid in completing a survey of the Adirondack wilderness and a map thereof. The appropriation was meager, and funds would be a long time coming. Nonetheless, Colvin turned north.

The fieldwork began in July 1872 near Lake Pleasant, Hamilton County. Colvin's plan was to advance the triangulation in a northeasterly direction toward Lake Champlain. The survey party ascended and measured Speculator Mountain and Rift Hill, then plunged on through the forest to Snowy Mountain, Cedar River, and Moose Lake. September found them at Indian Pass. Colvin opened his field-book to note their progress. It was absolutely splendid. They were moving with celerity among the dizzy crags. Bread without water, their lunch. Treacherous descents overtaken by darkness. Tree roots chosen as pillows to pass the night. The weather went sour. Benumbed with cold, Colvin stood shivering in a gray icy mist swirling over the top of Mount Marcy. Reluctantly he ordered a retreat. Down. Down to a place with dry spruce. Colvin, wrapped in any army blanket, shouted for his guides to renew the fire. And slept.

There was a little lake lying in a chasm between the mountains. Colvin discovered it one afternoon about four o'clock. He stood on its shore, his boots full of water, his pants torn and dripping. There had been some mistake. An inaccuracy of the maps, Colvin called it. The waters of this lake did not flow north to the Ausable, as had been represented, but south to the Hudson. It is, wrote Colvin, the *summit water* of the state, a "minute, unpretending tear-of-the-clouds—as it were—a lonely pool shivering in the breezes of the mountains."

They pressed on. The guides knew little of this part of the wilderness. Now Colvin was guiding *them*. Up Ragged Mountain. Through the Place of Shadows—the Ouluska Pass. Down Mount Seward. Then westward to Beaver River waters and Little Tupper Lake. October passed in the forest, and much of November, too. At last Colvin sat at his desk in Albany, summing up the first season afield:

"The vastness and wildness of the region is the better appreciated when, at this late day, we are able to find within it mountains from 3,000 to 4,000 feet in height, nameless, unascended and unmeasured. . . . It is now a question of political importance whether the section covered by this survey should not be preserved, in its present primitive condition, as a forest-farm and source of timber supply for our buildings and our ships." *Easy now, Colvin. Keep it practical, man. Look to the utility of it.* "The deprivation of a state of its timber," he went on "is a grave error in political economy, and at this time when the western states of the Union, feeling their deficiency, are laboriously planting forests, it behooves us to see to the preservation of those with which we are spontaneously blessed."

Summer and fall 1873. The second season in the wilderness. Between July 12 and December 2, Colvin would employ five survey assistants, fifty-one guides and packmen, and such assorted teamsters and boatmen as would boost the survey's total roster to ninety-seven men. Extracts from his journals:

August 13. "Leaving to others the gathering of supplies for the commissariat; the day opening clear, I drew together the survey party to the foot of Hopkins' Peak, which, together with the famous mountain, Giant-of-the-Valley, I proposed that day to climb and measure. [Giant] took more time then we had anticipated; windfalls of timber, dense thickets, descents and ascents along a broken ridge rendered progress slow. . . . It was a quarter to 7 P.M. when we reached the summit. Before us was spread a vast and grand but gloomy depth of scenery. At our feet, cliffs a thousand feet in height fell away. No chirp of insect, no cry of bird or beast broke in upon the awful silence of the scene, and as we beheld mountain on mountain stretching into infinitude, the knowledge that through and over them, beyond the reach of sight, our labors led, and would lead us, chilled all hearts and made us silent also. By the time we had completed the barometrical observations, the sun had set. Off the trail—in darkness—descending cliffs—across holes and chasms—on dead fallen timber—feeling, not seeing, we made our way down. It was one o'clock in the morning when the moon came to our aid and we emerged from the forest."

Daylight on the fourteenth threatened storm. One of the guides quit; another contrived to be absent for Colvin's roll call.

August 19. "Raining slightly and very threatening. Determined, nevertheless, to set out upon the ascent of Nipple Top Mountain, on the eastern slopes of which we were encamped. Climbed steadily. Dense white cloud enveloped us. Suddenly it was swept away at the east and Mount Dix, scarred and savage rock, rose before us. The gorgeous sunshine streaming on the distant cirrocumulus clouds below produced a rare effect. On the breast of the cloud, each saw his own form, the head surrounded by a rich anthelia, a circular glory of prismatic colors, the renowned 'Ulloa's rings,' which that philosopher beheld from the summit of Pambamarca. Not one of the mountain guides had ever seen or heard of such a sight before. It was gone all too quickly, yet it seemed as though nature today were reveling in splendors, for the clouds vanishing in the west, a sierra of mountain crags was uncurtained, torn, rugged, and wild, above all of which rose Tahawus, 'Cleaver of the Clouds.' "

August 20. "The last ration of flour baked, and breakfast over, we commenced our climb to the summit of the next mountain eastward, which the guides had named Mount Colvin. The knowledge that it was a mountain heretofore unascended, unmeasured, and—prominent as it was—unknown to any map made the ascent the more interesting. Reaching at length the height, its last approach a cliff almost impregnable, we drew ourselves up over the verge to find a seat upon a throne that seemed the central seat of the mountain amphitheatre. . . . It was after 4 P.M. when we left the summit. Twilight, and still marching despite the wish of wearied men to camp. Dark, and still marching. Night, marching, and our goal gained."

October found Colvin's party west of the High Peaks in the precincts of Saranac and Raquette lakes. November brought freezing weather. On the eighth, ice at Oven Lake stove in the bow of a guide boat. On the sixteenth, Colvin spotted panther tracks in the snow and resolved to chase and destroy the monster. The monster escaped.

Of his inner person, his private self, so little was known. Even his surfaces were deceptive. William Chapman White described him as "broad and strong, like an Adirondack spruce." A ragtime photograph or two reveal, above the starched wing collar, a stout neck and a stubborn chin, walrus mustache, high brow, lonely eyes. There is a kind of measured symmetry about the face, as though his living flesh had been triangulated.

His was a life of lists and entries. Contracts and permissions. Progress reports, payrolls, vouchers, and accounts. Requisitions and returns. Tables and appendices. Special instruments (Form 14, Manual of the Survey), including, but not limited to, theodolites, transits, gradienters, sextants, sidereal chronometers, rods and levels, heliotropes, scales and rulers, T-squares and protractors, tripods, compasses, aneroid barometers, differential thermometers, rain gauges, wind vanes, evaporation measures, pyrheliometers, signal cards, copper bolts, magnesium ribbon, plumb-bobs, and paint pots. Provisions and supplies (Form 20) of flour, potatoes, beans, crackers, salt, tea, coffee, pork, cheese, candles, and matches (trout and venison, on the cuff). Computations of traverse (Form 21). Transit lines of location (Form 22). Hypsometric observations (Form 27). Etcetera.

For all the bureaucratic jots and mathematic tittles, there was this other part of him, the poet who could gaze into the dark waters of a tarn and see a tear-of-the-clouds shivering in the breezes

of the mountains. Colvin, listing 180 newly mapped Adirondack lakes, could take pleasure in the nomenclature of discovery:
Ampersand, Bad Luck, Cowhorn, Darnneedle, Empty, Fish-
pole, Hotwater, Irish, Johnny-Mac, Mud-hole, Speck, Twin-
Lily, and White Cedar. O, the poles of antithesis. Hypsometry
versus Hotwater Pond.

He was—in the hindsight view of Mills Blake, his top assistant through all the survey years—"the most amiable man that I
ever met, but a very firm man in his exaction of work." Other
members of Colvin's wilderness coterie probably held less chari-
table views. After all, what could a young and footloose surveyor
make of a boss who insisted that field-book entries be made
with "Siberian lead of medium hardness"—and, mind you,
none other? And what was a robust grandfatherly guide from
Keene Flats to make of a superintendent whose rule-book prescribed "retiring" at 9 P.M., and for hunting or fishing—never
on Sundays? And there was something else: No booze. Colvin, preferring the purity of God's own drink, which is water,
had no tolerance for liquor. From the start of his first year afield, he had decreed that not a tittle of alcohol would be carried by any member of the party. "It was a rule," he noted with
characteristic certitude, "against which some of the men employed murmured, but they were only able to break it surrep-
titiously. The result has been subordination, steady work,
health, and success."

The poles of antithesis. They met most felicitously in his quest
for creation of the Adirondack Park.

Hear now the poet, purpling those treeless peaks among the
frosty clouds. Wild beasts looking forth from ledges. The voy-
ager by canoe, beholding waters in which the forests are reflected like inverted reality. Haughty crests. Mountains rising in
dark and gloomy billows. Landscapes brightly gemmed with
lakes. Crystal pools. Savage chasms. Dread passes. A place of
mystery. The wonder and the glory of New York.

Hear now the pragmatist, for the wonder and the glory of
New York was—wood fiber. "These forests will show a state tax-

less and debtless," he wrote, "exchanging its wooden wealth with the vast treeless West."

Yet timber production was only a part of Colvin's vision for the great northern wilderness, and as time went on, a diminishing part at that. Far more important were the salubrious Adirondack waters, the "cold, healthful, living waters of the wilderness," which he predicted would soon be essential to the future of the cities of the Hudson Valley. He had done some figuring. He had figured that the Upper Hudson watershed could deliver an annual streamflow of sixty billion cubic feet. He had calculated that "a stone dam thrown across the Hudson above its junction with the Schroon, while securing water free from deleterious substances, would afford the head of water necessary for aqueduct purposes." And should it ever become prudent to increase even that prodigious supply—say, to enhance canal navigation downstate—why, you could simply plug Smith's Lake into Tupper, and Tupper into Long, and Long, by dam and by canal, into the Hudson. *Voilà!*

In his second report to the legislature as superintendent of the survey, Colvin advanced his most eloquent plea for a forest preserve to protect the wonder and glory of water as well as wood. "Unless the region be preserved essentially in its present wilderness condition," he wrote, "the ruthless burning and destruction of the forest will slowly, year after year, creep onward after the lumberman, and vast areas of naked rock, arid sand, and gravel will alone remain to receive the bounty of the clouds—unable to retain it. The rocks warmed by the summer sun will, like the heated pot stones that serve the savage to boil his food in a kettle of bark, throw back the rain as vapor; and the streams that now are icy cold in the shadows of the dark, damp woods will flow exposed to the sun, heated and impure.

"The coolness of the evergreen forest in summer," he went on, "condenses . . . the warm, moist southern breezes. The moist, mossy, peaty soil receives the fresh rain and readily permits it to pass down into cavities amid the rocks. The dense forest . . . prevents evaporation. In spring, moreover, it shields the accumulated snow of winter from the sun's direct rays, and prevents it from rushing suddenly off in furious floods."

Noting the vast extent of burnt-over lands in the Boreas River mountains, Colvin urged reforestation to stabilize the soil and shelter the winter snows from the sun. The life of the individual, he wrote, "is too short to permit him to contemplate the planting of such a forest. The man who plants the pine will, in all probability, be dead when it is fit to be cut." But the state, he observed, "lives forever. It is the state, therefore, which should undertake this great work. . . . Here, under the shade of the young trees, the forest moss would grow again, and soon these vast areas of arid and burnt rocks would be covered with fresh loam."

The park. Always there was—and is—a confusion regarding the park as distinct from the forest preserve. In his own writings, before either entity had found its statutory place, Colvin did not try too often to separate the two; indeed, the terms were interchangeable. In his cracker-barrel conversations, his report to the regents after the first ascent of Mount Seward, his recommendations on behalf of the first state park commission, and in conclusions appended to the early topographic surveys, Colvin, whether speaking of park or forest, focused on what he called "the heart" of the Adirondacks, the High Peaks area in particular, with a few of the central lakes, such as Saranac, thrown in for good measure. And always, too, though varying in degree according to his audience, Colvin took great pains to justify these pleas for preservation by promising practical benefits. Utility was much in vogue among Victorians.

It was probably Colvin, for example, who placed the utilitarian stamp upon the park commission report of 1873. Save the Adirondacks? Yes indeed, as a riparian recharge area, to keep the barges floating down the state's canals; *not* as another Yellowstone Park, then but a year old and already described as a pleasuring-grounds for the people. Pleasure was not to be promoted in the Empire State in those days—though almost everyone but Colvin shamelessly pursued it. The very idea of such "an unproductive and useless park" as Yellowstone, the report asserted in strong Colvinian prose, "we utterly and entirely repudiate." Well, not *exactly*. But what could one say in the awesome presence of John Adams Dix, former U.S. secretary of the treasury, major general of the Army, president of the Union-Pacific and Erie railroads, and then governor of the wonderous and glorious State of New York?

And it was indisputably Colvin a year later who, superintending the survey, reported that timber and iron were the only "commercial advantages" to be found in the heart of the Adirondacks. Yet the trees, clinging to rocks with rope-like roots, were too poor for timber, and the forest was more valuable *growing* than as charcoal for the manufacture of the ore. So what was left? In sum, a region of wonderful beauty and picturesqueness. At that point, Colvin must have remembered his audience—the clodhoppers of the New York State Legislature; and, remembering, promptly shifted his literary gears. Yes, save the heart of the Adirondacks—and for its scenery, too—because, preserved from desolation, it could become "as profitable to this state by travel and traffic as Mount Washington and the White Mountains are to New Hampshire."

By 1889—four years after the birth of the forest preserve and three years yet before the park's—Colvin could speak and write more comfortably of scenery. In a letter to the editor of the *Essex County Republican*, the great utilitarian speculated that it might now be time to turn to questions of public interest beyond mere economic ones. What the repetitious forest fires had spared, he wrote, "is now, at picturesque points, fenced in with barbed wire and made the subject of admission and tolls unauthorized by law, over routes that have been public highways since the days of the Aborigines." The Adirondacks, he went on, "should be made free for every citizen to enjoy." One imagines Colvin pausing now at his desk, the pen (or perhaps the Siberian lead of medium hardness) hesitating above that curious word *enjoy*. O, rubbish! The writing hand comes down and moves across the page with certitude. "The kind of exercise obtained among these mountains,"—*yes, yes!*—"the camp life and the marching, the fearlessness and independence,"—*O, yes!*—"the facility of resources and skill in the use of the rifle are all valuable as military training to a people who may, at any time,"—*what? what now? yes, yes!*—"be called upon to defend their country."

With a decent title, the *Seventh Annual Report* might have become a real best-seller, like Preacher Murray's *Adventures in the Wilderness*. As it was, Colvin's Albany printer, Weed, Parsons and Company, could hardly bind and ship the book fast enough to fill the orders. The work, covering the years 1874–78, ran to nearly five hundred printed pages, but Colvin's public would not be put off by either the volume's bulk or its title page:

STATE OF NEW YORK.

SEVENTH ANNUAL REPORT

ON THE PROGRESS

OF THE

𝕿opographical 𝕾urvey

OF THE

ADIRONDACK REGION OF NEW YORK,

TO THE YEAR 1879.

CONTAINING THE CONDENSED REPORTS FOR THE YEARS 1874-75-76-77 AND '78.

WITH LATE RESULTS IN

GEODETIC AND TRIGONOMETRICAL MEASUREMENTS, MAGNETIC VARIATION, HYDROGRAPHY, RIVER SURVEYS, LEVELING AND BAROMETRIC-HYPSOMETRY, METEOROLOGY, RAIN-FALL, BOTANY, ZOÖLOGY AND GEOLOGY.

𝖂ith 𝕸aps, 𝕰ngrabings and 𝕮hromo-lithographs.

BY

VERPLANCK COLVIN,

SUPERINTENDENT OF SURVEY.

TRANSMITTED TO THE LEGISLATURE MARCH 7, 1879.

ALBANY:
WEED, PARSONS AND COMPANY, PRINTERS
1880.

The brittle pages turn. It is 1874. Colvin is furious. He is absolutely livid. There has been a mistake. He has discovered that the height of the Dudley Observatory Barometer at Albany—the station of reference for much of his fieldwork over the previous two years—is erroneously listed in the annals of that institution. *Damnation!* The magnitude of the error is *thirty-six feet!* An entire season is lost, hidebound to a desk, recomputing the mountain measurements. No matter. The legislature has denied the funds necessary to get to the field in any event.

It is 1875—but October already and the survey work just getting started, no thanks to the niggardly solons of Albany. Colvin has advanced from Keene Flats into the wilderness, up the valley of John's Brook and the backside of the Gothics Range. There is snow at timberline, and ice grizzling the frosted granite cones. Ah, yes, the great peaks gathered in grand magnificence and wild sublimity and (Colvin would write later) "no sound save the shuddering hiss of the chilly blast as it swept over the fearful ridge of ice that must now be [their] pathway." Now, "with spikeless boots, and no alpenstock save the tripod of the instrument," they essay the final ascent, gaze down in awe at the Lower Ausable Lake, "black as ebony," conduct the prescribed measurements, and set out along the icy ridge to seek some means of descent. On every side yawn glazed precipices, all the more grim and dreadful for the gathering darkness. Suddenly—*yegads!*—one of the guides slips and finds himself suspended at the edge, a thousand feet above the drifting clouds. And then is saved—by the sheer strength of his muscular arms.

The pages turn. "The black cliffs of Haystack are grim with monstrous yellowish icicles."

"Our old mountain guide counsels me to desist, and asks leave to return, fearing lest we may be entrapped in the deep snows in the gorge. I resolve, however, to carry the line forward to the summit at all hazards."

"The wind swept the summit at an estimated rate of seventy miles an hour. . . . The cold was so intense that one of the men froze his ears."

November 1. "Our old mountain guide left us today."

It is early July 1876. The *Seventh Report* does not indicate that Colvin is taking note of the nation's centennial on the fourth day of this particular month and year. Apparently Colvin is too busy. He is shuttling theodolites among the mountaintops. And he is not feeling well. It is excessively hot at the Upper Ausable Lake, but he is shivering with a fever brought on by fatigue. Wrapping himself in a blanket, he sends his guides off in search of a missing signal party. And promptly recovers his health by the strength of his muscular psyche.

It is 1877. Mid-February finds Colvin near the Fulton chain-of-lakes. Triangulating? But of course. And also rhapsodizing over the deep-blue of the winter sky, the snowy mantling of an earth "arabesqued with trees." Ahah, and what is *this?* The fresh tracks of a panther! The mutilated carcass of a deer! Pursuit! Rushing forward, Colvin comes upon the monstrous creature, coolly defiant, standing at the brow of a precipice on some dead timber, and—*Bang!*—sends a bullet through its brain.

February 28. "On the following day I returned to Albany, bringing with me the frozen body of the panther, which was placed in the rotunda of the State House for inspection by the legislature then in session." (Ever since, it has been said that Colvin's panther was the very last one ever tracked and killed in the Adirondacks. So it goes.)

And how time flies. It is 1878. October, atop Whiteface Mountain. Once more, a sighting of Uloa's rings, though it is not quite the same as before. The center is roseate. The first ring, purplish-blue. The second, yellow. The third, a narrow band of green. Then, yellowish-red, and deep-darkish-red, and blue, and green, and yellow, and red. Colvin is moved. Colvin writes:

"Cast against the surface of a dense frost-cloud this strange appearance excited awe and admiration; while the dim figure of the observer, with arms extended, appeared reproduced at the center of the anthelia, like a shadowy cross standing upon the faint, ghostlike figure of the mountain."

It was coming. One could feel it coming any day or year now. People almost everywhere were placing much stock in their public parks. There was Yosemite, in California. There was Yellowstone, in the Rocky Mountains. There was the Central Park of Manhattan, "the lungs of the city," they called it; and Frederick Law Olmsted, the traveling man, had other fine greenswards still up his sleeve. Soon, even the falls at Niagara would become a park. And the Adirondacks?

The Adirondacks decidedly had some mighty strong voices speaking in their behalf. There was young Theodore Roosevelt, in the New York Assembly. There was Morris K. Jesup of the American Museum of Natural History. There was Charles Hallock and, somewhat later, George Bird Grinnell, the influential editors of *Forest & Stream* magazine. And there was Governor Alonzo Cornell, the Western Union heir, who, in 1882, spoke highly of Verplanck Colvin's work in the Adirondacks and then sharply rebuked his own state for squandering the wildlands of the North. Some of the giveaways were scandalous. In the following year the legislature restricted the sale of state lands and appropriated fifteen thousand dollars to launch Colvin on a second round of Adirondacks surveys, this time to verify or correct the metes and bounds of some four thousand parcels of state property.

Now it was 1884. Grover Cleveland was governor. Unlike Cornell, he was not much enamored of Colvin. No matter. There was a new committee of experts appointed to investigate a system of forest preservation in the Northlands. Among the commissioners was Charles Sprague Sargent, the Harvard horticulturist, director of the Arnold Arboretum, and a bona fide tree-hugger, for certain. The report by Sargent and the commission, filed early in 1885, appeared to echo much of what Colvin had been preaching for nearly twenty years. In a nutshell, the commission recommended that all lands owned by the state or hereafter acquired in the northern counties be designated a forest preserve and therein "forever kept as wild forest land."

In February of that year the prestigious New York Board of Trade and Transportation invited Colvin to address its annual banquet. Colvin the spellbinder was to eschew the wild sublimity of Adirondack scenery. Instead, he would sing the rhapsodic praises of Adirondack water. God's own drink, it was. The mother's milk of the New York canals. Why, by Jove, there would be a day when great ships would float past the Erie Canal on mountain water, ascend a lock or two to Lake Champlain, and, by way of the St. Lawrence and the Great Lakes, sail on to the Cathays of the American West. Colvin called it the New Northwest Passage. One had to think of his audience.

In May, at the statehouse in Albany, Chapter 283 of the laws of 1885 made it official: a forest preserve of some 680,000 acres in the Adirondacks (and a smaller one in the Catskills). To be kept forever as wild forest, and never sold or leased or taken by any person or corporation. Unfortunately, the law said nothing of the taking of the timber.

Colvin was in the mountains that spring, kicking duff out of rotten trees in order to uncover the axe scars of colonial patents and survey lines. They say he was good at it. But he was getting tired. Not yet forty, and he was tired already of the skinflint bureaucracy, the do-nothing legislature, the cynics, the engineers who laughed at him behind his back, the paucity of packmen and guides who, like the superintendent, could be tolerant of frostbite and hunger and midnight descents.

Meanwhile, Colvin's idea of an Adirondack *park*—something a bit more than a forest preserve—had found a supporter in the new governor, David B. Hill. By 1891 the overseers of the preserve, the forest commissioners, were tracing a "blue line" on their maps to suggest the boundary of such a park in the mountains. And by 1892 there was a bill in the statehouse, Chapter 707. In effect, the park statute drew a blue line around that part of the forest preserve where state acquisition of private inholdings might be concentrated. But the law was a mixed blessing, for while it created this park "to be forever reserved . . . for the free use of all people," it weakened some of the earlier protections for the preserve as a whole.

At the time one did not have to be a zealot to understand that the Adirondack forest could ill afford *any* loss of protection. The forest was a mess. Those "vast areas of arid and burnt rocks" which Colvin had deplored in the 1870s could now be seen from every cloud-cleaving mountaintop. Fires raged from time to time along the railroad rights-of-way and outward from the lumberman's slash heaps. Timber thieves tiptoed past the trespass signs. Forest commissioners came under suspicion. There was talk of official skullduggery. How could a place be forever reserved for the people as wild forestland if the people allowed the forest commissioners to sell off the timber?

Colvin was troubled. Writing his annual report on the progress of the state lands survey early in 1894, he warned of a serious scandal. Bad enough that the suspect forest commission was conducting its own surveys without the precision and care to be found in *his* work; bad enough that a certain former state engineer was guilty of erroneous views in this matter. But now—worst of all—the forest commission proposed to sell timber from public lands adjacent to the properties of private owners. If, through inept surveys (Colvin argued), private timber were to be cut over and boundary lines destroyed, the state would surely incur great cost and expense and be compelled to pay damages running to the hundreds of thousands of dollars.

So it came down to the constitutional convention of 1894— nearly thirty years after Colvin's first trek into the wilderness. Fired up by the rhetoric—and the logic—of Colvin and his peers, fed up with vacillating legislators and inept forest commissioners, the people of New York State finally demanded forest protection through amendment of the state constitution. The vote in favor was overwhelming. Henceforth the trees of the Adirondack preserve would be held as "forever wild" as the lands and the waters.

There are so *many* trees. It is awesome to stand here at barely four thousand feet of elevation, here on the tamer side of the forty-fifth parallel, in the picked-over precincts of an original colony, and look out upon such a sweeping, undulate expanse of forest. And practically all of it, as viewed from here, forever wild, and no exceptions to the hands-off rule but for the mandate of two successive legislatures and the vote of the people.

Over the more than ninety years since "forever wild" entered the constitutional language, countless measures of one kind or another have been introduced in Albany to tame the Adirondack preserve for some popular or venal purpose. Only a handful were ever submitted to the people's vote. In 1911 the question was: Shall it be proper to use three percent of the forest preserve for water-supply reservoirs? The people said, Yes. In 1922: Shall it be proper to use three percent of the preserve for hydroelectric power? The people said, No. In 1930: How about some recreational facilities in the preserve with "the necessary clearings of timber therefor?" No, said the people. In 1940: Shall we construct ski trails on Whiteface Mountain that will be eighty feet wide? Yes, said the people. In 1958: Surrender three hundred acres for construction of I-87, the Northway? Yes, said the people, though barely. In 1967, at another constitutional convention: Should we not relax to some degree the forever wild provision, so that some of the land might be put to better use? And the people said, No, we should not.

There were other proposals, and some, such as construction of a motor road up Whiteface Mountain, passed; but for the most part, the people of New York State since Colvin's day have been reasonably protective of their forest preserve. They have held the line. But with the opening of the Northway in the mid-1960s, that other part of the Adirondack Park—the private lands—came under attack, for here was all this prime acreage up for grabs, and nary a land-use control on the books in all of the North Country.

And so it was said in the summer of 1967 by Laurance Rockefeller, brother of the governor and chairman of the State Council of Parks, that the only way to save the blue-lined North Country was to make of it a 1.7-million-acre Adirondack Mountains National park. At this point, there was to have been a pause in the announcement to allow for the hearty cheers of tree-huggers and other dilettantes of the preservations persuasion. Instead, there was a chorus of boos—not just from developers lusting for loot and rapine, but from the tree-huggers, too, the Forever Wilders who had the audacity to believe that somehow the wonder and the glory of New York would be better served under state management than federal. "The proposal had its curious aspects," wrote my colleague Frank Graham, Jr., in his splendid 1978 political history. *The Adirondack Park*. Among the more curious was the reaction of a staunch opponent of the for-ever-wild philosophy who noted that since two dedicated *proponents* of that precept—namely the *New York Times* and the Asso-ciation for the Protection of the Adirondacks—were naysaying the Rockefeller plan, well, then, there must be "something good" about the prospect of a national park in the Adirondacks.

The prospect originated with Laurance Rockefeller. Accord-ing to Graham, "Laurance himself was never quite comfortable with the dedication of a vast area to the principle of forever wild." Laurance was comfortable with mass recreation. Lau-rance leaned strongly toward parks-for-the-people. Sure, and he had his own mind on such matters. But wasn't his predecessor at State Parks the one and only Robert Moses who (according to Graham) had "chafed under the constitutional provision" that had prevented park-builders from turning the Adirondacks into a "gigantic playground"? And did not Laurance's co-prospec-tors include none other than Conrad Wirth, who had served as director of Dwight Eisenhower's road-building national-play-grounds-service in the 1950s? Well, no matter. As Graham re-calls it, the proposal "never got off the ground, but it exerted a lasting influence on the entire region of upstate New York. It forced all sides to examine the reality of . . . the pressures of de-velopment, the lack of effective restrictions on potential run-away development on the private land within the park, even the subtle threats to the supposedly invincible status of . . . forever wild." And the end result, that lasting influence, if I may tele-scope the succession of events a bit, was and is the Adirondack Park Agency.

Brainchild of a study commission appointed by Governor Rockefeller, the Agency was established in 1971 to classify the public parts of the park—the forest preserve lands—according to their capacities to "withstand use," and to promulgate for the private parts a comprehensive land-use and development plan. For the public sector, the Agency designated about one million acres, or 45 percent of the preserve, as wilderness, with management guidelines closely resembling those of the National Wilderness Preservation System. Here on the summit of Colvin, I stand at the threshold of *two* state wilderness areas—Dix Mountain Wilderness, underfoot, and High Peaks, at 226,000 acres, the largest of them all, yonder across the Lower Ausable Lake. Of primitive and canoe areas, there are some 100,000 acres so classified; a speckle of "intensive use" (for campgrounds and such) here and there; and for the rest of it, a bit more than half of the forest preserve, what is known as a "wild-forest zone," where the resource is said to permit "a somewhat higher degree of human use than in wilderness."

And for the private sector, there is an Adirondack Park Land Use and Development Plan, first advanced by the Agency in 1973. It is a fairly restrictive plan, as it should be, though not exclusive of reasonable levels of development. It factors the 3.4 million acres of private lands within the blue-lined park into six land-use categories, each with its own guidelines for density of development and compatible uses.

The Adirondack Park Agency has had its ups and its downs over the years, but, like the voters of the state confronted with yet another challenge to the integrity of the forever-wild idea, it has hung tough at the line more often than it has played possum. Part of the Agency's own integrity flows from the non-governmental Adirondack Council, intervenor in court and administrative proceedings as watchdog of the Agency and of the Department of Environmental Conservation, which administers the forest preserve. The Adirondack Council, frequently acting on behalf of such affiliates as the National Audubon Society, The Wilderness Society, the Natural Resources Defense Council, and the Association for the Protection of the Adirondacks, is an underfunded but highly effective membership organization operating out of Elizabethtown, New York. Its executive director is Gary A. Randorf, who once was employed by the Park Agency. He knows its strengths and weaknesses. For several years, Randorf spent a good part of his time convincing the Agency and the Department of Environmental Conservation of the weaknesses in their interpretive programs. "Most of the park's visitors," Randorf was heard to say, "don't even know what the park is." He was right, too. And he was effective. In 1989, the state opened a big, bright interpretive center near Paul Smith's. With many of the exhibits designed by Randorf himself, the center is regarded nowadays as equal to or better than some of the very best efforts of the National Park Service.

Randorf for a time shared the Council director's chair with George D. Davis, a onetime executive of the Wilderness Society and planner for both the U.S. Forest Service and the Adirondack Park Agency. Davis's efforts for the Council (and later for Governor Mario Cuomo's Commission on the Adirondacks in the Twenty-first Century) were aimed at expanding, through direct acquisition, key wilderness segments of the Forest Preserve. There has been much concern, for example, about protecting the southern flanks of the High Peaks Wilderness. Here lie the vast holdings of Finch-Pruyn, the Glens Falls timberlands owner. Here lie the Boreas Ponds area and part of the watershed of the Upper Hudson River, including the rim of a scenic gorge and the waterfall known as O.K. Slip, the tallest vertical drop in all the Adirondacks. In fact, it might be said that the most desirable private lands in the park are these Finch-Pruyn holdings under the winter shadow of the High Peaks. And it probably *would* be said, if it weren't for the "Bob" (and the Council's reluctance, along with the state's, to play one priority against another).

The Bob is short for the proposed Bob Marshall Great Wilderness, which lies west of Finch-Pruyn's Upper Hudson lands, beyond Long Lake and the Racquette River. The Bob would honor the memory of Robert Marshall, the Adirondacker widely acknowledged as the Father of Wilderness. There is a Bob Marshall Wilderness in Montana. Now the idea is to have one in New York—400,000 acres embracing more than four hundred lakes and ponds, three existing wilderness areas (Five Ponds, Pepperbox, and Pigeon Lake), three state primitive areas, a mix of other Preserve lands, and private lands scattered among some twenty different landowners. Unlike the High Peaks, the Bob isn't mountain country, but rather a rolling terrain more typical of the Adirondack lakes region. In fact, it is an integral part of that region. The largest block of private lands in the Bob, some 50,000 acres, is owned by the family of Cornelius Vanderbilt Whitney, of museum and horse-racing fame. The estate straddles a network of wilderness waterways that once formed essential links in the region's classic canoe-and-guideboat circuit.

"Some of those old routes have been closed for decades," says Richard Beamish, the Adirondack Council's communications director and himself a canoe-trip guide of considerable reputation. "If they could be opened by acquisition or easement, you could add a hundred miles of waterway to the hundreds already existing here."

Council people tend to be bullish about the Bob for another reason. Its sheer size, if all the elements could be put together in toto, might provide the depth of habitat needed to reintroduce a couple of extirpated natives. Namely, the wolf and the panther. "That's the only place you could really expect to bring them back with any success," says Gary Randorf. "It's our richest wildlife area already. It's our wild island of hope."

Colvin no doubt would have approved of Randorf, Beamish, Davis, and the Adirondack Council; would have cheered its efforts to expand the metes and bounds of the wilderness (though *not* its wild hope to reintroduce the wolf and panther); would have praised in particular its long-fought battle to roll back the acid rains that have poisoned hundreds of Adirondack ponds and corroded the purity of God's own drink, and of Colvin's. I mentioned this one day to a friend in Washington, D.C. He is about as close to the wilderness scene as one can get without actually being in it. He knows the historical mileposts, the heroes and heroines of the wilderness movement better than he knows the whiskers on his own face. So I told him I was going to the Adirondack Mountains to honor the memory of Verplanck Colvin. And you know what he said to me? He said: "Verplanck *Who?*"

Time now to go down from the mountaintop. The light is fading and there is ice on the trail. It would have mattered little to Colvin. He would have lingered over his notebooks and his instruments, descending in the dark. Dark, and still marching. Night, marching.

And the goal gained. The remembrance of a man, almost forgotten, vibrating in the plane of its own meridian.

There is little to say of his final years in the public light. The annual reports to the legislature grew briefer and drier—the last, in 1899, not published at all. After the constitutional convention he became conspicuously silent on the subject of the forest preserve. His hours seemed filled instead with nitpick and pique. There were monies appropriated yet never paid him. The office of the state engineer—under the fastidious Silas Seymour and his successor, Elnathan Sweet—jealously attacked Colvin's findings and political independence. Seymour accused Colvin of running a "parasitic" bureau, and then proceeded to belittle the conceptual linkage which Colvin had forged between water supply and forest protection. Sweet found it deplorable that, over the years, Colvin could spend $100,000 to secure surveys of the Adirondacks and then produce no map "of any value" whatsoever. Even Colvin's basic data were called into question. As Ebenezer Emmons had been found in error (by 123 feet in the case of Mount Marcy), so too were some of Colvin's calculations askew. In 1921, barely a year after Colvin's death and apparently basing his information on material in the archives of the state engineer's office, Alfred L. Donaldson would write in his *History of the Adirondacks:*

"The years have shown [Colvin's] work as a whole to be of uneven scientific value. . . . His office in Albany, indeed, looked more like the dressing-room of a sporting club than the repository of valuable records. These, if there at all, were apt to be buried beneath a picturesque profusion of snowshoes, moccasins, and pack-baskets."

Indeed. The years have shown Donaldson's work to be of uneven value as well. "His picture of Colvin," writes Norman J. Van Valkenburgh, a contemporary chronicler of Adirondack events, "was warped."

But, alas, the Colvin superintendency was not destined to endure beyond the first year of the twentieth century. The United States Geological Survey was the new boy in town. Governor Theodore Roosevelt (who as the vacationing U.S. vice-president one year later would dash down from Colvin's Lake Tear-of-the-

Clouds to assume McKinley's toppled throne) signed into law in April 1900 a measure abolishing the office of the superintendent of the state land survey. Colvin was fifty-three, a tender age even then for a man forced to contemplate early retirement.

He turned his attention to threadbare schemes. Garnet mining near Gore Mountain, in Warren County. And a railroad through the heart of his beloved mountains. He was fascinated by trains. Almost everyone, then, was fascinated by trains. Over the years, Colvin had served as engineering consultant to several railroads. He had been president, in the 1890s, of the short-line Schenectady and Albany Railroad. In 1905 he became president of the New York Canadian Pacific Railroad, which had ambitious plans to punch a rail line from New York and Albany straight through the mountains to Ogdensburg on the St. Lawrence River. More than a quarter-century earlier, Colvin had appended to one of his Adirondack reports an evaluation of possible rail routes through the high country. Most of the theoretical options skewered the wildest passes: Hunter's, Elk, Ausable, Avalanche, Indian, Ampersand, Ouluska. It was a curious measure of Colvin's double vision. He would glorify the wonders of the wilderness and then tame them with ties and rail. Glancing over the field of his life's labor, he would note with sadness the changes following the footsteps of his explorations: First "the blazed line and the trail; then the ubiquitous tourist. Where first comes one, the next year there are ten—the year after full a hundred. The woods are thronged" and—heaven forfend!—"ladies clamber to the summits of those once untrodden peaks. The genius of change has possession of the land; we cannot control it. When we study the necessities of our people, we would not control it if we could." And now Colvin's necessity was a railroad through the mountains. He devoted five intensive years to the project, but nothing came of it. By 1911 the scheme was dead.

Colvin's personal life, especially in the later years, ran toward a certain opaqueness. He never married. One Harriet Langdon Pruyn of Albany was said to have caught his fancy for a while. He wooed her with field-book poems and tall mountain tales recited by the fireside, then lost her to a one-time subaltern to

Governor Cleveland. His closest friend was Mills Blake—boyhood chum, chief assistant through all the survey years, housemate in Albany, a man (wrote mountain historian Russell M. L. Carson in 1924) "entirely the opposite of Mr. Colvin, a quiet, retiring little man who was content to live his life in the reflected glory of his chief." (It was Carson who, with the blessing of the State Board of Geographic Names, affixed Blake's name to a promontory directly south of Mount Colvin. At 3,960 feet of elevation, Blake's Peak is ranked forty-third in order of height in the Adirondacks.)

Point of reference: Toward the end it was said he was losing his mind. William Chapman White, in a poignant essay, painted a picture of Colvin slowly passing from "idiosyncrasy to delusion," muttering to himself as he aimlessly wandered the sidewalks of Albany.

Point of reference: Or perhaps the beginning of the end was more clinical than that. Norman Van Valkenburgh traces it to a blow to the head suffered by Colvin in the winter of 1916–17. Colvin, running for a trolley in Albany, slips on the ice and suffers a concussion from which he never recovers He is reduced to an invalid, cared for by Mills Blake. January 30, 1919; declared incompetent and remanded to the mental ward of the Albany Hospital. February 22, 1919: declared a lunatic and transferred to the Marshall Infirmary at Troy.

Point of reference: May 28, 1920.

It is dark on the trail now, I am feeling my way.

The Marshall Infirmary. Beneath the bedsheets, his upthrusted toes are perpendicular to the plane of the mattress. The bulge gives the effect of a mountain, miniformed; the sheets, a glitter of snow. Suddenly, upon the summit, there appears a circular glory of prismatic colors, a rich anthelia. It seems as though nature today were reveling in splendors. The observer extends his arms and is reproduced—a shadowy cross standing upon the mountain. Torn, ragged, cleaving the clouds. And, O, *yes!* One final request, a desideratum: that his copper bolts, like the forest wild, might last forever.

YANKEE FOREST FOR SALE:

BY THE BTU (1981)

T his is a story about trees and people, and about a forest where both grow in such profusion that some of the people are looking at trees in a different light. What the people see *is* light. And heat for a cold winter's night. And possibly a non-Arabian star-spangled fuel for the insolent chariot. In trees, they see a transfer of energy most Americans are too young to remember, yet of a kind so old its roots run back through human history to the mouth of the cave. It is the energy of the sun that they see. Not the direct radiance of it, or the fossils of its buried bright power, but the stuff of cellulose and lignin locked in the fibers of living wood, then cut and dried and ignited and released in a sunburst of orange pyrolysis. This is also the story of a question that some people have not yet learned how to ask. And what they should be asking right now is this: To what extent—given demand for lumber and veneer and particleboard and paper, for purity of watershed and diversity of wildlife, for public recreation and private amenity—given these, to what extent can people have their forest and burn it, too? The question will find its answer soon enough, though likely not to everyone's satisfaction; and likelier still, in the long run, to the satisfaction of absolutely no one at all.

Of all the forests of the United States, none is so close to the cutting edge of the question as the woodland of New England. Whatever the ultimate answer, it is certain to be discovered first in this land of white-steepled churches and wayside inns, of stony fields and seaside cities, and of a human density so extravagant to the square mile that one would hardly expect to find any space whatsoever left over for trees. Outlanders with memories for history might well perceive the region as bald. Was it not shorn of its pines by His Majesty's shipbuilders, then trimmed into pasture and orchard; the fields soon abandoned and the pilgrims gone west; the second-growth cut, and cut, and cut once again? Yes, indeed, this is true. But the forest kept bouncing back. And now, except in their northern reaches, the woods of New England have been bouncing freely for seventy-five years.

By any measure, it is the most uncommon forest in America. It covers 80 percent of the land area of its six indigenous states, a measure that makes New England by far the nation's most forested region, in proportion to regional size. Maine, New Hampshire, and Vermont rank first, second, and fourth, respectively, among states with the highest percentage of forested area. And tiny Connecticut, Massachusetts, and Rhode Island, for all their humanity, are so densely wooded as to exceed the forest factor of any three contiguous states outside the Old South, shouldering more timber, proportionately, than Michigan, Minnesota, and Wisconsin; more, too, than Idaho, Oregon, and Washington, to which the outlander mind invariably runs at the mention of forests.

It is an uncommon forest also in that, while it was bouncing back this last time around, the forest industry was preoccupied elsewhere, and largely ignored it. To be sure, there was and is substantial harvest of timber for pulp in the northerly precincts of New Hampshire and Maine. And here and there boards have been milled for pallets and furniture. But, for the most part, the woods of New England fell into nonindustrial uses when the loggers moved west and south. The forest became a place for leisure, for weekend homes to provide escape from the stifling cities, for reservoirs to slake the prodigious urban thirst. And, penultimately, the forest once again became what it had been from the time of first settlement to the emergence of coal as the fuel of choice in the winding-down years of the nineteeneth century. It became a woodlot.

The use of wood for fuel has traced a curious curve for itself on the energy ledgers of New England, and of the nation, too. Logs fueled half the country in 1880. Then the curve took a dive. By 1900, the coal pile was four times higher than the woodshed. By 1940, as oil began to replace coal, most of the nation's woodsheds stood empty. But not in New England. That year New Englanders pitched eight million cords into fireplace and stove. And soon switched to oil, like everyone else; so that by 1970, the number of cords burned in the region barely exceeded a hundred thousand. It was the Year and the Day of the Earth. April orators earnestly exhorted their campus listeners to look to a bright clean future of solar and geothermal technology. Some even spoke of obtaining energy from garbage. But hardly anyone spoke of securing it from wood. Then, one saved a tree for e-col-o-gee, at least until 1973. That was the year, more or less, when back-to-the-earth flower children of all ages rediscovered the cast-iron stove. And that was the year that Arab oil producers reinvented the embargo. Whereupon everything fell into place— the petroleum panic and the woodstove revival. And the forest, waiting.

It would not wait for long. Before you could say "Yankee Doodle Dandy," or "Camelot" for that matter, hundreds of thousands of New Englanders were pledging allegiance to wood. In many households, there was a classic and legendary quality to it all—the woodstove as round table, the chain saw as sword Excalibur, and a seasoned stack of oak or hickory as the Holy Grail. Soon, too, technicians were tinkering with central heating systems retrofitted for burning logs, or chips, or pellets; and there were plans on the desks of electric-utility executives calling for construction of fifty-megawatt wood-fired plants. In the spring of 1975, one such executive rose to address the Northeastern Loggers' Congress at Rockport, Maine. "I stand before you," he said, "with my Morbark Chiparvestor, my bag of rancid chips, and a book of safety matches to proclaim that we have more wood than the Arabs have oil, and I think we're going to burn it." And burn it we would. By the early 1980s, nationwide, eight of every hundred households burned wood for heat. Thirty-three of every hundred burned it in New England. Wood fiber soon occupied almost as much space in America's energy ledger as nuclear fission. "Split Wood—Not Atoms," proclaimed the bumper stickers in Vermont. And split it we would.

But there is always a catch. Splitting wood is arduous sweaty labor. And cutting it is ten times more dangerous than driving a car. If you do not cut and split it yourself, assuming the wood is yours from scratch to use, then you must pay someone else to do that for you. In southern New England, the price of a full cord— 128 cubic feet, including the airspaces in the pile—doubled in two years; and some suburban householders began paying almost as much for a BTU from the woodstove as for one from the oil furnace. Given the escalating value of wood, we found a new breed of chamois-collar criminal among us: the cordwood rustler, home on the range in our public forests and parklands. The volume of stolen timber multiplied yearly. And then there were those who would lawfully have turned a park into a plantation. At Narragansett, Rhode Island, a town official proposed that a local pleasuring ground be planted to hardwood species for harvest fifty years hence. The good man figured that was about the time we would run out of oil. Some folks take it one step further, believing there are limits to all things, including renewable resources. They figure that fewer than fifty years is all the time we'll need to run out of wood.

If the region or the nation should ever approach that absolute point of no wood at all, or little to speak of, if the forest should die, it is hardly likely that the chain saw and woodstove will be named in the obit as the causes of death. The backyard woodpile is too small a grave for so large a corpse. True, there are private woodlots here and there already destined, at their owners' mindless behest, to become biological junkyards by the end of the decade. But this is destruction on a microscopic scale. What is far more worrisome to environmentalists and foresters and wood-products businessmen, at least to those who have paused long enough to ask the burning question, is the prospect of macro-destruction; of harvest technologies capable not only of large-scale clearcuts, not only of slurping up whole trees and chipping them into vans, but of vacuuming *all* of a forest's biomass into the ever-expanding energy bag; of public utilities that know everything of generating kilowatts but absolutely nothing of regenerating trees; and beyond it all, the prospect of oil corporations waiting for the breakthrough that will bring wood-based methanol to the dried-up gas pumps of America.

If and when that finally happens, when the oilmen trade in their drilling rigs for chiparvestors, then there will be a pushing and shoving in the forest beyond our darkest fears. For here will be a Weyerhaeuser pushing for pulp and boards, and there will be a Commonwealth Edison shoving for kilowatts, and yonder an Exxon aggressively stumping, as always, for liquid fuel for the insolent chariot. Though there are strong opinions on the subject, who now is to say which of these will represent the best and highest use of the forest in the Year 2000? By then, perhaps, we will have navigated this time of transition between the burning of fossils and the trapping of radiant light. But how many times can a forest bounce back? Perhaps someday the best and highest of all possible uses will be to leave the forest alone, for the worms and woodpeckers. If anything is left.

I. THE BIG GREEN MACHINE

In a timber tally a few years back, the U.S. Forest Service looked at New England and counted thirty-one million acres of trees. And nearly half a million forest landowners, twice the number that had been counted a quarter-century before. Suddenly it seemed that everyone and his uncle was holding a deed to a piece of the woods. Public ownership, in state and national forests and municipal open-space lands, took a slim 6 percent of the acreage pie. Forest-industry lands stood at 32 percent, mostly in Maine and New Hampshire, where the industry plays a large role in the northern economy. And Mom and Pop held the rest of it, more often that not in parcels of fewer than fifty acres. All of which helped to explain to the foresters why, after all these years of bouncing, the New England forest might be heading for some kind of serious trouble.

For the most part, foresters do not look at trees as the rest of us do; they simply measure the timber. And when their measurements show that the annual growth in a stand of timber is far in excess of the volume removed by harvest or thinning; when they note a certain abundance of standing trees that are "rough" or "rotten"; when they see potential sawlogs turning to duff on the forest floor—then there is a wringing of hands and a sigh of regret that the landowner lacks the wherewithal to exercise sound forest management. It is bad enough, from the management perspective, that so much of the forest is fragmented into small individual holdings; but perhaps it is even worse that the largest single bloc of landowners, and the largest holding of private, nonindustrial land, should fall under the demographic rubric of "professionals and executives," meaning doctors, lawyers, and assorted chiefs—people who probably grew up in the suburbs and cities (where only wastrels chop down trees), who likely believe that thinning the woodlot destroys the scenery, and who would as soon entrust the back forty to a logger as hire a burglar to appraise the estate.

This was the way it worked for much of the woods through the fifties and sixties; annual growth exceeding removals by a factor of two to one—two cubic feet of new wood, growing, for every foot cut and taken away. At the same time, something else was happening in the forest. The rate of mortality, of trees dead or dying in competition for space and light, was increasing faster than the rate of new growth. And while all of this added up to bad news for most of the foresters, it could be construed only as a blessing by a new breed of would-be forest managers, the alternative energy technocrats who would now measure wood not by feet but by thermal units.

The energy types took their first panoramic look at the woods in 1977. In a report on "The Potential of Wood as an Energy Resource," the inter-agency New England Federal Regional Council noted that large volumes of "unmerchantable" trees and logging residues in the forest could (and therefore should) be used to fuel energy projects. "Removal of this material," the Council observed, "would increase forest productivity and improve the appearance of our woodlands. In addition, wood is low in sulfur and nitrogen, and its development as a source of energy is supported by environmental groups." (Well, sort of. Some environmental groups do not necessarily perceive the removal of unmerchantable trees as enhancement of forest esthetics; nor does woodburning hindsight much support the illusion of cleaner air.)

In any event, the Council suggested, the New England forest was going to waste. Here were 44 billion cubic feet of wood in growing stock and "rough and rotten" trees; and if you threw in the bark and the tops and the branches, normally untallied by the Forest Service, then here were 60 billion cubic feet of wood with a BTU-equivalency of 700 million tons of coal or 3 billion barrels of oil. Having made the energetic connections, the Council quickly explained that by no means did it intend to imply that "we should denude New England of her forests," only that "a resource of this magnitude should not be left standing idle."

Still, my own mind sometimes wanders perversely and improbably toward New England nudity. I see those 60 billion cubic feet of wood cut into logs, and the logs into two-foot woodstove lengths, and the lengths stacked in piles of four feet by four feet by eight, making about 720 million cords, and the cords laid end to end around the equator. Not once or twice, but *forty-four* times around the equator. Wood enough to fuel New England for a quarter-century, though perhaps not quite. For with all that Yankee wood stacked up around the equator, it would take some fancy heap of electric Kool-aid air-conditioning just to compensate the Yankees for the loss of their summer shade.

As a rule, wild things—forests, for example—have never paid much heed to boundaries conceived by cartographers and kings. Heeding isohyets is a different matter, for these, in their own peculiar linear way, describe volumes of moisture; and contour lines, for they define elavation and slope; and sometimes wild things, especially trees, pay overriding attention to the lines encircling soil types, for these are either the markers of welcome or of trespass, to be ignored by seeds at their own peril. But political boundaries? Not by a long shot. So when we speak of the New England forest, we should consider first not only how it blends with the landscapes around it, but also how oscillating lines within it define not one forest but probably as many as six.

New England is a vegetational intersection. It is where the Appalachian hardwood forest, trending northeastward, meets the Canadian North Woods. In the meeting, types tend to get tangled or drawn out. A woodlot in southwestern Connecticut, for example, may demonstrate strong silvicultural kinship with a hillside in central Pennsylvania, yet its sugar maples will suggest an allegiance to northern Vermont. Balsams at two thousand feet on the flank of New Hampshire's Monadnock Mountain are the same firs that tolerate sea-level life in New Brunswick or perch in the clouds in Tennessee. Scratch the canopy of the Adirondacks, in upper New York State, and you will feel the treetop texture of northern New England in its needles and leaves.

As the forest types meet, so do the extremes of weather: hot puffy air scudding up from the Gulf, fronts like open refrigerators tumbling out of Canada; such outrageous weather, in fact, that the region can count on up to fifty inches of precipitation spread equitably over the twelve months of the year. Thus, with the wet sky above and glacial-till soils below, New England is probably as good a place as any in the cooler temperate world for growing trees. If you don't mind diversity.

In general, one might conceive of this forest as a cake with six layers—Long Island Sound being at the bottom, and Canada at the top. One must be extremely flexible about this, however, for the layers do not run directly from west to east across the regional cake; rather, they wiggle and dance and soar, and sometimes they roller-coast up one side of a river valley only to fall away down the other.

So, then. Starting in the south, we encounter what foresters call the central hardwoods. It is a forest dominated by red oak, though black and white and scarlet oaks are mixed here and there with hickory (bitternut and pignut and shagbark), black birch, tulip poplar, ash, hemlock in cooler sites, red maple in wetter ones. Of all New England's vegetation zones, this is the most densely settled, the one most likely to lose substantial ground to future urbanization, and the one most susceptible, right now, to backyard chain-saw exploitation

Next, moving north, we enter the pinelands—a zone characterized by eastern white pine, mostly scattered among other species but occasionally found in pure stands on abandoned fields. Basically, it is still a central hardwoods situation here, though hickories are beginning to fall behind, and some of the oaks, too; while among birch, the yellow creeps in to usurp the black. Southeastward of the pinelands is the sandy-ground forest of Cape Cod, a vegetation zone that has more in common with Long Island and the Jersey Pine Barrens than with anything in New England. Mostly pitch pine and the scrubbier species of oak, this was the forest first encountered by the Pilgrims, which explains why those early stalwarts fared better the farther they pressed inland from Plymouth Rock.

North again, above the pinelands, are the transition hardwoods. These have something for everyone. They have oak from the south, but they also have sugar maple, beech, and white birch from the north. And beyond this lies the northern hardwood zone, the fifth forest. It is a thing of islands and reefs scattered across New England from the Berkshires to eastern Maine. Here, oaks are in full retreat before an onslaught of maple and birch. It is a wet forest, and a colorful one in the autumn, the best and brightest across the land.

Beyond a final line looms the dark serrated canopy of the North Woods, the spruce-fir forest that covers half of Maine, jumps into the White Mountains, and then leaps into the Northeast Kingdom of Vermont and the loftier ridgelines of the Green Mountains. For acreage, this is the largest of the six zones. It is not a purely coniferous forest. There are northern hardwoods here, too. Still, balsam or red spruce are dominant most places; maybe white spruce, getting toward Canada; maybe black spruce, on the swampier sites.

So there it is—the zones defined, the species identified. But what does it all mean in the human scheme of things? I have poked around in the literature and found many answers, all of them complex. I have spoken with professors and foresters and loggers and landowners, and each has his or her own theory about forests, though most tend to sound the same. To my own way of thinking, maybe the best summation came from a forester in Bangor named Lester DeCoster. He said the woods of New England were a great big green machine. He said there is this big green machine with five hundred thousand people pushing its buttons at the same time. Considering all that it has been through, he said, it was some big miracle that the green machine should still be running at all.

Carl H. Reidel is a man who would like to believe that the people of New England can have their forest and burn a bit of it, too—up to a point. He does not presume to know exactly where that point is at, and he's pretty sure that no one else yet knows where it's at. He only wishes—or seems to wish—that some of his peers in the forestry practice would devote to the search for an answer at least part of the time they now spend covering their traditional butts.

I found Carl Reidel at his desk in Burlington, where he presides as director of the University of Vermont's Environmental Program and as Sanders Professor of Environmental Studies and Forest Policy. Reidel is a veteran of the U.S. Forest Service, with considerable field experience in the West, and a past president of the American Forestry Association; and for all the academic pedigrees and hidebound affiliations, he is a bit of a maverick in matters of the woods. He sees wood not as a commodity, but as part of a working landscape of forest and village and farm. It just might be that he is one of those rare individuals who *can* see the forest for all the trees.

We talked that day in Burlington about "The Yankee Forest"—Reidel's phrase. He coined it as the title of a report that appeared under his name in 1978, a report that some Yankee foresters have been mulling ever since. Reidel, then, was a visiting lecturer at Yale University's School of Forestry and Environmental Studies. His report was in response to an appeal by the dean of that school, Charles H. W. Foster, for a "basic strategy" that would put the region's forests to work once again, and at the same time save them from a new wave of exploitation that Foster perceived cresting along the horizons of New England. While Reidel and his research associates did not attempt the master plan suggested by Foster, they did present a persuasive case that the forests were "not yielding anything near their potential in terms of forest products, services, or environmental amenities." And they identified an alarming number of issues that, in aggregate, raised serious doubts about the feasibility of fielding a region-wide remedial action program.

For openers, they found "serious gaps in essential information about the forest resources of the region." The U.S. Forest Service's Forest Surveys, for example, when reduced to the scale of a county, showed "sampling errors for selected forest types, growth, removals, and mortality" that exceeded "reasonable limits for management planning." Moreover, the federal data failed to account for "increasing use of whole tree harvesting systems and expanding firewood utilization."

For second openers, they found that while there were "a vast array of public and private agencies concerned with some aspect of the forest resource, their efforts [were] fragmented and generally uncoordinated." In several states, for example, forestry agencies had been absorbed by super-bureaucracies more concerned with environmental regulation than with resource management. As a result, some state foresters got lost in the shuffle. As for the private sector, overall it was found to be "poorly organized and ineffective at the regional level," and, unlike private associations in the West and the South, unable "to exert powerful influence on forest policy."

And for thirds, the public had been left woefully uninformed. Traditional information programs were "ineffective," and even these were "failing to reach the increasing number of nonfarmer woodland owners." Extension forestry programs at most land-grant colleges were "dominated by agricultural interests." While the "few extension foresters, and many county agricultural and 4-H agents, [had] done a creditable job," there were "simply too few of them with too little financial or program support." Equally serious was "the inability of many traditional foresters to serve owners who [did] not consider wood production the major objective for their lands. Thousands of management plans prepared for small woodland owners [would] never be implemented because of their often narrow and single-minded approach to forest management."

In short, the Yankee Forest was in one helluva mess. And as Reidel and I reviewed these gloomy findings, I caught my mind wandering off to the image of that great big green machine, out there beyond the office window, clanking along with five hundred thousand people pushing its buttons, some buttons for ON and some buttons for OFF, and hardly a pusher knowing the difference.

Reidel and I talked that day about some other matters, including the big fifty-megawatt wood-fired plant that Burlington Electric Department was hoping to build down in the intervale of the Winooski River. The plant would demand a prodigious amount of wood to generate such power, enough almost to double the whole state's annual consumption of fuelwood. "And I'm just not sure," Reidel was saying, "that it's going to be economically feasible to harvest that volume of wood selectively. So then you get into clearcuts. And there's nothing wrong with that, if it's done right. I just don't know whether there's enough concern for the forest as a resource, as part of our working landscape."

We talked, too, about some of the small firewood operations roundabout, the opportunistic ones that were high-grading the woods, taking the best specimens of oak and ash, and leaving the junkwood behind. "Surgery is the solution to some of the things that go wrong with people," Reidel said. "But you send for a surgeon, not for anyone who happens to have a knife."

And finally we talked of priorities, of the highest and best of all possible uses of wood. I told Reidel that I had been hearing from others that the most energy-efficient use of wood was not in combustion but in structures. By using wood structurally, the theory went, you displaced energy-intensive building materials such as steel. Thus, the highest and best use, aside from leaving the trees to the woodpeckers, was probably in lumber and reconstituted particleboards. And the second highest, according to a pecking order supplied to me by Ernest Gould, administrator of the Harvard University Forest at Petersham, Massachusetts, was in paper. And then, maybe, in third place, was the use of wood for direct space heating, as in stoves. And fourth, in the generation of electricity. And finally in fifth place, as a component of gasohol, or methanol.

Reidel heard it all out, sitting on the edge of his antique desk. It was a huge desk. It had seventeen drawers, and except for some brass fittings, was constructed entirely of wood—a tropical hardwood, he explained later. Possibly the desk had first belonged to some colonial dignitary in empire days. Now Reidel ran his fingers lightly over the wood and said: "Do I chop it up and throw it in the fireplace and heat this room for two days, or do I put it in a truck and send it down to New York City and sell it to an antique dealer for two thousand dollars? For two thousand dollars, I could buy enough oil to heat this room for five to ten years. Or do I leave it where it is, and enjoy it, and watch it appreciate in value? That's what I wonder about sometimes when I see an oak growing by a roadside within fifty miles of the Burlington Electric Department."

Homeward through Vermont, I stopped by the little village of Grafton, up Saxtons River a piece from Bellows Falls. Grafton was a thriving agricultural community once, back in the days when farming was so tenable roundabout that half the countryside, or more, would have appeared stark naked but for the stone walls on the hillsides and the grass of the pastures in between. Then hard times came along, as they would to much of central New England; and the place went tumbledown flaky until, in recent years, the Windham Foundation moved into town and managed to tidy things up. Now Grafton is an alabaster showcase of restoration, and the surrounding hills are so fully clothed in May that one can hardly see the old stone walls for all the leafy second-growth maples.

In Grafton, I called on Mollie Beattie. At the time, she was a forester employed by the University of Vermont to supervise its Grafton Forest Resources Project, which specializes in research and demonstration of multiple-use management of private non-industrial woodlands. The project has access to some two thousand acres controlled by the Windham Foundation and several other landowners. It appears to be the kind of place that is as splendid for studying ruffed grouse habitat as for demonstrating how selective thinning for fuelwood can improve a stand of commercial timber.

To Carl Reidel's way of thinking, most foresters fall into one of two categories—those who, when things get rough, "pull the wagons into a circle," and those who are, to borrow someone else's phrase, "groping toward the humanities." But Mollie Beattie seemed to fit neither type. More the renaissance forester than anything else, she had already explored the humanities as a philosophy major at Marymount College, a newspaper reporter at the *Manchester Journal*, and an Outward Bound field instructor in the Rocky Mountains. Beattie went to forestry school in Burlington "damn well determined," as she explained it, "to subvert the system." Like many young men and women who came of age on the eve of Earth Day, she believed that the woodman should spare that tree. "I came at it with my eyes closed," she said. We had walked from her office to the South Branch of Saxtons River, crossed it on a covered bridge, and now we were heading uphill among maples on a truncated tour of the Grafton forest. "But the eyes got opened. Now I'm trying to use my subversive energy to help change the forestry profession. We are so far behind our own technology. We've been preaching multiple-use since the turn of the century, yet we're still managing mostly for timber."

What about fuelwood? How did she feel about that?

"It could go either way," she said. "It's a make-it or break-it situation. Done right, it could really improve the forest. It could be good for wildlife. It could take just the junkwood, and that would be good for timber supply. Or it could be done wrong, and that could take everything."

For a while, then, we slabbed across the forested hillside; paused in a stand of young beech to examine the mischief wrought by nectria, a bark fungus to which beech seems increasingly vulnerable in New England; passed through a deep-shaded sugarbush—the Yankee expression for a grove of maples prized for their sugary sap; and, at last, descended to an open flat along the river. In the open, we turned and looked back to the hill.

The maps call it "Bear Hill." I had taken note of that in Mollie Beattie's office, and had asked if the name was at all appropriate. She replied that it probably was, for a time, and might be still; but that Bear Hill in all likelihood had got itself on the maps through a phonetic mistake. It was the other "Bare" the Grafton people had in mind when they first named this promontory a hundred and fifty years ago. And local people still called it that. Bare, because for most of the last century that's all it was, not counting the walls running across the hillside and hundreds of sheep coverting the grass into mutton and wool.

"It's nice this time of year, isn't it?" said Mollie Beattie.

Indeed it was, with pine and spruce and hemlock darkly brooding along the brow of the hill above the lime-green hardwoods. And I said I hoped it would stay this way for a while yet, if only to keep the *e* after *B* in Bear, on the maps.

2. HURRICANES AND CHIPARVESTORS

Every good schoolboy knows, if he has been attentive to his lessons, that northeastern America was once covered by the forest primeval. The towering pines and the hemlocks. Why, the trees were so thick and overlapping that a squirrel could have traveled from Kennebunk, Maine, to Kinnickinnick, Ohio, and never a paw on the ground. So it is said. Fortunately, most good schoolboys grow wise enough to sift the tall tales from the realities. And those who do not—well, they become nostalgic preservationists. I know, for I am sometimes recidivistically tortured by that tendency myself. In any event, the informed dry-eyed consensus seems to be that what we see today of the Yankee Forest is pretty much what the Penobscots and Mohegans saw before their heads were turned the other way by European sails four-sheets to the sunrise. More overall forest then, to be sure, and more of it old-growth, and maybe here and there a redistribution of the species; but nothing supportive of a treetop trip to Ohio, for certain. God or Nature did not suddenly invent the hurricane after 1492, though there was a pretty good one, smack through New England 1938-style, in 1650. Nor were lesser windstorms unknown to the region in early times; nor ice, shattering the treetops; nor pestilence and plague of a kind no less destructive than gypsy moth or chestnut borer; nor lightning, incinerating an entire hillside with a single strike. And then there were these Amerindians, the oldest established permanent floating arsonists in the world.

How they did like to prune with fire, torching the woods in November to bring on new growth in the spring. If there was ever a use of fire for land management on a scale such as this in any other culture, it goes unrecorded. The Indians of southern New England torched vast tracts around their villages, clearing the land for their crops, stimulating a successional bloom of berries, and of browse for game. By some accounts, the historic preponderance of oak and chestnut along the shore, and of white pine inland, might well be traced to these early and repeated burns; all three species are born-again winners after fire, though the chestnut, alas, has since fallen by the way. "The savages burn the country that it may not be overgrown with underwood," a visitor to Massachusetts, one Morton by name, observed in 1632. "The trees grow here and there as in our [English] parks, and make the country very beautiful."

Squire Morton's fondness for the pastoral beauty of the Native American commons was not often shared by other European observers, if only because it was not often seen. More than a century before, the sailor Verrazano had tacked along the shore with dour spyglass glances at a forest that he would later remember only for its shadows and gloom. In 1672, John Josselyn would write of the northward view from Sugarloaf Mountain in

Connecticut—the whole country "being filled with rocky hills" and "clothed with infinite thick woods." And his reaction? "Daunting terrible." Worse was the response of Puritan Michael Wigglesworth, who looked beyond the prayerful settlements of Massachusetts Bay to behold "a waste and howling wilderness, where none inhabited but hellish fiends, and brutish men that Devils worshipped."

The first-wave Yankees, and the second and third, made no secret of their contempt for the trees. I do not mean they had no *use* for trees. They had every use for trees. Buckets and bedsteads. Cribs and cabins, candlesticks and coffins. Ash for their oars, pine for their mainmasts, maple for gunstocks, hornbeam for handles. They used it all, and well. There was a reverence for wood, for trees taken singly by broad-axe and sliced into portable pieces. And pieces of wood kept the people warm. But *woods*—ash and pine and maple standing in aggregate—were something else. They were a howling wilderness. They were daunting terrible. They were things of shadows and gloom. Standing in aggregate, trees served no useful purpose. And what was not useful was "vicious," according to the brimstone gospel of Bostonian Cotton Mather. Such was the prevailing wisdom of the times.

Times change. By 1830, the howling wilderness had been pushed back to the edge of the North Woods. In Connecticut, Massachusetts, and Rhode Island, only a fifth of the original forest remained, and even that was being mined rapaciously for fuelwood. Then something happened. Or rather, two things happened that would lead a few New Englanders to look at their trees, standing in aggregate, in a different light.

The first thing was exodus. America was on the march, west. There was a canal called Erie. It dropped the cost of freight between New York and Buffalo from a hundred dollars a ton to five. In the markets of Manhattan, Chenango potatoes, at cheaper prices, were outselling Connecticut's. From out beyond the Alleghenies came tales of soils so rich and deep, and land so cheap, it just didn't pay any farming man to stay put in the East. So Yankees packed out to the Western Reserve; and before too long, on the maps of Ohio, there were towns with such names as Plymouth and Salem and Deerfield and Boston. And Vermontville, in Michigan, and Bunker Hill, out yonder in the Illinois. On a thousand hillsides in New England, the forest bounced back from the weeds of the left-behind farms.

The second thing was naturalism, though scholars might argue with that, preferring to call it the Romantic Movement. By whatever name, it was making palpable ripples in eastern America at the same time so many Yankees were turning their backs on the unromantic fields of home. Two years before the opening of the Erie Canal in 1825, James Fenimore Cooper's *The Pioneers* had opened a kind of watershed of its own. Nature was *not* our enemy, Cooper suggested. She was our friend. One had only to listen to Natty Bumppo, old Leatherstocking himself, describe the view from a Catskill crag. "What see you when you get there?" asks Natty's friend Edwards. "Creation," the scout replies, "all creation, lad. . . . How should a man who has lived in towns and schools know anything about the wonders of the woods? . . . And none know how often the hand of God is seen in the wilderness." For all of Cooper's "literary offences" (as Mark Twain would later churlishly claim), the creator of Leatherstocking nonetheless was more than a generation ahead of his peers in grasping the crude fundamentals of a conservation ethic. Of loggers and logging, Leatherstocking would warn: "If we go on this way, twenty years hence we shall want fuel." Twenty years hence, New Yorkers *did* want fuel. They got it by schooner from Maine.

Likewise alarmed by the exploitation of foresters was the muse of Walden Pond, Henry Thoreau. He admired the woodchopper's savvy of nature, but deplored the devastation so often left in the woodchopper's wake. If loggers were tall enough, Thoreau suspected, they would lay waste the clouds. They seemed to admire the log—"the carcass or corpse"—more than the tree. After his visit to the Maine woods, Thoreau would write that the "Anglo-American can indeed cut down and grub up all this waving forest, and make a stump speech, and vote for Buchanan on its ruins, but he cannot converse with the spirit of the tree he fells, he cannot read the poetry and mythology which retires as he advances. He ignorantly erases mythological tablets in order to print his handbills and town-meeting warrants on them. Before he has learned his *a b c* in the beautiful but mystic lore of the wilderness . . . he cuts it down [and] coins a pine-tree shilling."

Had Thoreau lived a bit longer than he did—say, into the late 1870s—he might have found the attitude toward trees more to his liking, at least in his native New England and in Cooper's New York. True, given the opportunity, most men would still cut down and grub up forests as quickly as they sprouted from the fields; but others now were speaking of conserving forests, too. By 1876, there was an Appalachian Mountain Club in Boston; by 1896, a Massachusetts Audubon Society; by 1898, a Forest and Park Association for the Bay State; and by 1901, a Society for the Protection of New Hampshire Forests. Increasing numbers of Yankees were immersing themselves at last in the mystic lore of the wilderness (or at least in the principles of multiple-use forestry). And none too quickly at that, for all the power of industrial technology would soon be available to supplement the woodchopper's axe.

The axe is surely the oldest tool in the world, and possibly the oldest weapon. One can only guess at the circumstances of the invention: This creature with the sloping brow, seated at the mouth of his cave, slapping two rocks together. One of the rocks fractures and thereby renders an edge sharp enough to slice the creature's thumb. One might also guess, however improbably, that the slapping rocks have caused a spark to shoot into a pile of duff, and that a thin blue ribbon of smoke suddenly curls around the creature's head. Thus, two discoveries for the price of one. Time trundles on. The rock's to become a whole-tree chipper; the spark, a fifty-megawatt burn.

In Colonial New England, the woods fell fast under axe and spark—the spark, because settlers soon adopted the Indian's torch to clear their own lands. Prudence was not a common virtue. In scattered locations, timber grew scarce. As early as 1647, the leaders of Springfield, Massachusetts, ruled that no logs, boards, or shingles should be carried out of town. In 1743, a law was passed restricting woods-fires in Massachusetts on the theory that they impoverished the soil and, out of control, destroyed people's fences. In the nineteenth century, prophets warned of a widespread timber famine. An iron horse was on the loose, whinnying down ten thousand miles of track laid on ties from New England's forest. The same forest furnished the steam-engine's fuel. Sparks from the engines fell in the forest remaining and burned up acres of uncut ties and free-standing fuelwood. Iron. It was at once the epidermis of America, and the cancer. For to have iron, one needed charcoal; and to have charcoal, one needed wood. Four cords of wood, slowly burned within a sod kiln, yielded the charcoal fuel to smelt one ton of iron. With hardwoods on the rebound, western Connecticut and Massachusetts became the charcoaling center of the country. Clearcuts could be seen upon the hills above the quaint white steeples.

As the century turned, the woodchopper stepped aside for the crosscut sawyer. It was only a small step for mankind, but a giant one for the logger. With a supple and toothy saw, two men could now fell twice the number of trees they might have taken before, with axes. But there was still the problem of transportation. Horses had to haul the logs to a river or sawmill (though some "portable" mills would be brought to the woods); and horses would continue hauling logs until the late 1930s, at which time tractors came into general use. Then someone discovered that if you welded teeth to a chain, and attached the chain to a small gasoline engine, and let 'er rip, you could fell maybe five trees in the time it took to drop one with a crosscut saw. The chain saw heralded a new age of mechanized harvesting.

The first big development was the feller-buncher with its powerful automated shears. In poletimber country, one man at the helm of a feller-buncher could accomplish the work of four with chain saws. The second development was the chiparvestor, an awesome machine, and wondrous, too. It is the meat-grinder of the woods. It seizes felled trees, of a girth up to twenty-two inches across the butt, and feeds them into its disk-knife chipper. The chipper takes all—leaves, stems, branches, bark, bole—and renders all into knuckle-size pieces. Then the chipper blows the pieces into a waiting van. With two feller-bunchers and two grapple-skidders to feed it trees, a chipavestor can spit out three hundred tons of chips in a one-shift day.

New England folk are likely to see a good deal of the big chippers in the years ahead. The machines are tailor-made for the pulp business; and as the structural-wood industry continues to shift its emphasis from lumber and veneer to reconstituted particleboards, the chippers will be in greater demand to supply that market, too. They will surely loom large in the woods when the electric-utility people start calling for more chips, if only to show the world that America has more wood than the Arabs have oil. What a splendid place for chipping, this Yankee Forest. All these rough young trees crowded in thickets—"puckerbrush," they call it Down Maine. No matter that there are ten to twenty species to the acre; no matter that most of them are what the old-time forester would call "unmerchantable." Just feed them all to the big chipper and they'll come out the same, knuckle-size. Good to the last BTU.

The Complete Tree Institute is located in a small office on the second floor of Nutting Hall, at the University of Maine's School of Forest Resources in Orono. Maximum use of those resources is the Institute's principle concern, and toward that end it issues occasional articles and reports on biomass inventory, nutrient cycling, and such other matters as may seem of consequence to the Institute's founder, director, and membership-of-one, Harold E. Young. A bibliography issued by the Institute lists some ninety relevant documents. Harold Young appears as the sole or principal author of most of them. The titles of some of his papers suggest a certain exclamatory style uncharacteristic of the research scientist, a desire, perhaps, to exhort as well as inform. One sees that, in 1974, he wrote a paper entitled "The Machines Are Coming, the Machines Are Coming." Not that Harold Young would exhort us to rebel against the machines. On the contrary, the founding director of the Complete Tree Institute is warmly enthusiastic at the prospect of machines designed to harvest complete trees. As oil-rich Texans are to Cadillacs and Lincoln Continentals, so is woods-wise Harold Young to feller-bunchers and chiparvestors.

Harold Young is a quantitative ecologist. Given his interest in biomass inventory, the first part of that pedigree needs no elaboration. As for the second part, Young is eager to explain to the inquisitive visitor that ecologists are scientists, and therefore not to be confused with environmentalists. And what are environmentalists? According to Young, environmentalists are those who "absolutely never read the scientific literature." The man's pervading pique, however, leans not in that direction. It leans toward foresters and ecologists who do read the literature—who, in fact, read Harold Young's own literature—and then presume to disagree.

Learned people have been disagreeing over Young's ideas since he first advocated complete-tree utilization in 1959. That idea was to take not only the merchantable bole but the slash that would otherwise rot on the ground. And the idea, too, if one could develop the proper machines for the job, was to take as much of the stump-root system as possible. After all, the bole was only a bit more than half the fiber volume of the tree. Why not go for the whole thing? "In forestry," said Young the day I called on him, "this was heresy tantamount to preaching atheism at St. Paul's Cathedral. And still is. You hear foresters talk today about using the 'whole' tree. Hell, they're just talking about the above-ground portion. That's not *whole*. That's only three-quarters."

From the Complete Tree, it seemed a logical step for Harold Young to move on to another idea: the Complete Forest. What he would do with the tree, he would do with a portion of the forest. Take it all. All species. All woody vegetation at least a foot high. All the stumps and the taproots. Take it all off. It would be a forest intensively managed for solid products, reconstituted products, solid and liquid energy, possibly fodder, and raw materials for the chemical industries. And there would be no waste to offend the lingering sense of Yankee thrift. Young said: "Using more of the tree, and more species in the forest—hell, it's like discovering new oil wells."

For all his enthusiasm, Young is not much impressed with the biomass energy effort in New England, or elsewhere in the United States. He sees it as "a lot of hot air, little smoke, and hardly any fire at all," and he regards wood-energy advocates in general as "doubtful experts," most of whom are too far removed from the science of forestry to understand fully the resource they would so eagerly tap. "You hear talk about energy plantations," he said. "Ridiculous! We've got *forests*. Four-hundred-and-thirty-five thousand acres of forest are harvested in Maine each year. The tops, slash, and stumps left behind in the woods represent about seventeen million tons of fiber. Now let's see what that means in energy. Maine uses twelve hundred megawatts of electricity. A megawatt is worth about ten thousand oven-dried tons of wood. Multiply the ten thousand tons by the twelve hundred megawatts. There's our power and light. There's twelve million tons of wood. And that's only part of what's lying out there in the forest, going to waste."

There appears to be some disagreement, however, over what might or might not be considered "waste." Some experts, and not such doubtful ones at that, regard the wholesale removal of logging slash, as in whole-tree chipping, a dangerous practice. For sure, you gain fiber. But you also lose nutrients needed for regeneration. Half the nutrients in a tree are concentrated in its leaves, twigs, and limbs. Take them away, by harvest, and you deprive the soil of that valuable feedback. Moreover, slash left behind in the forest enhances the soil's capacity to retain moisture, and serves as a cushion against erosion; and erosion, in the long run, leaches away nutrients already stored in the soil. Slash serves also as an umbrella of sorts, shading the ground from the sun's heat, which can be a vicious robber of the foodstuffs of forests. And finally there may be something to say for leaving the stump-roots in place, too, for these are the springboards of natural regeneration. Unlike conifers, most hardwood species sprout from their own root systems.

Harold Young is not altogether blind to the dangers of chip-and-run. "If we want more out of the forest," he said, "we're going to have to put more back. If we take the stumps, we have to replace them with seedlings. If we chip up the slash, we pay back with fertilizer. Pelletized wood ash might work. It lacks only nitrogen."

I asked Young if he believed the necessary paybacks would automatically follow intensive harvests by the big machines. Could the biomass-energy types, the ones of doubtful expertise in matters of forestry, be trusted to repay their debts to the harvested land? For the briefest moment, Young's eyes clouded over. I awaited an answer that would assure me that science and good sense would somehow prevail. I did not get it, for suddenly Young was saying: "Utilization is moving so far ahead of our biological knowledge. And there's no getting around it. Everything that man has ever devised has its destructive side. The automobile was never perceived in the beginning as a tank, nor the airplane as a bomber."

3. BEAUTIFUL BUT DIRTY

I remember the sound of the shovel on the cellar floor, winter mornings dark and early, like a fingernail clawing at a blackboard. And the pile of coal in the corner, chunky bituminous from West Virginia—you'd get a lump of it in your stocking at Christmas if you didn't behave—and the trail of soot leading to the furnace door, and the ashes spilling out from underneath; and later, out the back door toward school, looking up to see which way the wind was blowing. You could always tell, from the smoke. One day some men came with a big tank and put it in the corner where the coal had been. They monkeyed with the furnace and made noise with their tools. After they went away, we were burning oil. Mornings then were clean and quiet in the cellar. And hardly ever was there smoke enough above the chimney to read the wind.

As for remembering woodstoves, I came along too late and in the wrong place. No one bothered with them in Ohio, except for farm folk maybe, and fireplaces were just holes in the wall, grottoes for dried flowers in urns, though ours happened to be a crackling functional fireplace for Sunday afternoons and certain festive nights. And then there was a neighbor boy whose father's study seemed to flicker with firelight all winter long. I wondered from afar where they could possibly store all the logs—wondered until, admitted at last to the inner sanctum, I discovered that the logs were ceramic, and the flames, natural gas.

So it didn't take very long to catch up with us. Forty years of nothing to do in the cellar—about the length of a short rotation for the Yankee Forest—and now I have plenty to do in the cellar, with wood. And can read the wind, too.

The catching up, in my own case, was probably as much a circumstance of geography as anything else. I moved from a city place to the edge of the New England woods, to a drafty house in a hill town in Connecticut, with puckerbrush maples up front and oak and ash and hickory for flankers. And a functional fireplace in the livingroom. I cut a few trees, seasoned the logs, and burned them the second winter. Each time I lit a fire, the furnace kicked on; such is the price one pays feeding the flue with oil-heated air. Meanwhile friends and relatives from the North Country urged me to eschew the open hearth and order one of the new airtight, cast-iron Scandinavian stoves. It was the only way to beat the rising cost of heating oil, they said. And besides, it was good for the environment.

There was a feast of similar advice in the country magazines, the cracker-barrel catalogues, the back-to-the-earth books. Suddenly, since wood was small, it was beautiful. It was the "ecologist's fuel." It was renewable and could be grown "like any other crop." It was all of these, and it was "nonpolluting." With wood, one mass-market *how-to-beat-the-energy-crisis* book proclaimed, "we can clean up our air so that it is fit to breathe," because "any pollutants from wood may be said to be 'natural,' and, therefore, may be assumed not to be harmful to the environment." The author then went on to explain why all the benefits that are claimed for hunting "apply in spades to heating with wood—and you don't have to kill something in the process." Except a tree, she might have added, but didn't. "There is tremendous satisfaction in pitting your strength and skill against the elements," she went on. "Yet the demands are not so great that there need be any strain in doing it. At least no more than in landing a large fish, or playing eighteen holes of golf on a tough course." So one read it all with a large pinch of salt. And then went out and bought a woodstove, anyway.

Mine went straight to the cellar, for the cellar is where I happen to work; or, rather, tried to work my first two stoveless winters in Connecticut. The stove faces the cellar stairs. It has a fan. The fan blows hot air up the stairs to the kitchen, and beyond. Though not much beyond. I have no idea how much oil is saved as a result of this arrangement. Maybe ten percent of what I would otherwise use. Maybe half a dozen OPEC barrels. Last winter was mild. Still, I burned nearly three cords of wood, not counting what went into the profligate fireplace. I had to kill a few things on my place in the process. And bringing them in was not nearly so easy as landing a large fish. The stove I regard more as insurance than as money-saver. It will keep the water pipes from freezing the next time we are hit by a blackout.

The economics of wood-burning are getting tricky in New England, as elsewhere. I do not mean the cost of the stove, pipe, and installation, which isn't cheap; nor do I mean the value one places on his time, cutting and splitting and stacking and stoking. On my own time with wood, I place no monetary value whatsoever. It is therapy and exercise and, most important for me, it is fun. But for many people in New England, putting up a winter's supply of wood is either a miserable nuisance or it is out of the question, for want of a woodlot. According to one survey, New Englanders on the whole purchase from dealers about four cords out of every ten stacked in the regional woodshed. Some folks are paying dearly for it.

Yet even when the cost of cordwood begins to exceed the price of oil, as it will from time to time and place to place, some loyal wood-burners would rather freeze than abandon their stoves.

Perhaps it is enough for some to relish the sense of independence that comes from doing for oneself. It's a fine snug feeling after the first frost, with the cordwood stacked and ready, the chimney swept, the twiggy litter from summer storms laid up nearby in baskets, for kindling. Some places, too, it can run toward social things—a sharing of labor with neighbors in the woods, the communal use of a hydraulic woodsplitter, the togetherness of people basking in the warmth of an antique potbelly, tall tales from the rocking chairs, apple cheeks out of a Norman Rockwell cover for *The Saturday Evening Post*. Almost everywhere, it goes to a change of life-style for certain. "You put on more sweaters," says one Yankee, "and you close off more rooms."

The greatest casualty of the woodstove revival has been the fireplace; and for good reason. The fireplace does not work very well as a space heater. In fact, the same survey that found New England folk rushing to stoves like Gang Busters found them hurrying almost as fast to shut down the drafts in their fireplaces, especially in the North Country.

I suspect we can blame it on the English. Those stubborn Anglo-Saxons, standing around for centuries before the great stone hearth of castle or hut, the logs snapping and crackling, and most of the heat rising straight up the chimney—not only that, but pulling chill drafts to the fire besides. No wonder the English suffered a bum rap for being cold people. While apple-cheek Russians kept themselves toasty by tall brick stoves, and the Dutch and Germans did likewise with iron, the English came to the New World to spend their winters feeding open fires. Benjamin Franklin took dour note of this, saying that, to supply "great fires in large open chimneys," the English farmer in America needed "the constant employment of one man to cut and haul wood," that the draft of cold air to the fire was so strong as to freeze the heels of his family "while they [were] scorching their faces," and that this article of economy alone should, "in a course of years, enable the German to buy out the Englishman, and take possession of his plantation."

Genius that he was, Franklin came up with a solution. He called it the Pennsylvanian Fire-place. It was made of cast-iron. It fit into an existing fireplace, with an iron-plate shutter in front to control the draft, and a kind of baffle effect in the back. To be sure, one still viewed the fire—Franklin was high on the esthetics of firewatching—but one did not lose so much heat. His own common room, Franklin claimed, was "twice as warm as it used to be, with a quarter of the wood formerly consumed there." In time, the Franklin stove took on new configurations, but it never quite reached a level of efficiency held by other designs developed in the nineteenth century. And nowadays, with both the current leading Scandinavian and American manufacturers offering "combination" stoves, one can have his fiery esthetics and airtight efficiency, too. Well, almost.

Measuring the efficiency of woodstoves may be even trickier than figuring the economics, for efficiency is not only a variable of stove design, but of what kind of wood you burn, and how you burn it. I mean it does matter somewhat whether you burn oak or basswood; the heat from the coals of the oak will last longer. Nevertheless, it seems to me there is a certain trendy overemphasis, in woodstove literature, on charts showing the BTU heating values of tree species. So a cord of air-dried black locust has 12.2 million more BTUs than a cord of butternut. So the International Game Fish record for black marlin is 857 pounds heavier than for hammerhead shark. So what? There's nothing wrong with burning butternut. It just happens to be quite a bit lighter in weight than black locust; and, therefore, one has to burn more of it to BTU-match locust. The real trick is to burn it dry, whatever the species. And that can get to be a problem if one purchases a cord from a dealer and expects to burn it the same season. Generally, the product claims of the cordwood merchants are hoopla and hokum. Of three cords I acquired from three separate dealers last winter, only one turned out to be reasonably seasoned. And we all know what happens when we burn green wood. We get low heat efficiency in the stove, and creosote in the chimney.

Creosote—a residue of unburned gases and particulate matter, and a flammable residue at that—can build up inside a chimney even if the fuelwood is seasoned and dry. It happens like this. Misinterpreting the product claims of manufacturer or installer, the proud owner of a woodstove assumes that he is at last proprietor of a miracle, a miracle in which oxygen, somehow, is no longer essential to the combustion process. Here are these knobs, these draft controls. Fill 'er up and lean 'er down. Fill up the firebox, and lean down the draft, and what you have is a slow-burning fire that will be conservative with fuel and last all day. And fill the chimney with creosote. And eventually, perhaps, cause such a fire as to burn down the house. In just one year, fifty-three people died in Maine in fires attributed to wood-burning units (though most fires are caused not by creosote but by faulty installation of the hardware). "Small may be beautiful," says a friend in New Hampshire, "but it can be dirty, too." And dangerous, I hasten to add.

If the woodstove has brought a number of unpleasant problems into the home, it might be said, though more in the exception than the rule, that stoving has also brought a small measure of stewardship to the woodlot. A few folks are actually planning to manage their trees.

In poking around the Yankee Forest, I had heard about the other kinds of landowners, both the ones who were ravishing their woodlots with chain saws and the hands-off ones determined to let nature run the show. But I was not yet familiar with any Yankee who, through turning to wood for heat, had come to a way of looking at trees as a trained forester might, or who was learning to see them through the hired eyes of just such a person. So one day I picked up the telephone and put in a call to Jane Difley, a consulting forester up in southern Vermont, and asked, would it be all right if I tagged along on her appointed rounds and talked with a landowner or two? All *right*.

Like her friend Mollie Beattie over in Grafton, Jane Difley came to forestry out of the humanities, B.A. English, Connecticut College. She earned her masters in forestry at the University of Massachusetts, then worked as an extension forester, an analyst at the Resources Policy Center in Hanover, New Hampshire, and first editor of *Wood 'n' Energy*, a periodical of the Society for the Protection of New Hampshire Forests. Now Difley had gone freelance, and hung her consultant's shingle in Saxtons River.

We drove north from there on a drizzling vernal day into the hills west of Springfield and called on a young man named McGarry who was building a house with a wood-burning furnace in its basement. McGarry had hired Difley to appraise the timber on his seventy-five acres, and then to come up with a plan that would enable him to pursue three specific goals. The first goal was putting up firewood. For the furnace, and for a stove in the livingroom, he was going to need about fifteen cords a year; and he wanted to know from Difley how best to supply that need without messing up plans for the second goal, which was growing timber. McGarry had some fine old hemlocks on his place, and some pretty good maples and birches, too; and he hoped maybe he could select and sell enough sawlog timber over the years to cover his property taxes. There was some oak on the place as well, but McGarry told Difley he wanted to leave the oaks be, for they were essential to Goal Number Three. McGarry wanted to leave the oaks be for his own recreation, just for looking at, and for the acorn mast, for the deer. "The way things are going in this country," said McGarry, "people have to start looking at their own place for recreation, if they're lucky enough to have a place to look at. It's not going to be the way it used to be. Who can afford the gas?"

We walked up through the woods behind the half-finished house. Difley stopped beside an oak. From her pocket she took an instrument that resembled an overlong corkscrew, kind of Danish-modern. "An increment borer," she said, twisting it through the bark. "This way you won't have to cut down a tree to find out how old it is. The rings show up in this little core." Sure enough, when she withdrew the borer, she could count fifty-nine annual growth lines along the slender core of wood. "Good," said McGarry. "We'll leave it here for another fifty-nine, and for the deer."

In the late afternoon, Difley and I pulled up at the house of Neil Daniels, in Weathersfield, on a hundred and fifty acres of woods and with a hilltop view toward the Connecticut River valley. Daniels is a construction engineer with a big maintenance shop in nearby Ascutney. He heats both places with wood-fired boilers. The shop this winter will burn thirty-five cords; the house, eight. Daniels cuts and splits all forty-three cords himself, taking trees from his own woods, and places no monetary value on his time doing so. It is just as well. His time with wood is equivalent to two months at a five-day-a-week, nine-to-five job. Apparently, there's not a whole lot he'd rather be doing than putting up wood.

It was too late now to get around his property at any distance, so we sat with Daniels in his house and asked him how he did it, putting up forty-three cords of wood. "Motivation," he said. "In September, one should be motivated to get one's wood supply in order. If you can get ahead enough, the logs should sit twelve to eighteen months, seasoning. Now, what you see stacked up along the driveway, I started on that year ago January and then again this past fall. I'm thinning some places, and Jane here's going to show me how to do a better job at that, but mostly I'm just following some old abandoned woods roads across the place. Probably some of them go back fifty years because the trees growing in the roadbeds are ten inches in diameter. Split once, just right for the boiler. When I'm at it, I do about a cord a day. I cut a tree and buck it, and split the logs there, and put them in a trailer, and come on home and stack them up. Then it's time for a beer." Daniels said his preoccupation with putting up wood sometimes gets in the way of other pursuits. "Deer hunting, I'm just walking around looking at trees anyway. I see a good one, I mean a tree that ought to come down, I come back to the house and trade in my rifle for the chain saw."

In the cellar, Daniels showed us his forced hot-water heating system, with the boiler that takes logs up to twenty-four inches long and puts out up to 140,000 BTUs an hour. The unit, a smaller version of the one installed in the shop at Ascutney, cost Daniels $2,500. "And it paid for itself in its first year," he said. "The place to burn wood is central, not in woodstoves. I've got so many square feet in this house, I'd need *five* woodstoves. And look what happens." Daniels picked up a piece of hophornbeam from the cellar woodpile and turned it slowly in his hand. Hop-hornbeam has a shreddy kind of bark. Then Daniels twisted the log back and forth with both hands as he crossed the cellar. On the floor was a trail of gray flakes. "No, the way to go is central," he said at last. "Of course, one of these days I guess I'll get tired of cutting wood, or too old, so I'll probably have to go to a gas-ifer and burn chips, or pellets. And everything will be auto-mated. Can you imagine? *Automated!*"

4. THINKING BIG

The City of Burlington—with fewer than forty thousand peo-ple, the largest in Vermont—occupies a hill overlooking Lake Champlain and the Adirondack Mountains of New York. It is a venerable college town supporting varied small industries and a harbor that handles just enough tonnage to keep Burlington al-manac-listed as a North American port. Though waterfront ac-tivity is marginal nowadays, time used to be when this harbor was a real hustler—mostly of lumber and potash shipped to the barge canal at the foot of the lake, then on to the Hudson River and the saltwater ports beyond. For a period in the nineteenth century, when lakeside hills were being cleared for farming, Bur-lington exported a volume of wood products greater than that of any town in America. Now, the city is fixing to demonstrate that it is not always better to give than to receive. In a few years, Bur-lington could be importing—though strictly for energy—more wood chips than any city in the *world*. Which only goes to show that, even where small is beautiful, folks still lean tenaciously to-ward thinking big.

There were no small ideas, for example, in the seminal 1975 report of the Governor's Task Force on Wood as a Source of En-ergy. Headed by State Representative Sam Lloyd, the task force concluded that "enough surplus, unmerchantable wood fiber grows in Vermont forests each year to provide fuel for a substan-tial portion of Vermont's annual energy and heating needs," that the technology was at hand to convert wood fuel into steam for the production of electricity, and that large-scale removal of sur-plus wood could be undertaken without serious damage to the environment and with little, if any, negative impact on existing forest industries. One consultant to the task force, J.P.R. Associates of Stowe, opined that the annual surplus of wood in the forest was sufficient to generate the state's *total* electrical needs. Therefore, the associates urged, the use of wood for electrical generation in Vermont should be vigorously pursued.

Vermont's largest municipally owned electric system, the Burlington Electric Department (BED), was already raring to go. Its general manager, Robert C. Young, had long been looking for some indigenous and alternative fuel to add to the traditional mix of oil and coal, and of kilowatts imported from Vermont Yankee Nuclear Power and the Power Authority of New York State. Burning solid waste had been one of Young's ideas; but wood now seemed infinitely more attractive. Before long, at the behest of BED or the state, researchers from J.P.R. Associates and the Resource Policy Center at Dartmouth College's Thayer School of Engineering were turning out reports on just about everything anyone could possibly want to know about the feasibility of fifty-megawatt wood-fired powerplant. Regional employment, institutional contraints, environmental impacts, fuelwood availability, the economics of whole-tree chipping—you name it and there it was, all done up with charts and tables inside a bright blue cover. Some of the Dartmouth studies sounded cautionary notes, especially in regard to long-range impacts on the forest resource. But the analyses in general, and J.P.R.'s in particular, seemed to conclude that operation of such a plant was not only feasible but a happenstance devoutly to be wished for the commonweal.

The voters of Burlington saw it that way. In 1978, by a substantial majority, they approved an $80-million bond issue to finance construction of the plant on the outskirts of town, hard by neighboring Winooski. And Winooski? Predictably, Winooski winced. Meanwhile, BED had been taking steps to introduce its customers—and its critics—to the wood-burning process at its existing Moran Generating Station on the Champlain lakeshore. It would be a demonstration project of sorts, a dress rehearsal for the big one. Two of the Moran station's fossil-fuel boilers would be converted to receive and burn wood chips—up to fifty thousand green tons of chips a year, or a tithing of what BED proposed to burn at the projected McNeil Generating Station in the intervale of the Winooski River.

The woodburners at the Moran station were blazing away when I poked into the precincts of Burlington. Robert Young was out of town, so I spent some time with his public affairs chief, Tim Cronin. We went down to the lakefront and clambered around the old powerhouse with its huge pile of sweet-smelling chips cheek-by-jowl with an equally prodigious pile of bituminous coal, and we talked about procuring wood, and where the wood comes from, and at what cost, and of how the experience here, at Moran, might possibly reflect what would happen over there, in the intervale next to Winooski, if and when the big one is sanctioned by the Vermont Public Service Board.

Cronin said that wood procurement was the least of their concerns, for the time being. "For chips we're drawing on ten sites in Vermont, New Hampshire, and New York," he said. "Small landowners mostly. Under a hundred acres. A few are a little farther away than we'd like. Concord, for example." Concord, New Hampshire, is about 150 miles from Burlington. "From the Adirondacks, the wood comes by ferry from Port Kent and Plattsburgh. It's a good time for us right now. The suppliers aren't seeing a great demand from the paper mills. So we're benefiting. Of course, no one knows how long it will last. We just know that the wood's out there."

It was out there, all right; and it was relatively cheap. Fourteen to seventeen dollars a green ton, Cronin said, compared with forty-two dollars for a ton of coal. True, the coal burned hotter—12,000 BTUs the pound, compared with 4,200 BTUs per pound of chips. So it all came down to a wash, more or less, though the prices would no doubt fluctuate in the months and years ahead.

As for Winooski's concern about the McNeil project—well, that was something to be debated at permit hearings before the Public Service Board. Winooski's heaviest worry seemed to center on the trailer vans that would be hauling wood chips to McNeil right down the main street of the city. Each van would carry a payload of twenty-two tons, Winooski City Attorney William Wargo was arguing in a motion to dismiss BED's permit application. "Even an ideal transportation schedule," he wrote, "would present an unbearable burden, not only on traffic congestion, but on road conditions, on safety, on air quality, and on noise level as well." Moreover, there was this matter of the ambient air. Winooski would have to inhale the bulk of McNeil's emissions, given a pattern of prevailing westerlies and the city's location downwind. And what would BED do with its annual offal of sixteen thousand tons of ash? Dump it all into the wetlands along the Winooski River?

Cronin said, "We think we can deal with these concerns. Maybe we can deliver up to 75 percent of the chips to the plant by rail. We're looking into it. As for air pollution, with wood you don't have the big sulfur emissions that you have with coal. And you have fewer ashes."

What about the forest resource, I asked.

"It's renewable resource," Cronin said. "Coal isn't. Sure, there's a limit to what you can take. But our studies show that the forest can probably support up to three fifty-megawatt wood-fired facilities in the State of Vermont. And the way I see it, it's high time for Vermont people to take some responsibility for the energy they use."

To comprehend how many megawatts a forest might support, one must resort to images and figures. First, imagine an acre yielding fifty tons of wood. Energy people prefer their measures in tons, but tons do not lend themselves to imagery, so convert the fifty tons to twenty-five cords and stack them up in the middle of a clearcut acre. Now you have one piece of one megawatt. Next, consider the proposed McNeil Generating Station. Its sponsors say that McNeil will consume 500,000 tons of wood each year, an estimate considered immodestly low in some circles. Never mind. For the sake of round numbers, half a million tons it will be. That's 10,000 acres of forest, felled and chipped;

10,000 acres each year for at least twenty years. Sixteen square miles, each year. An area the size of Burlington itself, each year. Of course, this is only an image. The annual harvest will not, and could not, be taken in one fell block. Still, it is one helluva lot of wood. It more or less equals the volume of fuelwood burned in all of Vermont's woodstoves in a single year; equals, too, the volume harvested for *all* purposes in the northern half of the state. It is so much wood that one begins to wonder whether the Burlington Electric Department can indeed fetch sufficient chips from the forest roundabout without in some way depriving other users, such as tourists and lumbermen and paper manufacturers, of their own future stakes in the resource.

Among the more credible reports on this subject was a study of wood availability in the nine counties of northern Vermont. The study, commissioned by the state, was executed by Charles E. Hewett, a senior analyst at the Resource Policy Center at Dartmouth College. Hewett found that the net forest growth, above that already being harvested, could more than supply the fuel demands of a fifty-megawatt wood-fired powerplant (and, at the time, Hewett was estimating annual consumption not at 500,000 tons, but at 800,000). Moreover, he reported, there was enough "rough and rotten" timber, or cull, to supply such a plant for forty-five years—if only the cull could be harvested. If only there weren't all these physical and institutional constraints.

Having set up the straw men, Hewett proceeded to knock a few of them down. For openers, total reliance on harvesting cull would be out of the question. Crews would have to be working 540 acres—and selectively at that—every day of a 250-day harvest season in order to chip sufficient fuel for a plant the size of McNeil. The cost would be prohibitive. So on with the harvest, intensively. And what then? Then, harvest crews would encounter the constraints of slope and accessibility. Fully a quarter of the forest in the study area was situated on slopes of such a degree that feller-bunchers and grapple-skidders, the assault vehicles of whole-tree chipping operations, could not be used. Nearly half of the forest lay beyond a half-mile of the nearest road, a half-mile being regarded as the outside limit beyond which whole-tree chipping operators fall headfirst into red ink. Thus, adjusting for overlap between steep slopes and roadless inaccessibility, Hewett guessed that 45 percent of the forest of northern Vermont would not be available as supply base for the big one.

To make matters worse (or better, depending on one's bias), there was the human factor, this jigsaw of ownership patterns and of attitudes toward trees. More than 90 percent of the northern forest was privately owned. Statewide surveys already showed that 14 percent of the landowners controlled 51 percent of the private forest, and that they intended to harvest timber from it sometime over the next ten years; while 55 percent of the owners, controlling 12 percent of the forest, had no intention whatsoever of allowing loggers to harvest their trees. In general, a proclivity to harvest seemed to increase in direct proportion to latitudes north. That was the good news for Burlington Electric.

The bad news was that landowner acceptance of harvesting, presumably by the selective cut approach, began to erode when one brought up the subject of whole-tree chipping. In a Northland survey conducted by Hewett himself, the percentage of landowners "willing to harvest" dropped from about 75 to 50 percent when chipping became the only option, and, under the same scenario, the proportion of those opposed to harvesting almost doubled. Putting all of these factors together—the net growth and the cull, the constraints of slope and access, of landowner attitudes and marketplace economics—Hewett concluded that only a third of the private forest would definitely be available for whole-tree chipping. Even so, he wrote in summary (with co-analyst Colin High), the available resource "could produce about 90 megawatts of electricity annually. A 50-megawatt plant, therefore, will preempt most of the present surplus of low-quality wood in northern Vermont and will limit the use of this wood for small-scale power generation, domestic or commercial heating, or materials fabrication. . . . The potential impact on the environment, on existing wood markets, and on the recreation and tourist industry is substantial. . . . Because of the critical importance of obtaining wood from private, noncorporate landowners, whose attitudes toward mechanized harvesting are, at best, equivocal, the public response to real or perceived environmental impacts will play a vital role in securing the future wood supply, and therefore the economic viability of the plant."

And finally, Hewett suggested, perhaps a huge wood-burner would not be the best way to go after all. Perhaps Vermont could create more jobs and "more efficiently use the wood-energy resource" by encouraging, rather than one centralized fifty-megawatt facility, a number of small, three- to five-megawatt industrial boilers associated with manufacturing plants (known in the energy trade as co-generation). "Recent developments in assembly-line production of small boilers," Hewett went on, "combined with the reduction in wood transportation costs associated with scattered, smaller facilities, may return more energy for fewer dollars invested."

It sounded logical, but too late. There was no turning away from McNeil. And besides, the way people at Burlington Electric Department saw it, fifty-megawatts *was* small. At least, small enough.

The New England Wood Energy Advisory Council (NEWEAC) was, at the time of my encounters with it, an eclectic community of individuals dedicated to the proposition that one can have his forest and burn a bit of it, too. The perceived measure of just how much of it might prudently be burned varied from one individual to the next, depending on whether one was a forester circling his wagons or groping toward the humanities; or, for that matter, on whether one was not a forester but rather an electric-utility executive, a manufacturer of wood pellets, a regional planner, a paper-company panjandrum, a methanol advocate, a policy analyst, an environmentalist, or a huckster of wood-burning hardware. All such types, and many more, irregularly attended the occasional gatherings of NEWEAC, which, though lacking official status in decision-making circles, nevertheless provided the region with its own forum for the exchange of ideas about biomass energy and the future of the Yankee Forest. The principal figure in NEWEAC was Dennis Meadows, an expert in systems modeling, director of the Resource Policy Center, Dartmouth College, and chief architect of the 1972 Club of Rome Project on the Predicament of Mankind, out of which came the mind-bending book *The Limits to Growth*.

It was Mud Time in New England when I first ran into Dennis Meadows; a soft gray frizzled morning of a kind not inappropriate for woolen cap and thermal long-johns. At least Meadows was so attired. He had awakened early at his farmhouse in New Hampshire, no doubt fired up a woodstove or two (for his place has eight), stuffed some papers into a briefcase, and motored southeast across the granite hills to Boston, where some two dozen NEWEAC associates had assembled for a briefing on his latest project: a computerized modeling system designed to show the interaction of fuelwood utilization with the forest resource base. According to Meadows, the value of systems modeling is that it forces one to look for something one can't yet see. And in that sense, he would explain to me later, modeling becomes "social radar."

In Boston, in the library of the New England Regional Commission, Meadows shed several layers of wool insulation and took his place at the head of the conference table. He rummaged in his briefcase for some notes. He said that controlling fuelwood use would be the big problem in the 1980s. He said that all the various constituencies—and here he allowed his eyes to wander down the table among both forestry and energy types— were expecting a surplus of wood to be available to them. "And maybe," he said, "there won't be enough to go around. We may have to look to a future in which wood, heretofore a surplus, becomes scarce." Of course, there would be constraints. Such as? Such as pollution. "As pollution goes up," said Meadows, "the social acceptability of wood-burning goes down." And such as, chimed in a forester from Massachusetts, "the fear of burning down your house. Not much social acceptability there either."

Then Meadows proceeded to describe his design for a social radar that would analyze residential fuelwood use interacting with the forest resource. "We have constructed a causal loop," he explained, pointing to an image projected upon a screen. To my eye, the image, with arrows going in every direction, looked like the weather map of a storm that couldn't decide where it wanted to go. At the eye of the storm was a factor called Total Cut. Time and Area and Density, Environmental Damage and Net Growth, Logging Residue and Roundwood Utilized—all of these, with plus or minus values attached, seemed to assail each other on the screen, adding to and subtracting from the Total Cut. While, unseen by Boston eyes, back in the computer room at Dartmouth, Meadows's people were programming such additional factors as CUF (Capacity Utilization Factor), FOWS (Forest Owners' Willingness to Sell), and FOTS (Forest Owners Thinking of Selling). Despite the shorthand, I felt that Meadows might somehow be on the right track, though I could not be sure, since I am a life member of JUICE (Journalists Unable to Interpret Computer English).

Meadows was accompanied on many of his NEWEAC sorties by William T. Glidden, Jr., a Yale Forestry School graduate who, with Charles Hewett and Colin High, had been involved in much of the Dartmouth work in the forest-energy field. During a coffee break after Meadows's briefing, I asked Glidden how he perceived the schism between proponents of forest products and of BTUs. "The market force tends to generate disasters in the short-term," he said. "And right now, the market force is energy. The forest-products industry is getting worried. It sees the competition out there in the woods. A lot of foresters already feel that the energy harvest is getting out of hand; that maybe, instead of resulting in timber-stand improvement, it could turn right into a wholesale butchering job." And how did methanol fit into the picture, I asked. Meadows was standing nearby, and he fielded the question. "Methanol derived from coal, yes," he said. "But from the forest? What a crummy thing to do."

Once upon a time, the signs at the service stations called it gasohol. Actually it was gasoline, with a dollop of ethanol blended in to stretch the fossil stuff just a bit farther. Ethanol is an alcohol fuel made from corn or other grains. There is much confusion about its future, and though farm-state people tend to stand four-square in its favor, the Department of Agriculture seems to have no clear policy as to just how far it would like to see this synfuel go. As for the Department of Energy, why beat a dead horse?

There is somewhat less enthusiasm, and considerably more confusion, about the future of methanol, or methyl alcohol. Methanol is a volatile liquid used primarily as a chemical feed-stock for solvents and synthetic resins. Dry-gas is basically a methanol product, as is formaldehyde. For the most part, methanol is extracted from natural gas by a catalytic conversion process, but it may also be produced from such carbonaceous materials as coal or wood. Methanol conversion from coal or wood is more energy-intensive than from natural gas. Still, who knows? Tomorrow is already full of surprises.

One surprise, given appropriate engine redesigns in the automotive field, could be that methanol will ultimately replace both ethanol and gasoline as a motor fuel. To be sure, in early tests, its properties played havoc with an engine: vapor lock, cold starts, corrosion of plastic and rubber parts with which it has contact. On the other hand, methanol has a high octane rating. It allows for an advantageous compression ratio. It holds the potential to deliver, if not more miles-per-gallon than gasoline, more BTUs-per-mile at lower cost. And thus, a better performance.

But if there is to be a methanol fuel in our future, will it come from the coalfields, as Dennis Meadows and many others would prefer, or from the forest? No one has the answer, although some wood-energy advocates point out that, over the next twenty years, the uses of coal are likely to be even more intense and competitive than the uses of wood. In which case, most of the methanol will come out of the forest.

In New England there has been much talk of producing methanol from forest biomass. New England has no coal to speak of; and when the cars start queuing up again at the gasoline pumps in tribute to the mysterious laws of supply and demand, somehow the lines in Boston and Providence will seem longer than those of towns west and south. So the idea of methanol begins to sound very attractive indeed, although, for all the talk, there has been little action.

The New Hampshire Governor's Council on Energy commissioned a wood-methanol study some time ago that would seem to put that kind of fuel, and that kind of use of the forest, on the back burner for a while yet. Conducted by the Concord consulting firm of Whittemore-Abelson Associates, and a panel of experts on resource issues, the study suggested that New Hampshire was not ready to encourage methanol production from wood. Such was the state-of-the-art, some panelists felt it would displace less oil than if the same amount of wood were used in direct combustion for space heating. Moreover, with ethanol out in front at the time, the market for methanol was unknown. Also unknown was the amount of biomass available in New Hampshire for conversion to liquid fuel. Nonetheless, the study concluded that it was "quite possible under circumstances of a national crisis, or of an improvement in methanol and wood harvesting technology, that methanol may be identified as a high-priority forest resource product." In such an event, "the State should be prepared to commit substantial financial, social, environmental, and/or other resources in support of methanol development."

Colin High, who served on the Whittemore-Abelson panel and who conducted some methanol investigations of his own for the Resource Policy Center, told me he believes that the technological problems will soon be solved. "What bothers me," he said, "are the resource problems. If we should ever try to make deep inroads on gasoline with wood-based methanol, it's going to place a tremendous strain on the forest." I asked High if he believed the oil companies might ultimately become involved in methanol, once the new fuel had found its market. He smiled at the question—a sad kind of smile, I felt—and said, "It's unlikely they'll be kept out of it. They control the infrastructure."

It occurs to me that many people who espouse the environmental cause nowadays suffer from sylvan schizophrenia. They have this split personality in the presence of trees, and about who, if anyone, should cut them down, and for what purpose. For the most part, these people live in wood houses. They read books and magazines made of wood fiber. In parts of the country, such as New England, they warm themselves with wood as well. Yet if you ask them what is the greatest institutional adversary of the environment (after Big Oil, naturally), they are likely to tell you that it is the "Timber Beast," better known in polite circles as the U.S. forest-products industry. Such a puzzlement is best explained by Jerome F. Saeman, adjunct professor at the University of Wisconsin and research scientist retired from the Forest Products Laboratory at Madison. "All kinds of people who used to cry and weep when the trees came down for lumber," he says, "now stand by and cheer the chain saws come to feed the inefficient woodstove. It's hard for some people to hold two ideas in their heads at the same time."

Whatever the cranial capacity of New Englanders, the incidence of sylvan schizophrenia among them is certain to increase dramatically in the years ahead as the industry trudges home to where it started, two long centuries ago, in the Yankee Forest. It will be a closing of the great circle cut: first trending out of Maine, across New York, into the pinewoods of Michigan and Wisconsin, then west to the rain forests of the Pacific Northwest, and backwards, to Dixie. It might have held fast there into the next century if a number of things hadn't happened along the way. For example, if some of the timber companies hadn't overcut their own virgin lands in the West, and if their second-growth super-trees hadn't taken so much longer than expected, growing; and if this, in turn, hadn't forced industry to risk overcutting in the South; and, finally, if hardwood puckerbrush—species and grades of timber once thought unmerchantable—hadn't suddenly become attractive material for a whole new line of reconstituted wood products. But these things *did* happen. And because they did (among other factors too complex to explore here), the industry is about to discover a great truth: What Thomas Wolfe once observed of personal homecoming need not apply to all institutions. The forest-products industry not only can and will go home again. It *must*.

To be sure, hard times in general and a high-interest housing slump (circa 1981) helped to slow the industry's reluctant way home. Dozens of mills have shut down, mostly out West. According to one report in the *Wall Street Journal,* forest-industry jobs in the Northwest are expected to decline by 45 percent over the next twenty years—not just because of the sagging vicissitudes of economics; because of the hole in the available resource. By the mid-1990s, barring total economic standstill, removals on all commercial forestland nationwide are expected to exceed the net growth, which would put sustained yield, in practice, down the drain. The old-growth nationwide, those venerable sawtimber trees which we shall never see again except in wilderness, may be gone even sooner. So then what? For products, do we do without wood? Not by a long shot. For products, or at least for an increasing number and variety of them, we do it with puckerbrush.

The technology to do it with puckerbrush is available, both in the woods, with whole-tree chipping, and at the mill. With new blending processes, pulpwood operators are turning increasingly to hardwoods for part of the paper-making brew. With sawtimber scarce, mills are beginning to shift from lumber and veneer to the production of particleboards and oriented-strand fiberboard; and as time goes on, the new products will serve their purpose as well as the old. Some already serve it better.

There are those who say that New England has no place beyond its present one in the larger future of the forest-products industry; who say that this land of the small woodlot cannot possibly serve the long-range needs of a Weyerhaeuser or a Boise-Cascade. Yet Weyerhaeuser for several years now has had a real estate team looking to buy land in Maine. Boise-Cascade has been poking around in the Yankee puckerbrush, too. James River Corporation of Virginia has already claimed a big stake in New Hampshire. And for all the talk of a Sunbelt ascendancy and a Snowbelt decline, the fact remains that the Snowbelt embraces a forest that has hardly been touched for seventy-five years. New England, after all, is still a substantial marketplace. To move spruce boards from Oregon, or pine from Georgia, to market in woodsy New England consumes a good bit of energy. Trying to hold two ideas in the head at the same time, one tends to forget that nearly all of that energy comes from oil.

So it boils down once again to BTUs. And I hear the Bangor forester, Lester DeCoster, saying: "The forest-products industry is plenty worried that while this housing slump is holding forth, a huge chunk of the forest—a chunk it is going to need when the slump ends—will have been allocated to energy. There's a saying that oil is too valuable to burn, let's make things out of it instead. Well, that saying may soon enough apply to wood."

Perhaps it should apply already. Steel floor joists require fifty times more energy to manufacture than joists made of wood. Aluminum siding eats up twenty times more BTUs than its fiber counterpart. For energy intensity, bricks beat boards and shingles twenty-five to one. Not that the forest-products industry isn't itself fairly energy-intensive. It is said to consume nearly 5 percent of the nation's energy budget. But more and more nowadays, less and less of this industry's fuel is fossil. In fact, nationwide, the forest industry is close to 50 percent energy self-sufficient, cooking its own waste.

A while back I poked into Maine and stopped at the Scott Paper Company's Somerset pulp mill near Skowhegan. Somerset produces bleached Kraft pulp, about eight hundred tons a day, for the manufacture of Scott tissue products and S. D. Warren papers. The raw material is good old-fashioned Down Maine puckerbrush, one-third hardwood. It is a big operation, a $230 million plant, and its digester tower is said to be the tallest building in all of Maine. But I did not stop at Somerset to gawk at a skyscraper. I went there because 80 percent of Somerset's energy comes from burning its own wood waste, bark and lignin mostly, and because the capacity of its steam-turbine generator is such that, after supplying all of the plant's electric needs, there is an annual surplus of twenty million kilowatts available for sale to the electric utility that serves the public of central Maine. Co-generation. Two ideas in the same head at the same time. And it works.

Charles Cheeseman, manager of process systems and planning, said that about the only significant use of oil was to fire the kiln that processes lime in the chemical-recovery system. He said the next step was to move from 80 to 95 percent self-sufficiency. "With planned add-ons," he explained, "we'll increase the mix of bark in the hog fuel furnace and knock down oil consumption by 70,000 barrels a year. Right now we burn about 230,000 tons of bark. For every ton burned, we save a barrel of oil."

Two ideas were bouncing around inside my head as I drove away from Somerset. One idea had come to me courtesy of Charles Hewett, the wood-availability analyst on Dennis Meadows's team at Dartmouth. Hewett had once told a gathering of biomass-energy devotees that "wood-energy programs capitalizing on the expertise of the forest-products industry will be far more successful than programs which pit the established industry against newcomers to the use of wood." And that made me think of the Burlington Electric Department, which led to the second idea, courtesy of William Burch, a professor at the Yale School of Forestry and Environmental Studies. In a paper on "the Social Meaning of Forests," Burch had commented wryly on the prospect of burning a mature birch or maple forest solely "to fuel another night of Monday Football or Masterpiece Theatre." And that, he decided, would be shameful—nothing less than "the moral equivalent of firing up antique Chippendale furniture to toast a marshmallow."

Anyone who has spent some time pondering upon it, and who has room in the cranium for at least two ideas at the same time, can come up with a scenario for the Yankee Forest—a Preferred Case or a Worst, computer modeled or cast in concrete polemics. And why not? There are so many people out there already on the limbs of their own trees. What's wrong with one more? Here we go. Pessimistically at first, as I belong to the calling for which is best news is bad news; and because I believe that restraint is not yet a quality Americans feel comfortable with, not even in uptight New England. I mean the wood is *there,* and, one way or another, people are going to use it. Though not for long in woodstoves. I see no Jotuls and woodpiles in my crystal ball. I see retrofitted furnaces and piles of wood pellets—these little hard-packed balls of fiber, like rabbit turds, home-delivered much as oil is today, and burning hot as coal at half the price. Yes, and I see Burlington Electric turning chips into megawatts, and assorted other industries co-generating steam from wood, and timber technicians in the cabs of their machines no longer bothering to yell *"Timber!"* because the boles are so small, like matchsticks. And I see oilmen in the puckerbrush, smelling of methyl alcohol. And finally, I see the bare hills of New England bleeding away their nutrients through the granite stitches of the old stone walls. A warm, clean, well-lighted place, this New England. Though not very pretty.

And how pretty it can be when the hills are iridescent under maples in October, white-pine gothic against December snow, or lush in the fragrance of resinous summer. Prettiness is what most of the people take from the forest most of the time. Not logs and chips, board feet and BTUs. Yet amenity has this way of getting lost among the shuffling scenarios, as though it had no function or value, unmeasured and therefore immeasurable. Sure, and one can count the tourist dollars, the days afield, the miles of trails. But how does one tally up birdsong, or the texture of a dew-scrubbed fern? And who can begin to guess how much wild, unmanaged forest will be sufficient to fuel the stoves of the human spirit through the immeasurable rotations to come?

I remember wondering about such things, once in resinous June. I had dropped by Dartmouth College to call on the Gang of Four: Meadows, Hewett, Glidden, and High. Meadows and High were abroad somewhere following a beam of their social radar, so Hewett, Glidden, and I passed the afternoon with a causal loop or two, then hit out for the hills of Vermont, where Hewett had rented a cabin off a rutted one-track road. Hewett felt so much at home there, he had bought the fifty acres across the road from the cabin and planned to build his own place someday on a knoll where birch woods edge against open field. The sun was still above the hills. Glidden thought it might be worth our while to stretch the legs. And we did that.

We strolled through the tall grass of the landlord's field, climbed over a tumbledown wall, and came presently to a shelf of exposed ledgerock. A farmhouse and a barn had stood here once, all fallen down now, like the wall; hardly a trace but for foundations. Hewett said: "Practical people, those days. They built up here on the ledge because nothing would grow on it anyway." Beyond the ledgerock, white pine had invaded the field, and ferns of one kind or another; and then we were standing among ancient maples, and here were the ruins of a sugaring shed, and rusted buckets and boiling pans gone green with the years. An aspen had sprouted through the bottom of one of the buckets. Hewett pushed on.

At the top of a hill we entered a grove of old-growth hemlock—how did the loggers miss these?—and watched fractured golden light slanting among the tree trunks in such a way that one could stretch the mind and almost see a cathedral here in the forest, a nave with fluted pillars and needle-duff pews. Then the hill fell away steeply toward the road, and we went down skidding from scrawny poplar to slender ash—"Good stuff for chipping," said Glidden, "if you could get the equipment in here to do it." But you couldn't. And then we came to another stone wall, this one running straight through the woods, though once upon a time it had probably lined the edge of a pasture. "I wonder how many thousand miles of walls like these there are in New England?" Hewett said. "And I wonder," said Glidden, "how many million sweaty man-hours went into building them?"

We crossed the road and came at last to Hewett's knoll. He said he would face his house toward the field, to take advantage of the sunny exposure. He said he wanted to clear out some of the pioneer brush in the field, and maybe graze sheep on it, and raise some Christmas trees for income down at the far end. And I thought to myself: Hewett, if you do all of this, build the house on the knoll since you can't grow anything on it anyway, and run sheep in the field, and take your logs for the stove from the surrounding woods, then, in a sense, you will be closing some kind of circle yourself. And good luck to you, doing it.

The sun was sinking fast, redballing down the dark hills. I wished it luck, too, the sun, if only for growing things and for keeping folks warmer in winter, and for giving a bit more of itself in the solar times ahead. Hurry back, sun. The carbonaceous clocks are winding down just when we need you.

At the edge of the one-track road, with Hewett and Glidden gone ahead, I stopped and turned toward a faraway sound. It came suddenly from beyond the hills, somewhere out toward the sundown, a hard, rasping, low-pitched screech from the forest. It went *brap-brrrp-braapp* at first. And stopped. And started again. *Brrrrrap. Brrrraaap.* Now again, *brrraaaaaaaaaaaap.* Now steadily, like a one-note bugler warming up in the woods, for Taps.

YANKEE FOREST FOR SALE:

BY THE ACRE (1989)

I t seemed very clear not so long ago that the forest was here
to stay. That was the assumption. The forest was thought
to be Not-for-Sale. Besides, who but a lumberman would
want it? It was too big, too remote, too cold in the winter and
pestiferous after the ice went out of the spruce bogs. It was so
firmly clasped in the strong hands of a few good corporate
owners and familial stewards that the Appalachians might crum-
ble, Mount Katahdin would tumble before any market force or
migrating crowd could make a dent in the North Woods of New
England and upper New York State. Sure, there would be a taking of timber here and there, for that was part of the idea; that
was what helped keep the forest in reliable hands and many of its
scattered blue-collar denizens in groceries. And sure, despite the
scratchy edges that came with the territory and the long hours in
transit on two-lane roads, hundreds of thousand of outlanders
would flock each year to the Big North to partake of some of the
things the country had to offer, such as hiking and camping and
hunting and fishing and skiing and paddling and getting away
from it all. This was expected, that outlanders would come for a
fling with the woods, and then go home again. Making no dents.

Understand that this North of which we speak is not the nether coast of Maine or the ski-bunny slopes of New Hampshire's White and Vermont's Green Mountains or the spas of the Adirondack foothills, but a place of land and water beyond all that, as far north as you can get without trespassing into Canada. To measure the region properly, take out a map and put down your pencil somewhere down east of Bangor, Maine, and then squiggle a line west along U. S. Highway 2, past Skowhegan and Rumford, across New Hampshire in the winter shadow of the Presidential Range, across the Connecticut River into Vermont's Northeast Kingdom, then northwesterly until the pencil splashes into Lake Champlain near St. Albans Bay. Across that lake, in New York State, pick up the boundary of the Adirondack Park and follow it clockwise to a little town called Hinckley; then, taking care to include that great empty space that is known as Tug Hill, strike out for Lake Ontario near Oswego. And there you have it. Everything between that pencil line and Canada—three-quarters of Maine, a fifth of New Hampshire and Vermont, a third of New York, and thirty million acres all told, a forest the size of thirteen Yellowstone National Parks—is the Big North.

And it all seemed secure until, one British knight ago, something happened. In fact, a number of things happened that would throw the old verities right out the window, for now it could no longer be supposed that the hands of those big landowners were as steady as one would like them to be, or that blocks of the North would never be offered for sale. And it could no longer be said that the outlanders would have their fling with the forest and then go home again, for now they could buy right into the North, actually *possess* their very own piece of it. And if they could do that, they'd be damned if they'd go home again. They were here to stay.

Surely the most critical thing that happened was this: In 1982, a British takeover wizard named James Goldsmith (*Sir* James, if you please) acquired one of the region's timber giants, Diamond International of safety-match fame, and quietly proceeded to dismember the company and reshuffle its assets, reportedly making himself a 200 percent profit in two years. Diamond's holdings included more than a million acres of timberlands strung across the four-state bosom of the Big North and, by and by, some of these lands were packaged for resale. Speculators rushed to obtain them for the burgeoning market in wilderness ranchettes. Suddenly, the North was beginning to look more valuable for growing mortgages than trees.

In response to this threat to the status quo, the governors of the affected states were compelled to search for a way to hold the line. Even as you read this, their best people are looking for solutions. If you have never poked into the Big North yourself, seen it up close without leaving dents, you'd better have a poke before it's too late. I mean, what if the Big North is sold off before the governor's people find what they're looking for?

It wasn't too long ago that I took a poke at the Big North myself, picked up that pencil line in western Maine and followed it across to Lake Champlain; headed into the Adirondacks too. I saw a forest unlike any other on the planet, a meeting place where broadleaved deciduous types from farther south encounter pointy-top conifers from up north. Some people who take their forest provinces seriously call it the spruce-northern hardwoods community, while others parse it with different labels. By whatever name, the trees of the Big North appear in alternating patches of deciduous, coniferous, and mixed types: sugar maple and beech, yellow birch, paper birch, white ash and basswood, aspen coming up in some cutover places, black spruce and white cedar in the swamps, red spruce on the mid-slopes and balsam fir higher up, tongues of white pine and hemlock sneaking up the river valleys from the south. Way to the north, in farthest Maine, all hardwoods but the paper birch start to play out, so that you are left by and large with spruce and fir. That's *another* forest, the boreal one.

If you are in the business of growing trees in order to cut them down, and are in a hurry to bank the proceeds from the sale of the logs, the pulp, or the lumber, there are better places to be than the Big North. Trees grow much faster in Dixie; down there, you can get at least two rotations, or harvests, to a human lifetime. In the Pacific Northwest, the trees grow bigger, and just one rotation of sawlogs (often exported) is enough to keep you smiling all the way home from the bank. But the thin soils and long winters of the Big North won't permit that sort of growth. Harvest a fine strapping specimen today, and you'd better have patience. Its replacement won't be fine and strapping for sixty years.

But hold on, now. Tell the kids to stick around. This fiber here may take its own sweet time growing, but when it gets there, it's prime material. The spruce makes some of the highest-quality printing papers in the world. The hardwoods have a hundred applications—furniture and paneling and tool handles and . . .

"You just can't beat these northern hardwoods," Edward Johnston is telling me in Augusta, Maine. Johnston is director of the Maine Forest Products Council. He says: "We have one of the largest dowel manufacturers in the world, right here in Maine. Flexible Flyers—remember when you were a kid?—made right here in Maine. Number One maker of wooden clothespins. Number One for tongue depressors, say "*Aaaagh.*" Number One in the world for wood toothpicks. We have so much, so *much*. It's a real good opportunity for the landowner to practice good forest management, because he has all these markets."

For better or worse, landowners with sizable tracts in the Big North do tend to practice forest management of one kind or another. Of the region's thirty million acres, more than a third are owned by corporations prominent in the forest-products industries. Most of this land lies in Maine, the nation's most-forested state (89 percent of the landmass), where some two million acres are held by Great Northern Paper Company, one million by International Paper, and nearly six million in aggregate by such woodland giants as Boise Cascade, Champion International, Georgia-Pacific, and Scott Paper, among others. Private nonindustrial forestlands (large family or "club" holdings and active tree farms of substantial size) comprise another 35 percent or so of the Big North's pie and, along with the corporate holdings, help to fill out the checkerboard of the region's working landscape.

And a hardworking landscape it is at that. Forest products in Maine, New Hampshire, and Vermont account for at least a quarter of the total value of all manufactured goods shipped from those states, and for an employment base commanding a full fifth of the region's manufacturing payroll. In some northern precincts, the economic importance of the forest is even greater. In Penobscot County, Maine, for example, woods or mill work accounts for one out of every two jobs.

The remainder of the territory falls under either the rubric of public lands (about 11 percent of the regional total) or of private holdings so small and fragmented they could hardly be counted working parts of the whole. Most of the public lands are to be found in New York's 2.5-million-acre Adirondack Forest Preserve and in Maine's 670,000-acre state-owned domain. A few state parks and forests, tiny by Adirondack standards, are sprinkled across the topsides of New Hampshire and Vermont. As for the presence of Uncle Sam in the Big North, it hardly counts— one small lobe of the White Mountain National Forest in New Hampshire and a couple of national wildlife refuges in Maine and Vermont. The gulf between this shortage of public forest and the vast holdings of the timber companies accounts in part for the positive image the forest industry enjoys in New England. Where there are national parks and forests galore, as in the Northwest, people can afford to complain of clearcuts on the corporate lands. But in the East, the cuts are less visible, and the corporate lands are needed and enjoyed as de facto public playgrounds.

There is one more presence in the North that must not be discounted, though it owns no land itself. This one stands offstage, in the wings, prompting, sometimes even interrupting, the players who *do* own land, and the largest blocks of it at that. The presence is Wall Street.

In a report for The Fund for New England on emerging threats to the character of the North Country, economist Perry Hagenstein warned in 1987 that the national forest-products firms are under greater pressure to-day to rationalize their investments than at any time in the past two or three decades. A kind of mob psychology rules securities analysts, who in turn put pressure on corporate leaders. The theme in the forest-products industry now is "asset management." Although they are under pressure, forest-products firms have not wholly abandoned the idea that timber growing is profitable. But their commitment to continued ownership of large tracts does not extend to keeping their ownerships just as they are. Sale or development of separated tracts and of tracts with especially high recreation and development values are increasingly likely.

According to Hagenstein, the larger forest holdings in northern New England are now viewed as "profit centers" by their corporate owners. The lands, in effect, are expected to earn their keep. Trouble is, many of the forest companies with a stake in the Big North also have substantial holdings in the South or the West, or both, where timber values are relatively more attractive and therefore likelier to be enhanced by investments in timber-stand-improvement programs. Given these circumstances, the northern profit centers might appear to be out in the cold. And they would be, too, except that, when it comes to recreation and development values, the Big North clearly has it all over the West and the South. These woods are within a day's drive of forty million people in the northeastern U.S. and metropolitan Canada. "It is the difference between the value of this land for growing timber," Hagenstein writes, "and its value for recreation and development that leads owners to consider selling."

And of course, in the forest industry nowadays as in any other business, the corporation that fails to manage its assets for maximum short-term profit risks the corporate raid. For a western example, witness the unfriendly takeover a few years back in which the Maxxam Group Inc. gobbled up a California company, Pacific Lumber, and then proceeded to liquidate its trees. By the rules of the game that is now played on Wall Street, Pacific had perhaps shown too much interest in sustained yields and not enough in cash-'n'-carry clearcuts. Now the fear in the Northeast is that some of the forest companies may decide to cash in on subdivisions and jump into the business of liquidating land. On Wall Street, the analysts already are wondering, "*After Diamond, who's next?*"

Mollie Beattie is one of those people on whom the governors of the North Country are counting to find a way to hold the line. Beattie would seem to be a good one to count on, because she is savvy and articulate and has served as the commissioner of the Vermont Department of Forests, Parks, and Recreation. In my travels to the edge of the Big North, I sat one evening across a table from Beattie in Montpelier and we talked about the timber economy in Vermont's remote Northeast Kingdom and to what extent it might someday be supplanted by the kind of tourism that seemed to be rolling over the hills and hollows southward.

"I'd hope we could have both timber and tourism," Beattie said. "But not the junky kind of tourism. We have to try something else, a kind of tourism in which the tourists know where they are and understand what's happening around them, a kind in which the people aren't just passing through the landscape." Tree farms in Vermont like dude ranches in the West? Why not, she said. "We're not talking about replacing the forest economy. We're talking about *maintaining* it. Because, you know what? It has a value of its own. It deserves to be maintained for its own sake."

Heading over Beatties's way, I had detoured off my pencil-line route to look at some of the romper-room developments in the touristed precincts of the Granite State, and to call on her colleague Paul Bofinger, who is president of the Society for the Protection of New Hampshire Forests and whose vision of the North is much like Beattie's. Bofinger had spoken of the need to preserve the country's character.

"It's not just the trees," he said. "It's not just the pretty scenery and the flowing waters. The character I'm speaking of is a way of life—the people in their checkered shirts and their boots and their pickup trucks. You know what I mean. We have to preserve that. We don't want to bring in a lot of conventional tourist facilities and put those people to work as chambermaids for minimum wage. We've done enough of that, other places, right? Let's face it. What we have here is a wonderful wood resource, and to preserve the character of the North Country we have to learn how to use it better. We have to create the markets and jobs right here to protect that way of life."

Access to the Big North is the interstate highway that was only a dotted line on the map just a few years ago. Now it's four lanes, siphoning traffic out of the cities of Down Below, halving the travel time between the crowded coast and the remote Canadian border. Good-bye, Manhattan; hello, Memphremagog! Access is New York's Northway, the Maine Turnpike, I-89 and I-91 and I-93 and I-95. Good-bye, Boston; hello, Mattawamkeag, Molunkus, and Macwahoc. Access is also that loggging road off the main drag, maybe ten thousand miles of logging roads that have been built in Maine alone just in the past twenty years.

Excess, alas, is sometimes the product of access, as in Lincoln, New Hampshire, down in the North that's already used up. Lincoln is the town over which old-timers shake their heads so sadly, the kind of town we shall someday see in the *Big* North, if we don't behave.

I was last in Lincoln in 1982. It was a quiet little place then, though I-93 had already arrived (Boston: 2 1/2 hours). There was this sandwich shop with flowers in a window box and the Kancamagus Highway winding off toward the Pemigewasset Wilderness and Passaconaway. Now it is the discontented winter of 1989 and I see a different sort of place. I see *Condominiums*! I see *Luxury Townhouses*! I see Cinemas Four and The Depot and Mansion Hill and Star Ridge and The Village at Loon Mountain and The Nordic Inn. I see 8-by-24-foot privacy decks and cable hookups and six-panel solid pine doors and outdoor private-storage ski lockers and raised brick hearths and panoramic mountain views. Or so it says right here in the fancy brochure.

Is this what's in store for Mattawamkeag, Molunkus, and

Macwahoc? Will the new arrivals who inhabit these places in Lincoln (weekends and vacations only) wake up some morning and notice that their panoramic views are getting cluttered with other people's condominiums? Then what? Time to move on, to replay the great American folk migration, only this time toward a manifest destiny that lies not in the West, but in the North? If so, then who shall our Horace Greeley be, to point the young men in the proper direction?

One candidate is Harry S. Patten, head of the Patten Corporation of Stamford, Vermont, with branch offices in every convenient marketplace of the Big North and beyond, with classified ads appearing regularly in almost every metropolitan newspaper in the Northeast. Wilderness for sale. Trout streams. Lakefronts. Unspoiled acreage "overpopulated with big game." (Let's put this one in *Field & Stream*, someone must have said, so they did that.) Panoramic mountain views (there it is again). Financing available. Call now for your appointment.

It wasn't too long before the attorneys general of several northeastern states were calling Patten for *their* appointments. They spoke of consumer fraud complaints involving hundreds of lots purchased from Patten in Maine, New Hampshire, Vermont, and New York. They wanted to know if Patten representatives had possibly failed to disclose all the facts. They wanted to know, for example, if prospective buyers had been subjected to "bait and switch" scams—the come-on ads promising one thing, the real item delivering something less. They wanted to know if Patten Corporation might voluntarily enter into what attorneys general like to call a dispute-resolution procedure, but which is actually a kind of settlement of claims. The final dispositions could eventually cost Patten $2 million. Or more.

I am sitting now in the salesroom of Patten Adirondacks, at the edge of the Village of Lake Placid. I am speaking with Jim La Valley, who is vice-president for acquisitions, and Thomas Goss, the company's new regional president, who is right off the boat, as it were, from Patten's Gulf-Atlantic operation in Lake City, Florida, the state where land sharking first got its carnivorous reputation. "Look," Goss is saying, "people call us developers. That's not true."

La Valley says, "What we buy is how we sell it, divided only."

Goss says, "We are marketers. That's what we do. We go out and prepare a package of land for the market."

So far, the packaging has wrapped up about fourteen thousand acres in the Adirondacks alone. Neither La Valley nor Goss was willing to tell me what the net proceeds might be from all this activity; sources less beholden to Patten headquarters estimate the company clears a 25 percent profit on every sale.

One of the most intriguing packages the Patten folks have prepared for their Adirondack market is a 1,900-acre tract in Lewis County with a potential, under rural-use zoning restrictions, for 235 building lots. But Patten sees a different sort of buyer for this back-country spread, a sort with the desire and the disposable income to get away from it all. Consequently, the Lewis tract is to be subdivided into only 11 lots, ranging in size from 30 to 393 acres, each restricted by deed covenant to the placement of one "rustic cabin" not to exceed 800 square feet and to be used "primarily for hunting, fishing, and camping" on a "seasonal" basis only.

Good grief, you say. Could this be Patten, or a subdivision conceived in Heaven by John Muir?

Watch it, I hear someone saying down the road a piece from patten's office. It is Mike DiNunzio, the forester who troubleshoots in matter of land use for the Adirondack Council, a coalition of nonprofit conservation groups. "Sure, 11 lots beat 235. But the real problem is enforcing the restrictions. As the generations flow, there is more and more tendency for the landowner to say, 'Well, we don't need to do *that*,' and so in little ways the covenants get compromised. Besides, that's wild country. I don't know how 'rustic' you can keep it when you have to build roads where there were no roads before, where suddenly you have dogs and cats and electric lights and snowplows in the winter."

And down the road another piece, at the office of the regulatory Adirondack Park Agency in Ray Brook, I hear Chairman

Woody Cole saying, "As values continue to escalate, we're going to end up with smaller lots on all these so-called large lots. People will simply go to court and seek to break the covenants. So here is Patten with these rustic hunting lodges. The way it's going, we just might wind up with more hunting lodges in the Adirondacks than there are hunters."

The idea of "hunters" buying retreats in the wilderness amuses many critics of the Patten approach. They point out that the likelier buyer for a Patten-type offering is the upwardly mobile urban professional. Such people tend to be the sort who approve of neither hunting nor logging, among other consumptive uses. It is not at all uncommon for new arrivals to show their disapproval by posting their lands against any recreational entry whatsoever, and closing their minds to the thought that it might be okay to cut down a few trees. Thus, a change in the ownership alters the character of the country: Private land heretofore available for recreation (especially if it was corporate forestland) is suddenly withdrawn from public use and timberland once counted part of the working landscape is snatched from the local economic base.

Patten, of course, is not the only Big Operator in the Adirondacks. For a time, and up-and-comer appeared to be the flamboyant New Jersey businessman Roger Jakubowski, billed in the press as the "Titan of Tilt," for his string of pinball and video arcades on the boardwalk at Atlantic City, or the "Hot Dog King," for his chain of fast-food outlets. But there were other sobriquets for Jakubowski when, announcing that the only game with a name in the Adirondacks was *land*, he proceeded to buy up a ski mountain, a historic camp, an island in Lake Champlain, a veritable paradise of lakefront properties, and then, surveying the millions of public and private acres he had not yet acquired, declared: "I want it all!" Since then, Jakubowski has been keeping a lower profile, sitting on his assets, as it were, in well-wooded seclusion. He is said to be working to correct an image problem.

Walter Moore, New Hampshire's Outstanding Tree Farmer in 1988, lives outside Lancaster, New Hampshire, on the edge of what I have defined as the Big North. His is a fine place on the river road, a comfortable white frame farmhouse, a big red barn, 350 acres of woods, white pine and spruce and birch and ash and maple. Pine is the prize crop. It is cut selectively and sold to local mills for lumber. The birch and the ash go for veneer. Good prices for ash now, Moore says. Increasing demand, declining availability. Seven hundred dollars a thousand board feet, up from two hundred dollars just a few years ago. Prices for spruce and fir for pulp are up as well. "With prices like this," he says, "there's a strong temptation for some people to cut their land heavy and then sell it all. They're sure not going to pay taxes on it for the rest of their lives, waiting for the next rotation."

You planning to cut heavy and sell it all? I want to know. Moore smiles. "No sir. Oh, developers have been after us. One outfit made us a very big offer and just couldn't understand why we weren't interested. We've had letters from Patten, too, wanting to see if we'd sell. I just ignore them. But I can see how some people might be tempted, older people having trouble with their taxes. Five years ago, 'round here, you'd be doing good to get $200 an acre. Now, last I heard, Patten's offering $1,000." (Over in New York State, Dick Beamish of the Adirondack Council tells me how Patten operatives have been known to offer $1,000 "finder's fees" for tips leading to significant acquisitions. Beamish says: "They've got loggers lined up all over the Adirondacks, loggers who are out there and know the land and know who owns what and who owes what and where the easy pickings are. Those Patten people are out there knocking on every door in the mountains.")

I ask Walter Moore if there are any tree farms like his left in this lower corner of Coos County. "Down here," he says, "there aren't many farms of any kind left. You see, we're so close to the interstate, and you know what that means."

There are lessons to be learned almost everywhere along the edge of the Big North, and within it, for certain. Consider the disposition of the aforementioned Diamond International lands, those one million acres that would stir up the governors to get their people cracking on a way to hold the line.

It was Mud Time in the North Country, 1988, and the disposable Diamond lands with their trout streams and lakefronts and panoramic mountain views lay upon the auction block: 800,000 acres in Maine, 90,000 in New Hampshire and Vermont, and 96,000 in the Adirondacks of the Empire State. From time to time, for this piece or that, there were offers—the State of New York, the Nature Conservancy, the New Hampshire Retirement System. Rejected, no sale. Then the Vermont and New Hampshire lands were sold to Claude Rancourt of Rancourt Associates, Nashua, New Hampshire, operatives in the merchandising of condominiums and mobile homes. And then, a few months later, the Adirondack lands were sold to Henry A. Lassiter of Lassiter Properties, Inc., Atlanta, Georgia, buyers and sellers of the good earth. (Over time, Diamond's vast Maine acreage was sold as well; and though most of this land was acquired by other forest-products companies, at least one of the new owners has let it be known that it intends to resell certain properties that may be more valuable for growing mortgages than trees.)

By year's end, however, the situation with the former Diamond lands looked more promising. After months of intensive negotiations, conservationists and public officials in New York and New Hampshire had managed to "buy back" critical resource lands from both Lassiter and Rancourt. In New York, the salvage operation worked like this:

Initially, Diamond/Goldsmith interests had been asking $193 an acre. The state had offered $145. Lassiter had beat that easily with a bid of $177. Sold to the higher bidder. But New York could hardly afford to throw in the towel at that juncture. Tolerating threats to the integrity of the Adirondacks tends to be risky politics in the Empire State. Besides, as the Adirondack Council kept forcefully reminding Governor Mario Cuomo, some of the Diamond/Lassiter lands were pivotal in the Council's master plan for a proposed Great Wilderness north of Old Forge, and a Boreal Heritage Preserve north and west of Saranac Lake. Development now would scuttle those plans forever. So a buy-out was finally arranged: New York would purchase from Lassiter some 15,000 acres outright, acquire the development rights on 40,000 acres that would forever remain unbuilt on, open (for passive recreation), and a functional part of the working landscape. It was a deal all around, especially for Lassiter, who made a million-dollar profit without lifting a finger. In round numbers, New York was to pay the man from Atlanta $10 million, or an average of $194 per acre. Hardly anyone wanted to point out that, at $194 an acre, the Empire State, for lack of earlier fortitude, wound up paying $1 an acre in excess of the original asking price, but ended up without full fee-title to much of the acreage. No matter. Half a loaf is better than none.

In New Hampshire, the stakes were also high; the negotiations just as tricky. Here Rancourt held some 67,000 acres of the former Diamond estate. (There were 23,000 acres in Vermont as well; of these, the Nature Conservancy, on behalf of the state, would manage to salvage about 8,000.) Unable to buy up everything that Rancourt had acquired, New Hampshire soon narrowed its options to focus on the 40,000-acre Nash Stream watershed in Coos County, near Groveton, and about 5,000 other acres scattered about the territory, including a number of holdings in the White Mountain National Forest. To clinch the deal, the state and the federal government would share the costs: a Congressional appropriation of $5.25 million, engineered by Senator Warren Rudman, and $7.65 million in state funds from New Hampshire's Land Conservation Investment Program. A bridge loan arranged by the Nature Conservancy and the Society for the Protection of New Hampshire Forests glued the papers in place while the government's check was in the mail.

So what does it all add up to? In sum, a lot of money goes a little way in the Big North. Here (again in round numbers) we have a bit over 100,000 acres of former Diamond lands protected in three states at an aggregate cost of $25 million, or an average of $250 an acre. Let us suppose, then, that the states could pull out all the stops and go for something bigger, the biggest buy possible. For the sake of this exercise, let us allocate to the buying of the Big North the $35 million available in the Maine state treasury for land acquisitions (even though pressures to preserve the coastline are much stronger), the $20 million in New Hampshire's Land Conservation Investment Program, $15 million out of thin air in Vermont, and $100 million (let's not get greedy) out of New York's $250 million in available acquisition funds.

So let's say we now have $170 million to spend on the Big North. At $250 an acre, right? At $250 an acre, that buys us 680,000 acres. And that's a lot of territory, though nowhere near as much as Sir James Goldsmith took from Diamond International to resell shortly afterwards. So let's go to the federal government and get a matching grant (not bloodly likely in these deficit years), and now we have 1,340,000 acres. In short, less than 5 percent of the Big North.

What's to become of the rest of it? I mean, if the governors' best people can't find some better way to hold the line?

Burlington, Vermont, sits with its back to New England's North Country and its front door wide open to the Adirondack mountain view. In Burlington, at the U. S. Forest Service Experiment Station on Spear Street, the Governors' Task Force on Northern Forest Lands was in conference, assembled to develop strategies that might somehow protect the existing economy, recreational access and physiographic ambience of the Big North.

The task force served as the steering committee for a study by the U. S. Forest Service of the northern Forestlands—a study authorized by Congress in response to the Diamond dismemberment and similar bad news from the North. In addition to exploring protection strategies appropriate to the region, the task force's mission was to identify lands with critical natural and recreational resources, and, if possible, arrive at a common vision for the future of the Big North as well.

Across such a range of political geography—these are, after all, states well known for their feisty Yankee independence—common *anything* would seem an elusive goal. Yet here were the various delegates sitting around a table not only behaving themselves but actually beginning to make some sense of a difficult mission. "This may well be the most cooperation we've seen in New England since the Revolutionary War," said Carl H. Reidel, a director of the National Wildlife Federation, head of the University of Vermont's Environment Program, and possibly the region's most knowledgeable generalist in forest affairs.

At Burlington, the task force spent the day focusing on two related issues. The first was a need to develop some kind of incentive program to keep current forest landowners down on the tree farm, as it were, managing their woodlots in ways calculated to protect the long-term integrity and traditional uses of the land. The disincentives, of course, were easy to identify. Most of the delegates fingered the 1986 federal tax changes. "The hit from capital gains is going to kill you on a timber sale," Ed Johnston of Maine was saying during a recess. "The government used to take 60 percent of capital gains and exempt that from taxation, and tax you only on the 40 percent. Now the tax is on 100 percent of the gain. See, the trouble is, on timber now they treat you like you're Donald Trump or Ivan Boesky."

Federal estate taxes also hurt, in that heirs must pay taxes on 50 percent of the market value of inherited land. "Suppose the heirs don't have the cash that Uncle Sam is looking for," said Johnston. "They may have to sell half the land just to pay the estate tax."

There was general consensus, however, that any frontal assault on national tax policy would be doomed to failure, no matter how noble the cause. That led one of the Maine delegates, J. Mason Morfit of the Nature Conservancy, to wonder out loud if perhaps there might be some way to pursue a policy of "damage limitation"—limiting damage, that is, to the federal treasury by providing tax relief for forest landowners only in areas designated as having high priority, as in portions of the Big North— or all of it. The idea is that the loss of federal tax revenue would be offset by the economic, recreational, and ecological values inherent in a preserved status quo.

And *that* idea, finally, led to the principal topic of the day, which was, as one visitor put it, "How do you save 30 million acres without really buying them?" The answer was: *greenlining*.

Among Americans accustomed to having their "parks" laid out in tidy blocks of public land, the concept of greenlining takes some getting use to. As defined in a seminal document on the subject—Charles E. Little's 1975 report to the U. S. Senate Subcommittee on Parks and Recreation—a greenline park "would be a resource area containing a mix of public and private land which is comprehensively planned, regulated, and managed by an independent agency set up specifically to preserve [the area's] recreational, aesthetic, ecological, historic, and cultural values." Since distribution of the Little document, the number of greenlined areas in the United States has grown from one to five, including the Santa Monica Mountains National Recreation Area in California, the Columbia River Gorge National Scenic Area in Oregon and Washington, and Pinelands National Reserve in New Jersey. If a greenline is the sort of park that ain't what she used to be, the departure is clearly illustrated in the Pinelands, where two-thirds of the 1.1 million-acre reserve is privately owned and some 400,000 residents go on about the business of living and working in their seven counties and fifty-six municipalities. All this and some significant ecological and recreational rewards too: The Pinelands not only sustain a woodsy playground in metropolitan Philadelphia's backyard, they embrace the greatest freshwater aquifer on the Atlantic coastal plain.

The grandaddy of all greenlines, of course, is the great Adirondack Park, across Lake Champlain. At 6 million acres, the Adirondack Park is the largest single park in the Lower Forty-eight, the largest even if you throw out all its private lands, which embrace about 58 percent of the area, and count only the 2.5 million aces of public land that comprise the Adirondack Forest Preserve. The preserve lands, more or less checkerboarded among the private lands, have been protected as "forever wild" by the state constitution since 1895. The private lands within the park—or at least those that have not yet been Jakubowskified or Pattenized—are devoted to forestry, agriculture, and recreation, and, since 1973, have been regulated under the relatively tough restrictions of the Adirondack Park Land Use and Development Plan.

Originally, the state's idea was to acquire *all* the lands within the park, owners willing and funds available. But that was back in ragtime-and-parasol days. Now there is a growing sense that, except for some essential (and extensive) additions to the forest preserve, the integrity of the park and the character of the region might best be served by obtaining conservation easements on some of the private lands (as in the Diamond/Lassiter buy-back), strengthening land-use regulations along streamsides and lakefronts where development pressure is most severe, and moving to protect what has come to be known as "the view from the road"—hundreds of miles of forested roadside punctuated here and there with sudden, open, scenic views. "If the wind-shield visitor loses his view," Dick Beamish of the Adirondack Council told me, "we will start to lose our political base—the constituents who consistently have voted for the funds and reg-ulations we've needed to hold it all together. And if we lose those people, then we've lost the park."

So, as some of the task-force people in Burlington agreed, at least there was some kind of promising framework in place in *one* part of the Big North. But what of the other parts? What of the region's midsection, that stunningly beautiful reach of little mountains and lakes that sweeps from the Northeast Kingdom of Vermont across the top of New Hampshire to the Mahoosuc-Umbagog wildlands of western Maine? Paul Bofinger of New Hampshire's Forest Society envisions *this* as a greenline park, but how in the world could you move the three states to agree on the details?

And what about the idea of a Maine Woods Reserve that the Wilderness Society of Boston and Washington, D.C., was tout-ing so highly—2.7 million acres running from Moosehead Lake past Baxter State Park all the way to Carr Pond Mountain? Now there was some bold thinking—a greenline bigger even than the Adirondack Forest Preserve. Only trouble is, folks Down East don't much like taking advice from Boston and Washington,

D.C., or from an organization known not for any special commitment to the *working* landscape, but rather to the establishment of statutory uppercase-W Wilderness, where even chain saws are disallowed. But then, whoever said that saving the Big North would be simple?

It was getting late in Burlington, and a Friday afternoon at that. Meeting adjourned. Have a good weekend. That's what everyone else seemed to want to have. Already the northbound traffic was thickening up on I-89; I could picture it over on the Northway and I-91 and I-93 and I-95. Goodbye, Boston; hello, Memphremagog. And here they come. Here they come with the keys to the condo or the ad from the newspaper, all hell-for-leather toward their trout streams and lakefronts and picturesque mountain views, racing sundown to the back-country hideaway of their wildest dreams.

IN WILDNESS
WAS THE PRESERVATION
OF A SMILE

A lmost always there was a mountain beyond the windows of his world, a turret of rock rising above the forest, and on any one of those days he was likely to climb it. He would stride through the evergreen conifers to stand alone against the wind and the sky, and through *that* window he would see yet another mountain, and feel a surge of joy—of happiness—to know that there was one more untamed mountain left to climb. You see, he had been so dreadfully afraid, so sure that he had missed it all, born too late ever to taste the freedom of wilderness as, he imagined, Lewis and Clark had tasted it long ago in the wilder West. He tried to be rational about the deprivation. He allowed as how, had he been privileged to join that "most thrilling of all American explorations," he probably would have been "bumped off" by Indians or typhoid fever before he was twenty-five. So he created his own adventures, shared his happiness by writing of them, and attempted as best he could to hammer his personal philosophy into public policy. And died before he was forty, bumped off at sea level by a bad heart in a darkened berth on a midnight train to New York City. For all his miles afoot in the mountains, the least he deserved was a boots-on finish. Such are the perils of the century he sought to avoid, and, living in it, faced so squarely.

I would like to have known Robert Marshall. Known him not so much for his achievements as forester, explorer, author, and first president of the Wilderness Society as for some other credentials barely tangible between the lines of his short life. I would like to have known him for his laughter, his wit—humor being such a rare resource within the conservation community, though not so precious then as it is today. I would like to have shared just a bit of his affection for humanity, for unlike some of his wildwood peers and latter-day disciples, Bob Marshall probably loved men and women even more than he loved mountains and trees. And then there was this curious motive idea he had about wilderness, and why it should matter in the scheme of things. Curious, because the idea was so pure and simple it had not occurred to anyone else for quite a long time. The cult of cost-benefits had crept upon the Movement and suddenly overwhelmed it with facts. Not that Marshall was *against* facts. He adored facts. He kept lists of facts that might have stretched end-to-end from the Adirondacks to Anaktuvuk Pass. But to justify wilderness? No. How could one quantify adventure, or, more important, the perception of beauty? For Bob Marshall, the measure of wilderness flowed from his own experience in the mountains. He was not caught up, not entirely, in the need for gene pools and biological diversities, in looking for answers to questions he had not yet learned how to ask. He would have wilderness simply because it was *fun* to be there. It made people happy. In wildness was the preservation of a smile.

Had circumstance been kinder to him, he might have saved one of his face-splitting smiles for 1985—and two anniversaries for the price of one. His Wilderness Society turned fifty. His first mountains, the Adirondacks, beginning their second century under the protective aegis of the New York State Forest Preserve. A felicitous coincidence, that one event should follow fifty years exactly after the other; though perhaps not so coincidental, for it was in the Adirondack Preserve toward the end of the last century that the wilderness idea, the concept of "forever wild," found its first solid footing in America—and not without the help of another Marshall, Bob's father, Louis, the constitutional lawyer. So there was that, and there was the protected view from Louis Marshall's camp on Lower Saranac Lake. Robert arrived for his first season in the sun in the summer of 1901. He was six months old. The eyes needed a while to adjust to the distance. South from the boathouse across the blue water, the eyes in time would take him to the far shore, to the unbroken Adirondack forest, through cedars and hemlocks, through birch and spruce, on an upward pitch to the swayback summit of Ampersand. The first mountain.

A dirt road winds through the woods to the last low hill before you reach the lake. KNOLLWOOD, the sign said, back at the pavement that runs on to Saranac. Five hundred private acres surrounded by forever-wild lands. Six families, all of New York City, summering in six separate camps, though dining had once been communal, when Bob Marshall was here, in a spacious edifice called the Casino. As for *camp*—well, that is one of those words from the previous century. This camp, the Marshalls', completed in 1900, is three stories tall, sided with dark cedar shingles, trimmed with a shade of robust green, stoutly beamed with spruce logs still retaining their scaly octogenarian bark. A photograph—from that ragtime year of the San Francisco earthquake and the Madison Square murder of Harry K. Thaw—shows more or less of the same sitting-room scene. Elk head over stone fireplace, moose horn on one wall, caribou rack on the other, door and windows facing down toward the lake. Only the rustic furniture has changed over the years since this picture was taken. Only the furniture and, of course, most of the people.

Then, the young people of Knollwood were multitudinous. Of Marshalls there were four: James, the eldest; Ruth, or Pootie as the boys called her; Robert; and George, three years Bob's junior. None of them in those earliest years was in any great rush to ascend a mountain. It was enough just to climb up the knoll from the lakeshore, to explore the paths by the fish pond and the place called the Temple where sunlight (as George would remember it) filtered down through hemlock colonnades. And then, inevitably, they discovered the pathless woods. To a little boy like Bob, the forest of the Knollwood compound was a "mighty tract" in which, with diligence, one could occasionally "get beyond the sounds of civilization." Always, even after his most remote bushwhacks in the wilds of Idaho and Alaska, he would remember this lakeside country: "Real wilderness to me, as exciting in a different way as the unexplored continent which I had missed by my tardy birth."

And there were games with the other Knollwood children. There was Hounds & Hare (in which a Marshall was always the Hare because a Marshall always knew the woods better than any other child). There was Chingachcook (in which, with no apologies to Fenimore Cooper, one side would attempt to land its boat on the shore without being detected by the other). And there was a great deal of sandlot softball (at which, James even now will testify, "We Marshalls all batted .700 or better, except for Pootie, though she was by far the best of the girls. Softball at Knollwood—we loved that game." James believes "that game" started Bob keeping close count on everything. Before the miles and the mountains, he would tally the hits, runs, and errors.)

If Knollwood loomed large in shaping the early perceptions of the Marshall siblings, so did New York City, where they lived three-quarters of the year. Home was a brownstone on Manhattan's East 72nd Street, just a hop, skip, and a jump from Central Park. And what better guide for a stroll through the park than their father—Pop, Bob liked to call him—whose hobby was knowing trees. Louis Marshall: co-founder of the American Jewish Committee, head of the New York State Immigration Commission (*his* parents having immigrated from Germany a generation before), humanitarian and civil libertarian, frequent litigator before the United States Supreme Court, defender of minority rights. And had he not also been a vociferous defender of the Adirondack Forest Preserve and of Central Park, not to mention his serving as chairman of the board of trustees of the College of Forestry at Syracuse University, one might never have guessed that Louis Marshall loved trees almost as much as he loved people.

The children were enrolled at the Ethical Culture School off Central Park West. Louis assembled them every morning at 8:20 sharp at the door of the brownstone, and off they would go, down 72nd Street and across Fifth Avenue into Olmsted's greensward; past Pilgrim Hill and across The Mall to J.Q.A. Ward's bronze statue of the Indian hunter with stalking dog, and on to the Sheep Meadow and the West Side beyond. Along the way, Louis would often provide a running commentary. The subject was silviculture. He pointed out the Siberian elms and the Chinese cork trees, the Nordmann fir and the bald cypress and the copper beech. And just beyond the bronze of Daniel Webster, heading out toward the Women's Gate, was a double row of silver bell trees. They overhung the path, forming an arbor. In the spring of the year, Louis and his children found the blossoms a delight. And why not? When Springtime came, could Knollwood be far behind?

Always, there was something new to discover in those Knollwood summers. Even indoors on a rainy morning, in the charted precincts of the sitting room, there were things to fuel the imagination as one waited for the clouds to pass. The bookcase, for example. George Marshall would remember in particular the reddish-brown volumes "obscured in shadow" on the bottom shelf of the bookcase, and how one day Bob pulled them out and browsed the pages and became "enthralled" with the writing of Verplanck Colvin, the eccentric superintendent of the Adirondack Survey, whose topographic studies of those mountains in the 1870s and '80s had provided the essential rationale for the creation of a forest preserve. To a youth already enamored of the Adirondack woods, Colvin must have seemed a hero to match old Meriwether Lewis himself. Maybe even outmatch him, for Colvin wasn't some musty character of the long-ago-and-far-away; he was a contemporary of Pop, of his time and of his place. And the narratives! Good heavens, what dashing narratives of first ascents and precipitous scrambles among the lofty Adirondack crags. What powerful descriptions of gleaming waters and haughty crests and dread passes. And what magnificent places, lying just beyond the mountains across the lake—Skylight and Gothics and Ouluska, the Place of Shadows, and Tear-of-the-Clouds.

They began modestly, with Ampersand, in the summer of 1916—they being Bob, George, and Herbert Clark, the woods-savvy Adirondacker who had been guiding for Louis Marshall's family for a decade of summers and was fast becoming the boys' closest friend; Ampersand being that humble peak across the lake, not even 3,500 feet of elevation but affording good views northwest toward the pond country, and, about-face the other way, their very first spread-out breathtaking view of Colvin's High Peaks. Bob was fifteen that summer, full of plans for his future. His biggest plan was to become a forester. But that would have to wait awhile, so he decided to pursue an interim career with brother George and woodsman Clark. Together, they would become the premier peak-baggers of the Adirondacks. They would see it all, stand above it all. They would out-scramble Verplanck Colvin.

The Marshall & Clark Expeditions bagged their first trailless peak—and in those days, most Adirondack peaks *were* trailless—in the summer of 1917, then struck into higher country, 4,000 feet of loft or more, the following season. To limber up for Marcy, Algonquin, Whiteface, and Iroquois (first, second, fifth, and eighth, respectively, in order of Adirondack height), Bob and George circled Lower, Middle, and Upper Saranac lakes afoot—a one-day stroll of a mere 41 miles. "It took us 698 minutes," Bob wrote with characteristic precision in one of his record books. "Taking out the [time] spent in stops [and here the stop time is broken down into ten categories of diversion] . . . we covered the 41 miles in 613 minutes at the rate of a mile in 14 minutes and 57 seconds." Thus began Bob Marshall's extraordinary odometric account over the years of all his one-day hikes of 30 miles or more. There would be several hundred, more than sixty in the Adirondacks alone, a few running on incredibly to 60 miles or more. The man liked to walk.

The man liked to walk uphill. Consider the eleventh day of August 1920. Having packed in from Placid by way of Lake Colden, the Marshall & Clark party encamped at Panther Gorge, awakened in a heavy fog, eschewed a wringing of hands, and boldly set out to traverse the great range from Mount Haystack to Basin to Saddleback to Gothics and back again. Twenty linear miles and 9,200 feet of cumulative round-trip ascent. In one day. In nine hours and forty minutes, to be bobmarshall exact. Sighting not one other two-footed soul the whole way. Bidding adieu to the fog. Seeing Marcy "with a halo," as Bob would describe it in an article appearing, posthumously, in the 1942 annual of the Adirondack Mountain Club. Looking down from Basin into Panther Gorge and perceiving, with Colvinian hyperbole, "that fiercest of all the wild places among the great mountains, besides which the celebrated canyons of Colorado look tame." In one day, Bob shamelessly professed, for Westerners then as now had this tendency to pooh-pooh the topography of eastern places, they "climbed a fifth again as high as the climb up Pike's Peak from its base." The mental calculator refused to stop. Pike's Peak Plus wasn't good enough. After all, Bob felt obliged to note, for every foot of ascent there had to be a corresponding foot of going the other way. In one day, therefore, this Marshall & Clark Expedition had traveled "more than 3 ½ miles just up and down." It had been, as far as Bob was concerned, about the hardest, wildest, happiest day of his life.

To the happiness of that day and many others, Herb Clark no doubt was a great contributor. In the eyes of his mountain companions he was nothing less than a marvel—"the fastest man I have ever known in the pathless woods," wrote Bob. Clark "could take one glance at a mountain from some distant point, then not be able to see anything 200 feet from where he was walking for several hours, and emerge on the summit by what would almost always be the fastest and easiest route." Though such mountaineering prowess would later bring Herb Clark a measure of fame, he was better known at the time for his flatwater skills—a champion at the oars of an Adirondack guideboat, a man self-proclaimed to have been "born fishing." And a weaver of whimsy and tall tales. The way Herb told it to the Marshall boys, that dented rock in the Lower Saranac was where Captain Kidd had bumped his head. That stillwater pool in the West Branch Ausable was where the Monitor and the Merrimac had gunned the other down to the last round. There were spontaneous ditties and garbled songs and mythic folk such as Joe McGinnis, who came down with the "fantod" and thereby shrunk to the size of a baseball, not to mention Old Grandfather Pickerel, that elusive fish with the eyeglasses and a mouth full of gold-capped teeth. Onward, lads! To the next mountain.

By the end of the summer of 1922, there didn't seem to be any mountains left; none at least that might qualify as an Adirondack High Peak (*high* for the Marshalls starting at 4,000 feet). The expeditionary three, with time on their hands, took a straw poll of their favorite views from the summits of forty-two high peaks ascended. They ranked Haystack first (though third in elevation); Marcy ninth (though first in elevation); and the lowly Nye booby-prized at forty-second. Later measurements disqualified Nye and three other of the high forty-two as being short of 4,000 feet, but found four new ones as replacements. By then, Marshalls & Clark had already climbed them. They had done it all. No one else ever had. Not Verplanck Colvin. Not even Mountain Phelps, the most famous bushwhacker of all the old-time Adirondack guides. Eight of the Marshall & Clark climbs were first ascents. Had they been around to protest, Colvin and Phelps could have honestly claimed only seven.

Now, as for the Adirondacks, the only thing left for the Marshalls was to run up the score.

July 1930. A telegram from Bob and George Marshall, Knollwood, Saranac Lake, New York, to Newell Martin, Huntington, Long Island. The message:

Thanks to your inspiration and kindly interest, we, yesterday, climbed, in order, Marcy, Skylight, Haystack, Basin, Saddleback, Gothics, Armstrong, Upper Wolf Jaw, Lower Wolf Jaw, nine peaks, total ascent over 10,000 feet; but this does not approach in merit your six peaks record with five of them trail-less. Best wishes.

O, the gallant self-effacement of the mountaineering fraternity. Newell Martin had climbed Marcy and five other high peaks in one day in 1894; and, with tongue in cheek, had instructed his executors to carve upon his tombstone the inscription: "He held the Adirondack one-day record, six hills." And now, this. In a statement for *High Spots,* the journal of the Adirondack Mountain Club, Newell Martin would have to set the record straight. "In my [1894] excursion," he wrote, "I rode three miles in a wagon and four miles in a boat and had two guides to carry spare clothing and other luxuries. The Marshalls had the help of no wagon, no boat, and no guide." Herb Clark presumably had been AWL, absent-with-leave.

"The Marshall record should stand for another 36 years, till 1966," Newell Martin graciously predicted, though erroneously, for Bob Marshall, solo, would break it himself in 1932. Still, Martin could not let it go without another twist of the tongue in the cheek. Erosion, he noted, had been at work night and day on "those bleak mountain tops" for the thirty-six years since his own achievement. "They [were] lower, therefore, than they were when I climbed some of them in 1894."

If one were to consider the life of Robert Marshall without strict adherence to the rules of chronology, one might then find his ideas and accomplishments positioned upon three landscapes: the Adirondacks, Arctic Alaska, and Elsewhere, the latter representing the wilder forestlands of the Lower Forty-eight in general, and of the northern Rockies in particular. I do not expect that the subject himself would have minded much if we stretched this method of parsing his life to say that his ideas on wilderness, first shaped in the Adirondacks and later refined by experience in the Brooks Range of Alaska, found their best forum Elsewhere, in the middleground of his public career. This part is for Elsewhere.

But first, the pedigrees. Bachelor of Science, New York State College of Forestry, Syracuse, 1924. Master of Forestry, the Harvard Forest, Petersham, Massachusetts, 1925. Ph.D., the Laboratory of Plant Physiology, Johns Hopkins University, Baltimore, Maryland, 1930. Junior forester and assistant sil-viculturist, U.S. Forest Service Northern Rocky Mountain Forest Experiment Station, Missoula, Montana, 1925–1928. Director of Forestry, Office of Indian Affairs, U.S. Department of the Interior, Washington, D.C., 1933–1937. Thereafter Chief, Division of Recreation and Lands, U.S. Forest Service, Washington, D.C. And Elsewhere.

A letter from Bob Marshall in Montana to a friend in New York, dated March 10, 1926:

I received your letter after returning from a trip over Washington's birthday on which I walked 70 miles, 14 on snowshoes, in 48 hours. . . . I followed the route of Lewis and Clark up to Lolo Pass on the Bitterroot Divide. . . . There is a road within four miles of the pass, but in winter, with five feet of snow and a young blizzard howling along the divide, it didn't seem as if civilization was approaching very close. . . . On the Idaho side was a wilderness of thousands of square miles, unpenetrated by roads, uninhabited except transiently by a few trappers. . . . There was a great temptation to forget everything for a week and drop down to one of the trapper's cabins only 24 miles away. What a wonderful time a person could have!

From Marshall in Missoula to the same eastern friend, July 3, 1927:

I spent eight dandy days scouting for suitable areas on which to carry on our [pine reproduction] study. During that time I walked 240 miles (not on eight consecutive days), including one day of 40 miles. Have seen 5 bear and 35 deer in 39 days. The best part of these walks was the fact that most were taken in wild and inaccessible areas. . . . Am enclosing a reprint of a recent article of mine . . . merely to indicate the type of stuff [and here there is a correction—a bold horizontal stroke deleting the phrase "type of stuff"] the line of bull which foresters turn out.

At the time, he was turning out bullish stuff about soil alkalinity and precipitation cycles and life histories of the western white pine. But he was also writing vividly of this big-sky wilderness country into which his career had so obligingly thrust him. Again and again he was drawn in particular to what is now the 1.2-million-acre Selway-Bitterroot Wilderness Area, a Douglas-fir-and-ponderosa-pine kind of place, so different from the Adirondacks that one might suspect that the two belonged on separate planets. Of that sweeping, serrated panaroma he would write: "There is not even a single remote trace of civilization. Needlelike peaks rising unscalably into the sky, spacious plateaus suddenly dropping into gloomy gorges, wooded basins meeting on irregular fronts with snag-strewn burns, deep-blue ponds and bright peaks alleviating the harshness of granite." Verplanck Colvin could not have said it better himself.

Almost at the start of his very first summer in the big-sky West, lightning stabbed Watson Mountain in the Kaniksu National Forest near Priest Lake, Idaho, igniting one of the worst burns in those precincts in half a century. The junior forester pitched in. One night, he wrote in a letter to the Marshall clan, they "climbed a knoll from where the entire fire was visible. . . . Over the entire mountainside hung a lurid, shifting, molten, fiery vapor, like the burning gases of a nebulous planet. It . . . was like some ghostlike picture without form or substance, showing the unconquerable, awful power of Nature."

And here, too, out of the Elsewhere of his life, emerged Bob Marshall the satirist, the wit, the preserver of smiles. Consider his "Contribution to the Life History of the Northwestern Lumberjack," researched in Idaho, posted home to Pop, sat upon by Pop in the belief that its publication might offend honest women, and ultimately dislodged and published in the journal *Social Forces* late in 1929.

"I have undertaken," wrote Marshall, "a quantitative study destined to chronicle certain of the more outstanding social peculiarities of the Northwestern lumberjack. The traits which I have chosen for mathematical analysis are: (1) the lumberjack's speed in eating; (2) his table manners; (3) the subjects of his conversation; (4) his use of profane and libidinous language."

On the first count, by stop-watch calculation, Marshall had discovered that there was "in each camp a fastest man or group of men who waste[d] but 21 minutes diurnally in the mad dash for sustenance." On the second count, his analysis revealed that only "12 percent of the eaters were two-tool men; that is, employed knife and fork to lift the food into the oral cavity. As regards bread spearing, 33 percent of the diners commonly depended upon their forks to harpoon the staff of life." For the third count, Marshall's documentation was tabular, in part as follows (the figures representing percentages of 1,800 minutes of "confabulation"):

Pornographic stories, experiences and theories	23
Personal adventures in which narrator is hero	11
Outrages of capitalism	8
Sarcastic evaluation of the late war to end war	1
President Coolidge, with mordant comments on pseudo-cowboys	1

As for the final count of his social study, Marshall discovered that, on average, 136 "profane and lascivious utterances" were enunciated by his subjects every quarter hour. Instances of profanity were found to outnumber sexual and excretory maledictions better than two to one. "Unfortunately," Marshall concluded, "various heritages from Anthony Comstock's activities make it impossible to mention individually these profanations and obscenities."

And then there was the other side of Elsewhere, and of Robert Marshall, the shaper of forest policy. You see, he was so dreadfully afraid that the American wilderness was going down the drain. His first important manifesto emerged from the Johns Hopkins years and appeared, under the title "The Problem of the Wilderness," in the February 1930 number of *The Scientific Monthly*. It has since been called "the Magna Charta of the wilderness preservation movement." First, Marshall defined his terms. Wilderness was a roadless area "sufficiently spacious that a person in crossing it must have the experience of sleeping out." It was a place for the nurturing of physical independence, of cogitation leading to original ideas, of psychological repose, of adventure, of the perception of beauty. Yet there remained in America perhaps only twenty such places of a million acres each "and annually even these shrunken remnants of an undefiled continent [were] being despoiled." Fundamentally, he argued, "the question is one of balancing the total happiness which will be obtainable if the few undesecrated areas are perpetuated against that which will prevail if they are destroyed."

He conceded, of course, that only "a fraction" of a minority would ever actually pursue a wilderness experience. "Far more people," he went on, "can enjoy the woods by automobile." But here Bob Marshall came to a full and logical stop, wondering if, "because more people enjoy bathing than art exhibits," we therefore "should change our picture galleries into swimming pools." There were roads aplenty, he noted, "traversing many of the finest scenic features in the nation," but only an "insignificant wilderness residue." Thus it was important "to concede the right of happiness also to people who find their delight in unaccustomed ways. This prerogative is valid even though its exercise may encroach slightly on the fun of the majority."

The clock was winding down, Bob Marshall warned. "Just a few years more of hesitation and the only trace of that wilderness which has exerted such a fundamental influence in molding American character will lie in the musty pages of pioneer books and the mumbled memories of tottering antiquarians." It was therefore imperative to undertake forthwith a thorough study of the nation's wilderness needs. And the calculation he urged was not to be cautious, but radical—"radical . . . because it is easy to convert a natural area to industrial or motor usage, impossible to do the reverse; because the population which covets wilderness recreation is rapidly enlarging, and because the higher standard of living which may be anticipated should give millions the economic power to gratify what is today merely a pathetic yearning."

Three years later, Marshall's most ambitious policy statement appeared between hardcovers—a 234-page tract called *The People's Forests*. And radical? Why, it was radical enough to curl the hair on the chinny-chin-chin of any red-blooded capitalist;

enough to make a lumber baron desirous of forking Marshall up like a slab of bread, chewing him up, and spitting him out in pieces. Good grief! In order to end what he called the devastation of America's woodlands, this man wanted nothing less than wholesale public acquisition of private timberlands. Two hundred and forty million acres he wanted, at an incredible cost of a billion Depression dollars. And to *nationalize* the forests! But why not? argued Marshall. It was a modest proposal when one considered that half a billion had been spent on the Panama Canal.

The modest proposal was but prelude to something else—something a bit closer to Bob Marshall's heart than sustained yield, something called forest recreation. As there were several kinds of recreation, so were there several kinds of recreational forest. There were the "superlative areas," so "surpassing and stupendous in their beauty," and most, he noted, were already preserved within national parks. There were "roadside" and "residential" areas, which perforce must be preserved as scenic corridors and service centers for the windshield tourists. There were "outing areas" for those whose hiking and camping proclivities fell somewhere between the windshield and the wilderness. And there were "primeval areas" and "wilderness areas," between which two Marshall would construct an interesting distinction.

Primeval areas were to be natural areas for the scientific study of the natural distribution of the flora of the world and the esthetic enjoyment of nature. "There are great differences," he noted, "between the beauty of the redwood, the Engelmann spruce, the western white pine . . . [and] each important type should be preserved in the museum of the forest." To qualify, Marshall said, a primeval area should be no smaller than 5,000 acres.

Wilderness areas were to be places for visitors to lose themselves, sufficiently spacious—say, 200,000 acres or more—"for a person to spend at least a week of active travel without crossing his own tracks." The difference, he said, is that the primeval area exhibits primitive conditions of growth whereas the wilderness area exhibits primitive methods of transportation. Of course wilderness areas may contain within their boundaries much that is primeval. Their chief function, however, is not to make possible contact with the virgin forest but rather to make it possible to retire completely from the modes of transportation and the living conditions of the twentieth century."

Marshall figured there were only about sixty-five areas in the coterminous United States that, in 1933, could still be set aside as wilderness without "serious sacrifice" of raw material or change in existing highway plans. And only nine of the sixty-five contained as many as a million acres. If someone wanted wilderness of that sort "that existed in frontier days," well, he'd just have to retreat to the great outback of northern Canada. Or to Alaska.

It was written that blank spaces on maps had always fascinated him. And here he was in Baltimore, in the spring of 1929, facing a scot-free summer before the final push for the Ph.D. There was an atlas on the shelf. He turned to the map of Alaska. Two big blanks. One on the Kuskokwim, southwest of Mount McKinley; the other at the headwaters of the Koyukuk, north of the Arctic Circle. The notion of a summer in the Arctic was alluring. But, wait. As a plant physiologist, he would need some scientific rationale to justify such an expedition. He would make a study of tree growth at the northern timberline. "I cannot say," he would confess after the event, "that I learned very much about tree growth or timberline. But I did come away with a vivid impression that the few white and Eskimo people who were scattered through this remote region were on the whole the happiest folk I had ever encountered."

So begins *Arctic Village,* Bob Marshall's literary *pièce de résistance,* a masterwork of observation and perceptive commentary on the human condition in a far and lonely place. Brought out in the same year (1933) as *The People's Forests,* the Arctic book became an overnight success, struck the fancy of the Literary Guild, which made of it a featured selection, and prompted high praise from taste-makers along the length and breadth of Publisher's Row. Hard-to-please H. L. Mencken himself called it "a very good book"—shrewd, civilized, and "genuinely eloquent" in its descriptions of the Koyukuk scenery.

For an outsider to accomplish this, one summer on the Koyukuk would hardly have sufficed. Consequently, to Fairbanks in August 1930 Marshall had packed himself, a phonograph, thirty records, and sixty-six books (an eclectic library as varied as *The Magic Mountain, The Decline of the West,* and *The Sexual Life of Savages*); and, with a break at last in the weather, flew some 250 miles north to the tiny gold-panning village of Wiseman. There, though with some time-off-for-good-behavior trips to satellite mining camps and the unexplored glaciers of the Central Brooks Range, Marshall ensconced himself in a one-room, sod-roof log cabin and, over the next fifteen months, proceeded to fill one notebook after another with the raw material of a sociological best-seller. His subject: the lives and times of his seventy-seven Anglo-sourdough, forty-four Eskimo, and six Indian, neighbors.

The Eskimo people called him Oomik Polluk, meaning big whiskers. He was their good friend. They trusted him. So did the Anglo old-timers who had come into the country with the glitter of a fortune of gold in their eyes, poor landlocked bachelor men now with broken connections to the Outside. Why did they seem so happy, these people of the long nights and short summers and empty pockets? Was courage a part of it? Like Old Poss Postlethwaite, seventy-eight and going blind, who "could still say after an entire winter which yielded four [mining] partners a total of $181, 'Discouraged? Christopher, no!'" Was irreverence a part of it?—this Eskimo telling Oomik Polluk that when you're real sick, "you want to cuss and swear and fight like hell" because "most the people who die give up cussing and start in praying too soon." Or was it laughter?—a certain unnamed Koyukuker telling O. P. his favorite recipe for cooking a porcupine: "Place the porcupine and a rock in some boiling water. Cook until you can shove a fork into the rock. Then throw out the procupine and eat the rock."

Courage, yes; and irreverence and laughter, too, brought happiness to the people of Bob Marshall's Arctic village. But he also found they were happy as well for their independence, their self-reliance, their freedom of thought and action, their exultation in adventure. All that, and their ability to enjoy life "as it passes along," no remorse for the past, no worry for the future. And finally, as Marshall perceived it, there was happiness for the stark beauty of the Koyukuk landscapes, for "the overpowering loveliness" of the Arctic wilderness. "As far as one can see," he wrote, "up and down the Koyukuk, the flat valley floor is flanked by pure white mountainsides, jutting into rocky pinnacles which catch the sunlight hours before the lowlands are out of shadow." And beyond the view from Wiseman, following the Koyukuk upstream toward its headwaters on the Arctic Divide, one could behold "precipices rising sheer for hundreds and even thousands of feet, with deep glacial canyons as sensational as Yosemite." This, of course, did not explain the happiness of the people of Wiseman, for few of them had ever been to the far Divide. But Bob Marshall had been there, and that, in part, explained *his* happiness. He was especially happy because, among those glacial canyons and soaring cliffs, there were still a few places where no man— not Meriwether Lewis, not Verplanck Colvin, not even Poss Postlethwaite—had ever set foot.

He had named the mountain Doonerak, borrowing the word from the liturgy of the Kobuk Eskimo medicine men. It meant devil or spirit, a thing that delighted in making big trouble. The Kobukers believed that the world was infested with thousands of dooneraks. But for Robert Marshall, there was only one, and because it was there he would have to climb it.

He had first seen the mountain in the summer of '29, slogging up the North Fork of the Koyukuk with the prospector Al Retzlaf and passing on through the Gates of the Arctic to Ernie Creek. It seemed to him as though he had been placed upon a pedestal in a great towering amphitheater. In almost every direction stretched a landscape beyond imagining—ragged peaks, giant needles of black slate, plunging waterfalls, canyons carpeted with moss. And then, this singular peak appearing to rise above all the others, this saw-toothed isosceles rending the sky. That summer he called it the Matterhorn of the Koyukuk, but when he returned on a second trek two years later, he renamed the mountain Doonerak and, with the aid of a hypsometer, calculated its height at 10,100 feet (the U.S. Geological Survey would later truncate that elevation to 7,610 feet). From afar, the summit appeared unscalable. He would challenge that assumption. But not this time. Next year, perhaps. He would go back to the Koyukuk next year, for Doonerak.

But he did not go back next year, or the year after. Urgent business kept him Outside. And fun, too. In July 1932 he returned to his beloved Adirondacks to run up the score. In a single day, starting at 3:30 A.M. and ending at 10:30 P.M., he scrambled up fourteen peaks for an aggregate ascent of 13,600 feet, taking the last 700 by flashlight.

He was writing now, too, shaping his thoughts on recreation into a chapter for the Forest Service report "A National Plan for American Forestry," and honing the uncut edges of his own two books. After their publication, he hoped to get back to Alaska to dogsled across the Brooks Range from Wiseman to Point Barrow, and to climb Doonerak. But after publication, he was mushing instead through the bureaucratic canyons of Harold Ickes's Interior Department and its Office of Indian Affairs. Or, as if that weren't enough to keep his mind off the Great Land, he was busy consorting with the likes of Benton MacKaye and Harvey Broome and writing checks to launch a new organization called the Wilderness Society. But—oh!—how he was homesick for Alaska. "I can't think of anything more glorious than to be on the trail with you again," he wrote to Ernie Johnson, his Koyukuk traveling partner from the summer of '31. "There is still much exciting country to explore there and it would be too bad not to take advantage of it."

Marshall's advantage—a leave of absence from the Forest Service, which had just stolen him from Ickes to run its new Division of Recreation and Lands—came in the summer of '38. August 4. Wiseman. The return of Oomik Polluk. "Oh boy, was it great to be back!" he wrote in one of his journals. But his first impressions after seven years' absence were not altogether delightful, for he "realized nostalgically that the Wiseman of 1931 had changed." Ten airplanes had touched its dirt runway in the more than a year he had spent there in 1930–31. "Now," he noted, "there were two or three a week." Then, only one tourist. In the past year, a hundred and fifty. Wiseman was "no longer . . . beyond the end of the world." Only Doonerak was.

In the early morning of August 10, 1938, Ernie Johnson, Jesse Allen, Kenneth Harvey, and Bob Marshall shoved their tub of a boat into the current of the Koyukuk for the start of a month of exploring "beyond the paths of man." They were headed "for Mount Doonerak and the sources of the Anaktuvuk." But since the Anaktuvuk's headwaters came first, it was early September before they arrived within striking distance of the mountain; and on the morning of their planned ascent, they emerged from their tents to discover that it had snowed heavily through the night—the snowline within five hundred feet of the valley floor. "Doonerak," wrote Marshall, "was hopeless for this year. It was time to get out."

Yet there would be one last attempt, one final trip to Alaska in the summer of '39. Once more to Wiseman, up the North Fork, through the Gates of the Arctic, past Ernie Creek to a new base camp beyond Hanging Glacier Mountain. July 5. A perfect day. Up the steep, green shoulder of a ridge. Suddenly face to face with Doonerak. An abutment rising straight up for two thousand feet. Not a chance. Cross over now to the northeast shoulder. Up almost vertical chimneys, around the edges of great cliffs, clawing with toes and fingers to the top of a rocky dome off—and below—the true summit. And still the great black face of Doonerak, less than half a mile away, jutting two thousand feet higher into the sky. And Bob Marshall, with his notebook, writing: "Some day, probably, people with years of rope-climbing experience will succeed in reaching the top. . . . We all knew that we never could." No matter. It had been fun.

The train to New York City left Washington's Union Station at midnight. In the Pullman cars, behind the green curtains, the berths were already made up, crisp sheets and pillows plump. All aboard.

It had been a long and busy week for him, all those arrangements for the extended tour of southern forests that would start on the far side of this weekend, a luncheon meeting with Robert Sterling Yard to thrash out financial and editorial plans for the Wilderness Society, and dinner just hours ago with Gardner Jackson at Chevy Chase. They had had a good chat, he and Jackson, though the principal topic was most unpleasant. The topic was Hitler. Good heavens, today was Armistice Day, twenty-one years to the last day of the war to end war. And now, this. Hitler. He must be defeated. There could be no tactical temporizing along the line, no straddlers, a fight to the finish. It would have to come to that.

The train rolled north through the night and it was dark in the berth, so dark that the curtain lost its color. There had been a time, once, when dark such as this overwhelmed him with terror. He hadn't known then that most little boys have this bout with the night. All that he had known—and what he still knew—was that you couldn't let a thing like the dark get you down. So he had fought his match with the night at Knollwood, stepping out before bedtime for a walk in the darkest of woods. No flashlight, no matches; only stars, sometimes, or a sliver of moon. A summer of nightwalks, scabs on his barked shins, and he was the winner.

He knew, too, that a person couldn't let a thing like his health get him down. He had fought that good fight almost from the very beginning, pushing himself on the long walks, building himself up, tough as nails, topping the peaks and the records. He would complain to friends that reports of his occasional illnesses were greatly exaggerated. In 1937 he had had to put down that story about sunstroke, saying instead that it was ptomaine poisoning that had knocked him out of his head for twenty hours. And then just this past month, stricken in the high country of Washington State, and flying East to see his doctor, and telling Bob Yard this time it *was* sunstroke lest Yard diagnose it as a flaw of the heart. Yard was on to something, for he had urged rest after even moderate exertion. And he had replied to Yard, without batting an eye, that rest seemed to be a very good plan, and then he hopped on a flight back to Washington State to continue his hikes in the high country.

Through town and country, the midnight train rolled north along the edge of the tidewater. Perhaps he slept. Or perhaps overwrought from lack of rest, he found his thoughts switching tracks toward darker places. Not uncommon, finding the mind doing that after midnight. In the dark, perhaps, memories of the long departed. His mother, his sister, Pootie, and Pop.

His mother, Florence, had died when she was only forty-three, and he, fifteen. His sister, Ruth, alias Pootie (though Bob spelled it "Putey"), dead but three years ago, age thirty-eight. *His* age, now. Dear sweet Pootie. "I guess probably I was fonder of Putey than any person I know," he wrote to his friend, the mountain historian Russell Carson. "Certainly she was as grand a human being as I can possibly imagine. She grew up under the terrible inhibitions which came from being the daughter of a prominent citizen of the Victorian age. She fought her way by sheer will through the misery which those inhibitions brought, and just about the time when she had completely escaped from them, she died." She had become "a sort of second mother" to him, helping him through "innumerable difficulties," helping him in particular to conquer his "abnormal fear of girls," as this not-quite-confirmed bachelor-to-be himself described it.

"I have never known anyone as courageous and as splendid as Putey," he wrote. He never would.

Pop had died in '29, an over-reacher at seventy-three. Of that death, Bob Marshall had written:

> Personally, I do not believe in any hereafter and my guess is that death means oblivion. Yet it is a perfectly inevitable event, and nothing which is inevitable seems tragic. The variable which to me seems to make the difference between a tragic and a normal death is the factor of happiness; a dual factor embracing both the personal happiness of the one who died and the amount he did toward making other people happy. In this particular case, Fa-

ther lived a remarkably happy life . . . (and) did a considerable bit toward making other people happy.

The old man, the son went on, had wanted to die in harness, and so had remained vigorous, walking each day and working long hours to the end of his life. To the son, that seemed an ideal way to die, with boots on and flags flying.

The son himself had almost cashed it in, in harness, the summer before in Alaska, coming down the flooded Koyukuk after the snowstorm had turned them back from Doonerak. Floodwaters had punched a tunnel through a gravelly oxbow, their boat sucked into it, a crunching of wood, icy water, total darkness, what a boots-on way to go, and thinking, however incredibly—wouldn't it be swell to recall, before dying, all the fine experiences of his thirty-seven years. Then, saved by the bell.

But what would have been swell to recall? Doonerak, that ragged black troublemaker, for certain. The lights of Wiseman winking on a winter's night. The long view west—Meriwether's view—from Lolo Pass. Haystack with George and Herb Clark in the gleaming dawn of an Adirondack morning. Rowing with Pootie, the guideboat slipping among the islands of Saranac Lake while the sky purpled up and the pines pasted tassles upon the red sunset. Seeing Ampersand across the lake, first time ever. Feeling the beginning of something. And perhaps knowing, then, finally, that he would be there long before morning.

INDEX

Adams, Sherman, 175
Adirondack, The, or Life in the Woods
  (Joel Headley), 184
Adirondack Council, 203–5, 267,
  269, 270, 275
Adirondack Forest Preserve, 23,
  182, 184, 262, 274, 280, 281
Adirondack Mountain Club, 283,
  285
Adirondack Mountains National
  Park (proposed), 201
Adirondack Park, 191, 198–99,
  201, 259, 274
Adirondack Park Agency, 202–3,
  267
Adirondack Park Land Use and
  Development Plan, 203, 275
Adirondack wilderness areas, 202–
  3
Adventures in the Wilderness: or,
  Camp-Life in the Adirondacks
  (Henry H. Murray), 186
Agassiz, Louis, 185

Albright, Horace, 144
American Forest Council, 49
American Forest Resources Alli-
  ance, 49
Appalachian Mountain Club, 181,
  227
Arcata Redwood Company, 148–
  49
Arctic Village (Robert Marshall),
  291
Association for the Protection of
  the Adirondacks, 202, 204
Ausable lakes (N.Y. State), 183,
  196, 197, 203

Beamish, Richard, 205, 269, 275
Beattie, Mollie, 222–23, 237, 264
Belous, Robert, 149–52, 155
Blake, Mills, 191, 208
Blennerhassett, Harmon and Mar-
  garet, 11–12
Bob Marshall Great Wilderness
  (N.Y., proposed), 204–5

299

Bob Marshall Wilderness (Mont.), 16, 204
Bofinger, Paul, 176–79, 181, 264, 275
Boise Cascade Corporation, 24, 28, 252, 261
Bollenbacher, Barry, 18, 21, 43
Brandemihl, Keith, 37
Brannon, Edgar B., Jr., 35–36, 45–47, 51
Brower, David, 145, 147, 176
Brown, Edmund Jr., 153
Burch, William, 254
Burlington, Vt., 240, 241, 272
Burlington Electric Department, 220, 241–42, 246, 254, 255
Burlington Northern Railway, 17
Burr, Aaron, 11–12
Bush, George, 59

California Department of Forestry, 154
Carson, Russell M. L., 208, 297
Cascade Range (Wash.), 56, 82–83
Central Park (N.Y. City), 280–81
Champion International Corporation, 24–25, 28, 30, 32, 37, 41, 261
Charlevoix, Pierre Francois Xavier de, 126
Civilian Conservation Corps, xii, 101; early plans for, 105; organization of, 106; supplies for, 107; daily camp routine, 109; and the Press, 112; and the U.S. Army, 113; phased out, 115–16; accomplishments of, 117–18
Clark, Herbert, 282, 283–84
Cleveland, Grover, 68, 198
Cleveland Cliffs Iron Company, 127

Colvin, Verplanck, xii, 182–83, 281, 284, 287; parents of, 184; early visits to Adirondacks, 186; first Adirondack report, 187; begins the Adirondack survey, 187; ascents and views described, 188–95; the man described, 190; tools of his survey, 190; as perceived by others, 191; on water supply, 192, 198; on reforestation, 193; his utilitarian views, 193; and "forever wild," 200; his final years, 205–8
Complete Tree Institute, 229–30
Cooper, James Fenimore, 226, 280
Communities for a Great Northwest, 39, 41, 49, 73, 75
Cornell, Alonzo, 198
Crescent City, Calif., 155–59
Cuomo, Mario, 204, 270

Davis, George D., 204
DeCoster, Lester, 218, 253
Depression, the Great, 103
Deukmejian, George, 153
Diamond International Corporation, 259–60, 270
Difley, Jane, 179–81, 237–38
DiNunzio, Michael, 267
Donaldson, Alfred L., 206
Doonerak Peak (Alaska), 293, 295
Drury, Newton, 144–45

Earth First!, 39, 41, 42, 46, 51
Eisenhower, Dwight, 202
Emachu U.S.A., Inc., 84–85
Emerson, Ralph Waldo, 185
Exxon Corporation, 213

Fechner, Robert, 112–13
Flathead Lake Region, 15

Flathead National Forest, 16, 19,
    21, 31, 45
Flathead National Forest Manage-
    ment Plan, 18, 34, 46, 54
Flathead River, 20
Follansbee Pond, 185
Forks, Wash., 62, 67, 71, 78
Foster, Charles H. W., 219
Franklin, Benjamin, 235–36
Franklin, Jerry, 94–95
Friends of the Wild Swan, 34, 45,
    46–47, 55

Garvan, Susan, 179–80
Georgia-Pacific Corporation, 24,
    148, 261
Glacier National Park, 19, 21, 69
Glidden, William T., Jr., 248, 255,
    256–57
Goldsmith, Sir James, 259–60,
    272
Goos, Ann, 81
Grafton, Vt., 221–23
Graham, Frank, Jr., 202
Grand Canyon, 23
Great Northern Paper Company,
    261
Green Hills of Africa, The (Ernest
    Hemingway), 138
Grinnell, George Bird, 19, 198

Hagenstein, Perry, 262–63
Hallock, Charles, 198
Hammer, Keith, 51
Hammond, Samuel H., 184–85
Harbor Springs, Mich., 139
Headley, Joel Tyler, 184
Hemingway, Ernest, 128, 132,
    135–38
Henry, James Everell, 174–76
Hewitt, Charles E., 244–46, 248,
    255, 256–57

High, Colin, 248, 250, 255
Hill, David B., 199
Hill, Warren, 101, 102, 108–11,
    116–17
History of the Adirondacks (Alfred
    Donaldson), 206
Hitler, Adolf, 296

Ickes, Harold, 294
International Paper Company, 24,
    261
ITT Rayonier, 65, 67, 77

Jakubowski, Roger, 268
James, William, 104
James River Corporation, 252
Japan, import and use of U.S. logs
    by, 83
Jesup, Morris K., 198
Johnson, Lyndon, 146, 147
Johnston, Edward, 261, 273

Kelly, Steve, 42–45
Kitchel, Phillip, 80–81
Koyukuk River (Alaska), 291, 292,
    293
Kuhl, Richard, 52

Larsen, Peter G., 80
Lassiter Properties, Inc., 270–71
Last Redwoods and the Parkland
    of Redwood Creek, The (intro-
    duction by Edgar and Peggy
    Wayburn), 146
LeBroke, Charles F., 100, 102, 116
Leopold, Aldo, xi
Limits to Growth (Club of Rome),
    247
Lincoln, Abraham, 16, 185
Lincoln, N.H., 265–66
Little, Charles E., 274
Litton, Martin, 146

London, England, 8–9
Longfellow, Henry Wadsworth, 185
Louisiana-Pacific Corporation, 30
Lowell, James Russell, 185
Lower Saranac Lake, 279

MacArthur, Douglas, 113
McKinley, William, 68
Maine, early logging in, 170
Maine Forest Products Council, 261
Manning, Dick, 32, 34, 41, 50
Marquette, Jacques, 126, 127–28
Marshall, Florence, 297
Marshall, George, 281
Marshall, James, 279–80
Marshall, Louis, 279–81, 297–98
Marshall, Robert, xii, 24, 204, 278–80; summers at family camp, 279–82; Adirondack ascents, 282–83, 294; education and career, 285–86; in the Rocky Mountains, 286–87; as humorist, 287–88; on wilderness, 288–91; on nationalizing forests, 290; on forest recreation, 290; in Alaska, 291–98; attempts to scale Doonerak, 293–95
Marshall, Ruth, 279–80, 297
Mason, Larry, 75–78
Massachusetts Audubon Society, 227
Mather, Cotton, 225
Maxxam Group, Inc., 263
Meadows, Dennis, 247, 248–49, 255
Michigan: Upper Peninsula of, 119–21; nothern timber supply, 123; ore mining in, 126–27
Mission Mountains (Mont.), 16, 21, 31

Missoula (Mont.) Missoulian, 27, 32
Montana Logging Association, 38, 50
Moore, Bud and Janet, 53–55
Moore, Walter, 268–69
Morfit, J. Mason, 273
Moses, Robert, 202
Mountain States Legal Foundation, 72–73
Muir, John, 23, 60
Murray, Henry Harrison, 186

National Audubon Society, 58, 76, 97, 203
National Forest Management Act of 1976, 13–14
National Forest Products Association, 49
National Geographic Society, 146
National Wilderness Preservation System, 173, 203
Natural Resources Defense Council, 203
Nature Conservancy, The, 270, 271, 273
Nelson, Randall, 84
New England: forest types described, 216–17; early timber depletion, 228; harvesting technology in, 228
New England Wood Energy Advisory Council, 246–47
Newsweek, 148
New York State Department of Environmental Conservation, 203
New York State Forest Preserve (see also Adirondack Forest Preserve), 278–79
Nixon, Richard, 147
Northern Pacific Railway, 16, 86

Olmsted, Frederick Law, 9, 198

Olmsted, Frederick Law, II, 144
Olson, Keith, 38, 50–51
Olympic National Forest, 62, 63, 69, 75
Olympic National Park, 61, 62
Olympic Peninsula, 60; champion conifers of, 61; land use of, 62; log exports from, 82
Oregon Natural Resources Council, 58

Pacific Lumber Company, 263
Parson, William J., 47–50
Patten, Harry S., 266
Patten Corporation, 266–67
Pemigewasset Wilderness (N.H.), 168, 171–74, 176–81
People's Forests, The (Robert Marshall), 289–90
Petoskey, Mich., 131, 136, 139
Pinchot, Gifford, 14, 22, 25, 45, 69, 167
Pioneers, The (James Fenimore Cooper), 226
Plowden, David, 121
Plum Creek Timber Company, 17, 25, 27–28, 31–32, 37, 41, 47, 87–90; log exports by, 84 –85
Porcupine Mountains (Mich.), 121

Rancourt Associates, 270–71
Randorf, Gary A., 203–5
Reagan, Ronald, 18, 54, 147
Redwood Creek (Calif.), 142, 145–47, 151–52
Redwood National Park, 141–42, 143, 148, 156
Reidel, Carl H., 218, 220–22, 273
Resource Policy Center (Dartmouth College), 241, 244, 247, 250
RIDGE, 89–91

Roadless Area Review and Evaluation (RARE II), 173, 178, 181
Robbins, Philip S., 110, 114–15, 116
Rockefeller, Laurance, 201
Rockefeller, Nelson, 202
Roosevelt, Franklin Delano, 103– 4, 105
Roosevelt, Theodore R., 23, 69, 198, 206
Roslyn, Wash., 84, 85–88
Rudman, Warren, 271
Russell, Ellsworth, 101–2, 107–8, 111–12, 116

St. Claire, Judith, 79
St. Ignance, Mich., 129
Sargent, Charles Sprague, 23, 198
Save-the-Redwoods League, 143– 45, 160–61
Scott Paper Company, 253, 261
Sierra Club, 35, 142, 146
Silcox, Ferdinand, 70
Simpson Timber Company, 96, 98
Sisco, Chuck, 97–99
Six Rivers National Forest, 156, 161
Smith Wild River National Park (proposed), 161
Society for the Protection of New Hampshire Forests, 176, 227, 237, 264–65, 271
Stillman, William James, 185
Stubblefield, Ted, 64–65
Sun Also Rises, The (Ernest Hemingway), 133
Swan Range (Montana), 16
Swan River and Valley (Mont.), 15–16, 44
Swan View Coalition, 35, 46–47, 51–52

Thoureau, Henry David, 165–66, 167, 170, 174, 185, 226–27

Twain, Mark, 226

Udall, Stewart, 142, 146
U.S. Fish and Wildlife Service, 58
U.S. Forest Service, 13, 25, 42, 57, 77, 213, 272
U.S. Geological Survey, 206

Van Valkenburgh, Norman J., 206, 208
Vatheuer, Hartwig H., 88–89, 90–92
Vermont Department of Forests, Parks, and Recreation, 264
Vincent, Bruce, 38–41, 73–75
Vineyard, Lucille, 148, 154
Voelker, John D., 128

Warnock, Douglas, 154, 160
Washington Department of Natural Resources, 65–66
Washington, George, 11
Wayburn, Edgar and Peggy, 146
Weyerhaeuser Corporation, 28, 65, 97–98, 149, 213, 252
White, William Chapman, 190, 208

White Mountain National Forest, 174, 176, 271
White Mountains (N.H.), 185; early logging in, 175
White Pine, The (Gifford Pinchot), 167
Whitney, Cornelius Vanderbilt, 205
Whitney, Jack, 33–34
Wigglesworth, Michael, 225
Wilderness Society, 58, 204, 275, 278, 294
Wild Northern Scenes: or, Sporting Adventures with the Rifle and the Rod (Samuel H. Hammond), 185
Wilson, Woodrow, 69
Windham Foundation, 221–22
Winooski, Vermont, 242–43
Wirth, Conrad, 201
Wiseman, Alaska, 292

Yard, Robert Sterling, 296
Yosemite National Park, 69
Young, Harold E., 229–32